LITERACY IN A LONG BLUES NOTE

LITERACY IN A LONG BLUES NOTE

Black Women's Literature and
Music in the Late Nineteenth and
Early Twentieth Centuries

Coretta M. Pittman

University Press of Mississippi / Jackson

Margaret Walker Alexander Series in African American Studies

The University Press of Mississippi is the scholarly publishing agency of the Mississippi Institutions of Higher Learning: Alcorn State University, Delta State University, Jackson State University, Mississippi State University, Mississippi University for Women, Mississippi Valley State University, University of Mississippi, and University of Southern Mississippi.

www.upress.state.ms.us

The University Press of Mississippi is a member of the Association of University Presses.

Copyright © 2022 by University Press of Mississippi
All rights reserved

Any discriminatory or derogatory language or hate speech regarding race, ethnicity, religion, sex, gender, class, national origin, age, or disability that has been retained or appears in elided form is in no way an endorsement of the use of such language outside a scholarly context.

First printing 2022
∞

Library of Congress Cataloging-in-Publication Data

Names: Pittman, Coretta M., author.
Title: Literacy in a long blues note : Black women's literature and music in the late nineteenth and early twentieth centuries / Coretta M. Pittman.
Other titles: Margaret Walker Alexander series in African American studies.
Description: Jackson : University Press of Mississippi, 2022. | Series: Margaret Walker Alexander series in African American studies | Includes bibliographical references and index.
Identifiers: LCCN 2022031547 (print) | LCCN 2022031548 (ebook) | ISBN 9781496843036 (hardback) | ISBN 9781496843043 (trade paperback) | ISBN 9781496843050 (epub) | ISBN 9781496843067 (epub) | ISBN 9781496843074 (pdf) | ISBN 9781496843081 (pdf)
Subjects: LCSH: American literature—African American authors—History and criticism. | African American women authors—History and criticism. | Race in literature. | Blues (Music) | LCGFT: Literary criticism.
Classification: LCC PN56.R16 P58 2022 (print) | LCC PN56.R16 (ebook) | DDC 810.9/928708996073—dc23/eng/20220921
LC record available at https://lccn.loc.gov/2022031547
LC ebook record available at https://lccn.loc.gov/2022031548
British Library Cataloging-in-Publication Data available

To my mother, Helen Theresa Pittman

CONTENTS

Acknowledgments ix
Preface: The Shifting Tides: Transformational,
    Transactional, and Specular Literacy Practices xi
Chapter One: Literacy, the Woman's Era, and the Literary
    Imagination: Anna Julia Cooper and Victoria Earle Matthews 3
Chapter Two: Literacy and Education: Katherine D. C. Tillman
    and Pauline E. Hopkins 37
Chapter Three: Literacy in the New Negro Era:
    Angelina Weld Grimké and the Classic Blues Pioneers
    Mamie Smith, Lucille Hegamin, and Alberta Hunter 72
Chapter Four: Literacy, Literature, and Classic Blues:
    Jessie Redmon Fauset and Gertrude "Ma" Rainey 112
Chapter Five: Literacy, the Folk, and Classic Blues:
    Zora Neale Hurston and Victoria Spivey 150
Coda: Spectacular Women 175
Bibliography 179
Index 187

ACKNOWLEDGMENTS

Many of my childhood memories about my stepfather are directly related to his two obsessions. These include social class and cars. He talked incessantly about who lived where, what car they drove, and where they worked. On car rides to the grocery store or on country roads, he explained the meaning of those differences. What I did not realize until my adult years is that his obsessions are now my obsessions. I think about social class and cars every day. The difference is that I don't typically discuss them with my loved ones, but I have found that my research focuses on some aspect of social class.

The idea for this book came to me because I wanted to know more about working-class Black women and their views on race, specifically, those living in the late nineteenth and early twentieth centuries. How did they participate in public debates regarding race and class? Did they address those concerns differently from their elite and middle-class Black women peers? My obsession led me to the classic blues singers of the 1920s and '30s. I realized they, too, had something to say about race and class during the New Negro Era in ways distinctive from their peers and predecessors in what is sometimes called the "Woman's Era" of the late nineteenth century. The classic blues singers came from working-class families, then rose to fame, but remained wedded to a working-class ethos. I am fascinated by them because they refused to moderate their ideas and behaviors to gain social acceptance from elite and middle-class Blacks and whites. This project highlights their contributions to important conversations on race and class even as they were marginalized by some of their New Negro Era peers.

The semester-long sabbatical I took in 2018 allowed me time to revise and write sections of this manuscript. I desperately needed the time away from campus to think and write. I am grateful to Baylor University for my research sabbatical. The feedback I received from the Pittman 6+ writing group proved quite helpful to me. Many thanks to Jerrie Callan, Sarah Ford, Tara Foley, Niffy Hargrave, Hope Johnston, Julia Daniel, Ryan Sharp, Stephanie Boddie, and Danielle Williams for their thoughtful and insightful feedback.

I want to acknowledge and thank the manuscript reviewers, Sarah Robbins and an anonymous reviewer. They believed in this project, and for that I am grateful. Their feedback was invaluable. I extend a hearty thank you to editor Katie Keene at the University Press of Mississippi who also believed in this project and thank you to copy editor Lynn Page Whittaker for her tireless work on this manuscript.

I owe a debt of gratitude to Jacqueline K. Fleming Hampton, Beulah Oldham, TiJuana Harris, and Ann R. Hawkins.

To Shelia A. Collins and Mona Choucair, I say thank you for being a sounding board when the academic world is too much.

To Adrienne A. Grant, I say thank you for always believing in and supporting my academic projects.

Thank you to Melissa Perry and Stephanie Eckroth for transcribing blues lyrics.

Many thanks to TJ Geiger Jr. for telling me politely that he did not like the original title of my book by providing me with alternatives. Thank you for the better pre-colon title: *Literacy in a Long Blues Note.*

Much love to the ALL the Pittman cousins on Preston Street, especially the first five: Lisa Tanner, Chris Pittman, Kevin Morgan, Tina Tanner, and Pam Pittman. I am who I am because of y'all.

I am eternally grateful to my maternal grandparents, Elehue and Ruthie Mae Pittman, who loved me quietly and housed and fed me so often.

Finally, I am awed by my mother, Helen Theresa Pittman, for waking up every day even when her body and mind tell her not to.

Preface

THE SHIFTING TIDES

Transformational, Transactional, and Specular Literacy Practices

Angelina Weld Grimké's play *Rachel*, first staged in 1916, was published in 1920. The play is centered on the lives of the Loving family, who are impacted by racial violence, forced migration, and economic hardships. The patriarch, Mr. Loving, is lynched along with one of his sons. Their lynching forces the rest of the family members, Mrs. Loving, Rachel, and Tom, to flee from the South to the North. There in the North they encounter still more problems. Rachel and Tom are overeducated for the only jobs that are open to them because they are Black. Rachel, an unwed daughter, intimates that marriage may not be the ideal means of providing protection and stability to her as a future wife and mother, which, in turn, places any future social and political action in jeopardy. Her brother, Tom, is despondent because he cannot find employment as an engineer. Thus, marriage and fatherhood do not appeal to him. Much grief permeates the play. It is a dark tale with a dark end. Its narrative belies the hope that education, marriage, and family embraced by nineteenth-century Black women uplift advocates can be formidable measures against racial injustice.

Mamie Smith's song "Crazy Blues" was released in 1920. By all measures it was a massive hit. There is passion and violence, all wrapped together in this one song. The female lover is mistreated by the man she loves. He eventually leaves her without saying goodbye. Upset, the jilted woman threatens to kill herself because she cannot live without her man. She ultimately decides against suicide; instead, she decides to take drugs and shoot a policeman. Smith sings, "I'm gonna do like a Chinaman, go and get some hop, get myself a gun, and shoot myself a cop." For many reasons, this type of music resonated with thousands of Black people. Soon after Smith's hit, blues music written and performed by Black women was being recorded at a dizzying rate. The songs addressed taboo subjects like sex and sensuality, love and revenge, crime and punishment, and same sex attractions. Moreover, the songs gave the Black women who performed the songs and the female protagonists at their center an agency that many lacked both in Black communities and in the broader American society. Furthermore, the songs affirmed feelings and behaviors usually policed by respectability politics.

These women's creative expressions exemplify two ways of solving personal and civic problems. One way is to turn inward and forsake desire and familial obligations; the other way is to turn outward and seek revenge. Neither was a viable option previously encouraged by Black women uplift advocates such as Josephine St. Pierre Ruffin or Victoria Earle Matthews during what is sometimes called "the Woman's Era," perhaps in homage to Ruffin's national newspaper *The Woman's Era*, which was written by and for African American women and was published from 1894 to 1897. Yet the restraints of religious piety and social custom that had governed the rhetoric of nineteenth-century uplift had shifted the ways some Black women writers and singers in the early twentieth century expressed how Black people might act against personal and civic transgressions. Grimké's play and Smith's record reveal divergent discourses about the ways Black women expressed themselves outside the usual boundaries of respectability politics in the New Negro Era. This turn toward different approaches in Black public expression suggests that Black women from the elite to the working classes were authoring alternative narratives against racial injustice that were different from each other. More specifically, it means that working-class Black women's concerns were no longer subsumed under the discursive auspices of their elite and middle-class peers. These ideological and discursive shifts are evident in the literacy practices utilized by many Black women in the Woman's and New Negro Eras. Equally so, their ideological positions and discursive and vocal choices on matters of race reflect their class status.

From the highly stylized written conventions of Anna Julia Cooper to the aural dimensions of the folk captured in the lyrics and voices of the classic blues singers, to the southern Black folk language skillfully recorded in the fiction of Zora Neale Hurston, these and other Black women of their eras used their voices as race theorists, creative writers, public intellectuals, and singers to guide the race, to contest racial injustice, and to provide entertainment as a healing balm. Their texts operated dialogically to give meaning to Black lives. In this book, I have chosen several representative women and their texts to highlight the ideological, discursive, and aural shifts among Black women in the Woman's and New Negro Eras. The women from the Woman's Era are Anna Julia Cooper, Victoria Earle Matthews, Katherine D. C. Tillman, and Pauline E. Hopkins; the New Negro Era women are Angelina

Weld Grimké, Mamie Smith, Lucille Hegamin, Alberta Hunter, Jessie Redmon Fauset, Gertrude "Ma" Rainey, Zora Neale Hurston, and Victoria Spivey.

My chronology begins first with Cooper's and Matthews's essays on the purposes of race literature, which argue that literature can be used to advance the race and engage the broader public on matters of race. Cooper and Matthews both articulated a vision for race literature, utilizing and affirming forms of transformational literacy—by which literacy and education transform Black individuals' lives for the better. An extension of their visions for race literature can be found, I argue, in Tillman's novellas *Beryl Weston's Ambition* and *Clancy Street* as well as in Hopkins's serialized novel *Of One Blood*. Both Tillman and Hopkins center forms of transformational literacy as an assimilative tool to build social capital through education and hard work, though Hopkins critiques Western-only forms of literacy and education. I recognize, however, that shifts in thinking and alternative forms of literacy emerge in the New Negro Era with the publication of Grimké's play *Rachel*, Fauset's novel *Comedy: American Style*, and Hurston's novel *Jonah's Gourd Vine*, as well as in the lyrics of classic blues music of the 1920s and '30s. These works illustrate extensions, disruptions, and critiques not against the value of race literature as a theory, but challenging the idea of the inherent usefulness of literacy and education as transformational.

These literary and musical daughters of the Woman's Era writers and public intellectuals critiqued uses of literacy that offer individual users rewards, but negate their communal responsibilities. Henry Louis Gates Jr. called attention to "the commodity function of writing" in noting that writing, for many literate enslaved people like Phillis Wheatley, "was a commodity which they were forced to trade for their humanity" ("Writing 'Race'" 9). This commodity function of literacy, based on what individual users gain for themselves from writing, is similar a form of transactional literacy. When transactional literacy, however, is not accompanied by attention to communal responsibilities, it negatively impacts the future successes of the race as addressed in Grimké's drama and Fauset's novel. Finally, what I see occurring in the literature and music of some New Negro Era writers and classic blues singers is a form of literacy that affirms and honors the oral and discursive practices of the folk in ways different from their Woman's Era predecessors as well as their New Negro Era peers. In so doing, this form of literacy, which I call *specular literacy*, reflects in the literature and the music the cultural traditions, values, and beliefs of a people whom these writers imagine in their fiction and in the fictive world of the blues to exist as they are. Such a chronology helps to point to disruptions not as critique but to illustrate that Black women from all social classes cared deeply about their communities even as they used different strategies to remedy the social dislocations and economic burdens brought on by oppressive conditions. Moreover, this chronology establishes how different uses of literacy afforded Black women the discursive and aural tools to speak to and on behalf of the race despite class differences.

THE WOMAN'S ERA

Henry Louis Gates Jr. has suggested that 1890–1910 could very well be named the "Black Woman's Era" because Black women from Cooper to Hopkins to a myriad others became published writers then ("Foreword" xxii). In part, Gates wonders if Black women were inspired to write during this period due to an essay written by an anonymous writer from Philadelphia (xviii). In 1886, a woman writer surmises that the great American novel might just be written by "a woman as well as an African" (qtd. in Gates, "Foreword" xix). Shortly thereafter, a number of texts written by Black women appeared. Fiction, poetry, prose, periodical writings, drama, biography, and autobiography were the genres Black women turned to as they claimed ownership of their lives as producers of stories and writers of truths meaningful to them and their race. In the nineteenth century and the early twentieth century, Black women were published in the *A.M.E. Church Review*, *The Christian Recorder*, *The Woman's Era*, *The Colored American Magazine*, and other publications and by other presses. As a collective body, these women used their literacy skills to make visible their theoretical positions on race.

This Woman's Era thus reflects a time when Black women, particularly those in the small emerging elite and middle classes as well as the religious-minded, adapted ideals about the home and womanhood from white culture that had, on the one hand, provided clear delineations for the ways white women might obtain what was then defined as true womanhood status and, on the other hand, made it clear that Black women could never obtain such status given their race and presumptions about their inherent sexual immorality. In that definition, Black women could never truly be ideal women. Such outright inventions of the white imagination were rejected by Black women who argued for and embraced a respectability politics and posture they thought would prove the naysayers wrong. Brittney C. Cooper describes why respectability politics was a key tactic for nineteenth-century Black women activists. She writes, "Black women's strategic deployment of respectability, on the one hand, and embodied discourse that pointed to the extreme racial and sexual vulnerability Black women experience, on the other, was critical to shifting public perception and opinion about the value of Black women's lives" (19). In many ways, Black women writers and activists were compelled to adopt this position for their very survival. In the Black women's club movement, many leaders of the late nineteenth century who adopted respectability politics as a strategy found opportunities "for autonomy and authority, and in turn, reconfigure[ed] African American public culture into a realm of deliberation and leadership" (Jones 175). Black clubwomen such as Ruffin and Matthews believed that the mission of Black women's clubs "could solve the 'race problem'" (Jones 176). One outgrowth of the club movement during this time was the opportunity for Black women to discuss among themselves how they might publicly respond to their oppressive conditions and false accusations against the race, specifically those that demonized Black women. Those with the literacy skills, time, and financial means to do so set out to mount their public rebuttals. In the mid-1890s, many Black clubwomen galvanized against attacks on their womanhood by joining a conference called by Ruffin to address those and related matters.

This important conference was the First National Conference of the Colored Women of America in 1895. Its tasks centered around Black womanhood, especially refuting lies proffered by white people generally but James Jacks specifically, who was "then President of the Missouri Press Association" and had called Black women "prostitutes, thieves, and liars" (Jones 177). The clubwomen also met to discuss the overall uplift of the race. As president of the Woman's Era Club of Boston, Ruffin addressed the national crowd of clubwomen who had assembled in Boston. She argued that silence and individual efforts were not sufficient tools to dispel the vile words being used against Black people broadly and Black women specifically. Black women had to defend their honor by speaking up. Ruffin declared:

> It is to break this silence, not by noisy protestations of what we are not, but by a dignified showing of what we are and hope to become that we are impelled to take this step, to make of this gathering an object lesson to the world. For many and apparent reasons it is especially fitting that the women of the race take the lead in this movement, but for all this we recognize the necessity of the sympathy of our husbands, brothers and fathers. (qtd. in E. Davis 24)

Ruffin and other Black clubwomen in attendance recognized that it was imperative that as a collective body of women they respond to the slights and offenses perpetuated in white print culture. They could no longer allow those voices to be the dominant source for defining Black womanhood. Thus, it is not unusual that a respectability politics organized around the elevation of Black womanhood and the humanity of the broader race was one method to advance a counternarrative. However, as the 1890s ended and the 1900s moved into its second decade, different kinds of alternative narratives and strategies emerged. These alternatives are revealed in literacies reflective of class dynamics often viewed as marginal and second-rate.

THE NEW NEGRO ERA OR THE HARLEM RENAISSANCE

The New Negro Era, also known as the Harlem Renaissance, reflects both a literary movement and a more expansive cultural era. Although scholars are not in agreement on the origin years of the New Negro Era or, within that, the start of "New Negro Movement in Literature" (Jimoh 489), I want to use Grimké's play *Rachel* as a starting point. I take my cue from Venetria Patton and Maureen Honey who trace "The New Negro literary movement's beginnings to 1916 and the production of Angelina Weld Grimké's play *Rachel* that year. Central to this revised periodization is the play's thematic focus on a woman's choice to remain childless and forgo marriage because of racial inequities and the terroristic violence of lynching" (qtd. in Jimoh 489).

The play was published in 1920, the same year "Crazy Blues" was released. A. Yemish Jimoh describes the New Negro Movement "as a time when New Negroes cleared a space for African American writers to inscribe their differences in viewpoint, thematics, aesthetics, and so forth into the literature of the United States" (492). Jimoh makes clear that "the emphasis here on literature in no way separates writers from other cultural producers such as painters, dancers, musicians, filmmakers, and photographers, working during the cultural moment many people frequently refer to as the Harlem Renaissance" (492). The cultural terrain upon which the ground began to shift included formations of newly emerging identity politics delineated in the fiction and music to come out of the New Negro Era.

Alain Locke, a leading African American critic and writer of the first half of the twentieth century, chronicled how shifts in identity politics came into being in the early decades of the twentieth century. In one sense, time was a causal effect and was followed by migration and by technologies of sound, photography, and film that led to Black people's and specifically to Black women's hypervisibility. In 1925, Locke's edited volume *The New Negro* was published as a collection of essays, poems, reviews, editorials, and art. Many of the writers published in *The New Negro* were already important voices on race; others would become leading literacy voices whose fiction, poetry, and plays marked an important cultural period. Locke's essay in the collection, "The New Negro," captured a dynamic cultural and ideological shift transpiring in the 1920s. The old Negro, Locke asserted, was being replaced by a younger new modern Negro not bound by the same psychological or geographical constraints that had kept his forefathers and foremothers locked in place. This New Negro had escaped geographically and ideologically from the South and had moved north to find new life and new ways of being in the world. In that essay, Locke wrote, "with this renewed self-respect and self-dependence, the life of the Negro community is bound to enter a new dynamic phase" (4). Locke's hopeful assessment led him to believe the New Negro would be afforded the opportunity to participate in American life. However, should race limit access to full citizenship, Locke offered a caveat: "if in our lifetime the Negro should not be able to celebrate his full initiation into American democracy, he can at least, on the warrant of these things, celebrate the attainment of a significant and satisfying new phase of group development, and with it a spiritual Coming of Age" (634). Although Locke was hopeful, he also recognized Jim Crow laws continued to impede the progress of the race; thus, the New Negro's dreams might be delayed but not denied.

Although Locke did not include the classic blues singers in his essay on "The New Negro," scholars Hazel Carby, Angela Davis, Erin D. Chapman, and others see them as an integral part of the New Negro Era. The classic blues singers added competing and compelling narratives employing literacies reflecting ideological shifts among the race so much so that Black public culture was made visible in new and disquieting ways. This visibility, however, obscured the dynamic and distinct ways the classic blues singers offered reflections on matters of race. In addition, the disquieting was part of an ongoing obfuscation that rendered the classic blues singers as merely audacious without recognizing their own contributions to the broader concerns of race in the early decades of the twentieth century. Their literacy practices, steeped in the vernacular traditions of a subset of the Black working class, are both a connection to an older order and a defiant act of resistance to white norms and Black middle-class sensibilities. Among their predecessors and contemporaries, I contend, were classic blues singers who were as invested in their communities' lived experiences and hoped for possibilities as other race women. The classic blues singers are part of a group of Black women whose creative expressions helped to establish the cultural milieu of the New Negro Era along with writers such as Grimké, Fauset, Hurston, and others. As women from working-class families who maintained a connection to the Black working classes even as their fame grew, the classic blues singers contributed their voices to important conversations on race on behalf of a subset of the Black working classes.

The genre of classic blues is defined by the group of Black women who performed this type of music from the 1920s until the 1930s (Carby, "'It Jus Be's Dat'" 231). Much of the early discussions of classic blues singers centered around the sexually suggestive and bold lyrics most associated with the blues. Carby's summation of the classic blues singers is apropos: "the blues singers had assertive and demanding voices; they had no respect for sexual taboos or for breaking through the boundaries of respectability and convention" (241). Carby, Angela Davis, and others highlight the classic blues singers' overtly sexual and audacious content. Any quick reading of their lyrics or playing of records like "Crazy Blues" provides evidence of just how much the blues women moved away from respectability politics. The kind of social advancement proposed by their predecessors and peers gave way to racial advancement that promoted self-acceptance that needed no radical reformation. A discursive, embodied, and vernacular self was wholly enough to occupy the psychic and physical spaces they inhabited.

There are, of course, scholars who question whether the classic blues singers were in control of their creative content. Ann duCille and Chapman, for instance, wonder if classic blues singers were controlled by white record producers and executives looking to monetize Black women's sexuality. In fact, duCille argues that the sexual content central to many classic blues singers' songs was not authentic to Black working-class women's experiences; thus, such mythologizing for material gain was less about reflecting their experiences and more about economic exploitation. She goes on to "suggest that the many colliding ideologies, colluding imperatives, and conflicting agendas of the era make it difficult to determine definitively who constructed whom in the cultural kaleidoscope of the 1920s and 1930s" (74). Despite duCille's concerns, I argue that the classic blues singers did have some agency, and it is this agency for which Angela Davis believes they occupy an important place in the cultural milieu of the New Negro Era. She writes that "affirmations of sexual autonomy and open expressions of female sexual desire give historical voice to possibilities of quality not articulated elsewhere. Women's blues and the cultural politics lived out in the careers of the blues queens put these new possibilities on the historical agenda" (24).

It is these considerations related to sex and sensuality but also to how Black women occupy public spaces while refusing to adopt normative behaviors and values that are important here. Their lyrical content, even as it participated in and profited from stereotypes, gave fictive voice to a people long encouraged to remain invisible and silent on matters of the body, mind, and spirit and relatedly on race. The racially disinherited now had a public face. Unfortunately, then and now the classic blues singers seldom receive recognition that, as purveyors of, participants in, and witnesses to a vibrant and important subculture, they too had something to offer their communities and the larger society even as their visions on race were articulated in vernacular language and folk expressions different from the norm.

THE SHIFTING TIDES: FINDING THE VOICES HIDDEN IN PLAIN SIGHT

To date, there have been important studies on literacy, race, class, and gender in the latter half of the nineteenth and twentieth centuries in a multitude of fields and subfields. Those in my own field of rhetoric and composition have been forward-thinking and inventive, including Shirley Wilson Logan's *We Are Coming: The Persuasive Discourse of African American Women*, Jacqueline Jones Royster's *Traces of a Stream: Literacy and Social Change among African American Women*, and Sarah Robbins's *Managing Literacy, Mothering America: Women's Narratives of Reading and Writing in the Nineteenth Century*, to name a few. Since my work is situated between 1892 and 1934, I have found their and others' scholarship focused on nineteenth- and twentieth-century Black women writers helped me to think about the voices hidden in plain sight. As their studies illustrate, the focus on Black women writers tends to be on elite or middle-class Black women, those who embrace middle-class values, or those who are formally educated. Moreover, these women's literacy practices almost always reflect middle-class writing conventions and styles—with some departures, of course. This is not a critique but merely an observation and a point of departure I want to attend to in my work.

I am interested in the voices who did not articulate modest views or embrace behaviors in the fictive worlds they create, yet they too offered important deliberations on the question of race. I am thinking specifically about Black women writers like Grimké whose play *Rachel* was intended to shift how readers understand unfulfilled dreams experienced by overeducated and underemployed aspirational middle-class Black families in the early decades of the twentieth century. This hidden voice in plain sight is an ambivalent one, struggling to reconcile the promises offered by literacy and education over the stark realities of their racialized experiences. Then I think about the other voices hidden in plain sight such as Ma Rainey, a classic blues singer whose lyrics (whether adapted from other blues verses or originally composed) fictionalized a world where approval from Black or white elites or the middle classes was not the goal and where racial and love matters are resolved by nontraditional and sometimes illegal methods. Rainey offered these possibilities while paying particular attention to oppressive conditions, male domination, and intraracial conflict. I think about Fauset, who offered a critique of colorism. It is the hidden voices in plain sight, those voices typically from the working or middle class who dared to critique their race and social peers, that warrant attention from Black women theorists, public intellectuals, writers, and singers. I am interested in the ways these voices used their creative energies to insert their views into public discussions on race in ways both different from and analogous to their predecessors and contemporaries, yet they have been less seen and respected. I am interested in the ways their literacy practices reflect a shifting dynamic made real in their fiction and music. As a function of their discursive aims, these women employed their literacies as defiant acts of contestation and occasional ridicule against traditional norms.

TRANSFORMATIONAL, TRANSACTIONAL, AND SPECULAR LITERACIES

Literacy is often difficult to define. I take my cue from John F. Szwed, who asks not what literacy is but what is the "*social meaning of literacy*: that is, the social roles these abilities play in social life; the varieties of reading and writing available for choice; the contexts for their performance; and the manner in which they are interpreted and tested" (422; emphasis in original). Szwed's definition helps to illuminate how the Black women in this book perceived literacy. Literacy has a social function as well as a political one. Literacy, as these Black women writers and classic blues singers came to practice it, functioned as a political act with sociocultural purposes. As individuals, their reading and writing skills provided them access to employment beyond sharecropping and domestic work as well as, sometimes providentially, discursive entry into ongoing public debates regarding race. Reading and writing also gave them a sense of pride and accomplishment. As a collective group armed with sophisticated reading and writing skills, they literally and figuratively mounted challenges against racial oppression on behalf of the race that lacked access to education and a wider public audience. Alternatively, as individuals, many of the classic blues singers who came from poor families utilized their skills to revise traditional blues verses or compose new lyrics to imagine scenarios in which propriety is decentered and audaciousness is appreciated. As a collective group of women, the classic blues singers embodied a shared working-class ethos among a stratum of people often the subject of ridicule and censure. Nevertheless, their politicized literacy imbued with sociocultural purposes is intimately connected to sets of writing conventions and styles, dialects, values, and traditions that demonstrate various groups of Black women were always engaged in processes of knowledge-making to help their communities survive.

Although there are many types of literacies circulating in the texts of the writers included in this study, there are three principal ones I see utilized by the women considered here. The three forms are transformational, transactional, and specular. Generally, users and advocates of transformational literacy practices hope to transform states of being personally, communally, and materially. This is enacted in five specific ways. First, transformational literacy is usually imbued with a moral code; second, it seeks to prove one's worth in the face of personal and/or interracial group attacks; third, it utilizes various discursive forms including but not limited to nonfictional and fictional prose as modes of protest; fourth, users hope to change minds and hearts; and fifth, users hope it provides a counternarrative against attacks aimed at the race. I see Anna Julia Cooper as an exemplar of this kind of literacy practice.

Users of transactional literacy, the second type, usually gain advanced literacy skills to accrue social and material capital sometimes intraracially and/ or at other times interracially. This type of literacy functions in three ways. First, literacy is acquired as a means to an end—specifically, those skills that are approved by the dominant racial group. Second, it is acquired to allow an individual to climb the social ladder without considering how the person may uplift others in the racial community, particularly those of a different social class or even hue. For instance, one may gain specific disciplinary literacy skills such as those acquired in a medical profession that confers status and money but do not encourage or pass on the acquired knowledge to members of one's own racial group. Dr. Christopher Cary Sr., the patriarch of the Cary family in Jessie Fauset's *Comedy: American Style*, typifies this kind of person. He thinks only of himself and his family until a tragedy forces him to think more about the race. Third, it is, however, possible to acquire advanced literacy skills that will eventually be useful to one's racial community members. This can be precipitated by several external and internal factors.

An emerging literacy practice I notice developing in the New Negro Era is a kind I call *specular literacy*. Specular is defined by the Oxford English Dictionary as "relating to or having the properties of a mirror." Consequently, the object or subject one sees reflected in a mirror is not a distortion of that object or subject. It *is* the object or subject one sees. Thus, specular literacy is the practice of reflecting back properties (e.g., writing conventions and styles, dialects, values, traditions) of one's racial and class community. This occurs in four dynamic and distinct ways. First, specular literacy is centered on affirmation of the self as it is; second, it pushes social boundaries and linguistic norms; third, it employs a multitude of genres including but not limited to prose, fiction, song lyrics, etc., as discursive and aural modes of protest; and fourth, it adapts cultural practices for artistic purposes, thereby reflecting back dialects, beliefs, and traditions that have been shunned by both the intraracial communities from which they come and interracial communities at large. One might imagine the classic blues singers and Hurston as exemplars of specular literacy. The characters in their fictional worlds speak in regional vernaculars and hold on to cultural traditions and practices as a reflective practice rather than a transformational practice.

RACE, CLASS, AND GENDER

Transformational, transactional, and specular literacies form a triumvirate reflected not only in the literacy practices employed by these women but also utilized by the characters in their plays, novellas, and novels, as well as the invented personas inhabiting blues songs. The hoped-for outcomes are similar, of course. As theorists, public intellectuals, and entertainers, these women argued for outcomes that would give the race the kind of full freedom granted to white people. With that, Black people could live out their dreams without the color of their skins inhibiting them from becoming their full selves. This invariably meant that Black people would not be subjected to unjust laws that prohibited them from active and productive citizenship as recognized by state and federal laws even as Black people were always already engaged in citizenship practices as theorized by Derrick R. Spires. Spires points out that early Black activists and writers such as Absalom Jones, Richard Allen, Frances Ellen Watkins Harper, and others were practicing and theorizing citizenship: "for these writers, citizenship (and blackness itself) emerges not as a destination, an enacted identity, or static relation to a state but rather as a self-reflexive, dialectical process of becoming" (3). I contend that the women in this book, including the classic blues singers, were also theorizing and engaging in acts of citizenship while at the same time arguing for state and federal recognition of themselves and members of their race as citizens who deserved just treatment. These arguments were expressed by way of their literacy practices and in the literacy activities employed by the characters in their fiction and in the personas occupying their blues songs.

As raced and gendered beings, these Black women writers and classic blues singers had much to contend with. Because they were racially identified as Black by legal decree and social practice, they were second-class, and as Black women they were marginal to white women and Black men. Yet they too wanted full citizenship rights; they wanted their voices heard alongside those of their Black male counterparts and among the throngs of whites who tried to negate their humanity. Without invitation but with dogged determination, they added their voices to a growing body of public voices concerning the race. Writing about race women, particularly those in the late nineteenth century, Brittney C. Cooper describes their gendered politics, writing that "race women took it as their political and intellectual work to give shape and meaning to the Black body in social and political terms, to make it legible as an entity with infinite value and social worth. In so doing, they hoped to create livable terms upon which Black women could be both known epistemologically, and upon which Black women could live and engage" (20). Of the challenges sung about by the classic blues singers, Daphne Duval Harrison says, "life for working-class black women in the United States has been especially difficult because of their bottom-rung status due to racism and sexism. The grief of a broken-love affair is always poignant; it is more so when cast within a racist system" (6). Hence, Harrison suggests a writer of blues "validates and reinterprets the experiences of the folk and acknowledges the blues as the embodiment of the black experience" (7). In writing about Black women writers, duCille maintains that their texts reveal "indices of power and material relations, as cultural products whose formal structures have inscribed within them the social, political, and economic conditions of the moments in which they were produced and the historical moments they echo" (9). These groups of Black women writers offered their communities as well as the broader society bold and inventive strategies on behalf of the race. The classic blues singers as writers and performers of the blues provided a subset of the Black working classes with dimensions of themselves that affirmed and acknowledged how race impacted their lives. Class notwithstanding, Black women had something to say about the race.

As is obvious by now, I have chosen to focus on Black women from the Woman's and New Negro Eras. I have done so to underscore the ways these women from various social classes and philosophical approaches hoped to solve issues facing the race. Theirs was always an uphill battle that they climbed as Black women. They realized early on that the race could not reach its full potential unless Black women were leaders in their communities. Hence, any consideration of the contributions to questions around race as part of these women's literary practice should acknowledge the intersections of race, class, and gender. For instance, as a brilliant scholar on race and gender among her other intellectual pursuits, Anna Julia Cooper clearly understood how race and gender negatively impacted Black women. Reading "Womanhood: A Vital Element in the Regeneration and Progress of a Race" before the "colored clergy of the Protestant Episcopal Church at Washington, D.C., 1886" (9) is early evidence that she raised this most fundamental concern then—as when she declared elsewhere, "The colored woman, then, should not be ignored because her bark is resting in the silent waters of the sheltered cove. She is watching the movements of the contestants none the less and is all the better qualified, perhaps, to weigh and judge and advise because not herself in the excitement of the race" ("Status of Woman" 138). In "Womanhood," Cooper asked repeatedly what the clergy were going to do to protect Black women and urged them to train those who needed instruction so they too could help solve the race issue. The church, meaning Black male clergy, had not done their due diligence to include Black women in matters of importance, she insisted. She forthrightly outlined their omissions in her essay.

Writing about Cooper's "rhetorical savvy" (36), Shirley Moody-Turner notes that Cooper appealed to the clergymen's chivalry and uplift efforts to encourage them to shift their thinking and activism. Moody-Turner stresses:

> She creates a rhetorical basis for her argument by enlisting both chivalric ideals and traditional Christian principles as a way to challenge the male clergy to make these abstract "universal" ideas a reality for their specific communities and families. She moves continually between the abstract ideals and the historically specific realities of black women, linking the theoretical concepts to which the clergy most certainly subscribed to the need for the practical action on behalf of African American women. (36)

Cooper argued before the clergymen, according to Moody-Turner, that "the fundamental agency under God in the regeneration, the re-training of the race, as well as the groundwork and starting point of its progress upward, must be the *black woman*" (28; emphasis in original). Black women must not be excluded. In fact, in Cooper's estimation, no movement toward full citizenship could happen without the Black woman. Thus, it would be to the detriment of the race if the church and, more specifically, the Black male clergy continued to exclude Black women from discussions of racial progress. Vivian May intimates that Cooper's activist vision "advocated an intersectional methodology of liberation. Across her lifetime, Cooper challenged the interlocking dynamics of race, gender, nation, and empire" (*Anna Julia Cooper* 49). Cooper was an astute scholar and writer who recognized and theorized early how social and political constructs like race and gender impacted the lives of Black women. Although Cooper did not use a specific term for her insightful observations on the intersections of race and gender as did her successors Pauli Murray and Kimberlé Crenshaw, she nevertheless recognized how deterministic these realities were in producing outcomes not just for Black women but all Black people. Cooper's early consideration of the intersectionality of race and gender is instructive and has been concretized in the twentieth century by scholars such as Murray and Crenshaw.

In the 1940s, Murray created the term "Jane Crow" to theorize how sex and race were twin oppressions affecting the lives of women of color. According to Rosalind Rosenberg, "In coining the term 'Jane Crow'... Murray had meant not only to emphasize the parallel nature of race and gender discrimination but also to convey the compounding effect of gender plus race discrimination for women of color" (309). In the 1990s, Kimberlé Crenshaw expanded Murray's theory of Jane Crow as she sought to explain how identity politics "frequently conflates or ignores intragroup differences" (357). Framing this discussion of intersectionality among domestic violence victims, Crenshaw explains that race and class cannot be extracted from the ways women of color experience domestic violence outcomes differently from white women. Moreover, she describes how the failure to recognize the impact of race and class on women of color domestic violence victims obstructs safety nets designed to ameliorate their suffering. Furthermore, Crenshaw says, the ways that feminists and antiracist theorists talk around these issues singularly rather than collectively obscure the real impacts they have on the lives of women of color suffering from domestic violence (358). While Murray's theory of Jane Crow is linked to discriminatory labor practices and Crenshaw's theory of intersectionality is initially focused on domestic violence victims, their theories are always already historical and expansive in that race, class, and gender are triads that were always impacting the lives of Black women and other women of color, as Cooper had astutely recognized much earlier.

The classic blues singers also understood the distinct challenges around not only race but gender and class. Many of their songs—both those they received writing credit for and those written by others—were informed by gender and class politics. In some songs, women are brutalized by men psychically and physically. In other songs, poor Blacks are unable to escape poverty or state-sanctioned punishments. In still others, racial caste pits lighter-skinned Black women against their darker-hued sisters. The class consciousness inherent in the music of the classic blues singers is reflective of a broader recognition that systemic racism had tendrils that extended well beyond the general and into the specific realities confronting the race. Thus, recognizing differences in class was also a recognition that class and gender could never really be extracted from race. Such recognition was bound together in Black women's day-to-day realities and in their artistic expressions.

Class distinctions among Black people dictated to some degree which art forms they embraced and those they rejected. It shaped as well as the values they upheld and those they derided. Since nineteenth- and early twentieth-century Black women writers and singers were occupied not just with states of freedom but also how and what freedom should look like among the newly freed, it is little wonder that class divisions among them were reflected in their different literary practices, values, behaviors, personal styles, and tastes. It stands to reason that, in their public addresses, literature, and music, class differences would emerge as each sought to use her platform for uplift purposes, to challenge racism, or just to reflect a way of life lived by people they admired and respected.

The women in this book certainly adhered to specific class practices. Some more than others leaned toward an elite or middle-class world view in which specific linguistic habits, manners, and dispositions were the best method for rising beyond race. Andreá Williams suggests that "African Americans emphasized class differentiation to show that their race could produce representative middle and upper classes distinguished from the uncultured figures who stood for black people in most Americans' imaginations" (2). Such distinctions were necessitated by a slave system that had itself made clear who were so-called "'good Negroes'" and who were considered "'bad Negroes'" (Gatewood 7). Others simply reflected a working-class ethos with vernacular speech patterns more akin to their own communicative practices or those they were intimately connected to. Willard B. Gatewood takes a historical look at the class divisions among Black people in the nineteenth and early twentieth centuries. Differences in social class were sometimes marked, he writes, by "wealth, family status (e.g., whether one was born free, one's significant family history) . . . [which] was in large measure bound up with blacks' experiences with slavery—their place in the slave system, their role in opposing it, and the extent to which their families had been born free from it" (9). Education, occupation, and complexion were also markers of social class, according to Gatewood. Moreover, personal beliefs and behaviors such as morals and manners practiced by certain types of individuals were indicators of one's social class particularly in the upper stratum. Facility with English was another marker of high social class. Gatewood provides an example from an 1891 newspaper article in which Ralph Tyler, a member of the upper class, describes its features. According to Tyler, "the black upper class spoke flawless English, while those blacks who sprinkled their conversation with 'dialect' expressions clearly belonged to 'the lower class of colored people'" (qtd. in Gatewood 27).

Freedom from slavery did not erase class differences. After the Civil War, Gatewood notes that the offspring of former white masters and their mulatto slaves benefitted from intimate connections with their white fathers, some of whom educated their sons, treated them with kindness, and gave them property. These sons were able to enjoy the benefits of such birth and gifts. This, in turn, allowed the sons and their future offspring to join the ranks of the Black upper class, which continued to see itself differently from the masses of Black people. He goes on to identify still other class distinctions in the lower and upper South as well as in the North, Midwest, and New England (12–14). Gatewood's study of social class among Black people is helpful because it shows not just that social class mattered, but that it influenced how advocates of racial uplift were enmeshed in class consciousness that shaped their sociocultural ideologies and uplift strategies. Some of the women in this book were born shortly before the Civil War, while others were born in the latter half of the nineteenth century. Some were born into relative privilege, while others were born into poverty. Some were considered elite or middle class, and others eschewed middle-class respectability politics. All these differences among Black people and the Black women in this book help to dispel the myth of a homogeneous Black community. It is within reason to extend the idea further that Black women from all social classes within Black communities would find different ways of articulating visions for the race in the aftermath of Reconstruction and in the face of Jim Crow realities.

Chapter one of this book focuses on two women and their views on the intersections of race and literature during the Woman's Era: Anna Julia Cooper and Victoria Earle Matthews. Cooper's 1892 essay "The Negro As Presented in American Literature" and Matthews's 1895 speech "The Value of Race Literature" serve as the foundational texts. I have chosen these essays as a framework because their ideas on the literary imagination, literacy, and education highlight a particular kind of vision for the race that can propel forward movement out of the nineteenth century and into the twentieth century. Toward these ends, both women advocated for a particular kind of literacy, namely transformational literacy, as a way to encourage future Black writers to write about the lives of Black people, to challenge racism, and to seek to change the hearts and minds of the broader white society. They hoped that a literate mind at work would have transformational power.

Chapter two examines how the literary call to arms put forward by Cooper and Matthews was realized in Katherine D. C. Tillman's novellas *Beryl Weston's Ambition: The Story of an Afro-American Girl's Life* published in 1893 and *Clancy Street* serialized in 1898 and 1899 and in Pauline E. Hopkins's novel *Of One Blood; Or the Hidden Self*, which was released in installments in 1902 and 1903. The Black characters who inhabit Tillman's novellas are transformed by literacy gained through home, school, and church. As exemplary characters, they serve as models for the kinds of lives Black people can live if given access to education and its concomitant rewards. Hopkins's characters also illustrate the transformational possibilities of literacy and education, specifically for those who are instructed in a combined African and Western worldview. However, Hopkins makes it clear that, even with an African and Western educational worldview, oppressive systems must continue to be challenged; otherwise, literacy and education merely become tools for individual advancement rather than communal uplift.

Chapter three focuses on the years from 1920 to 1922, when more diverse and divergent approaches to issues related to race and the race emerged than among the Woman's Era writers and even among the Black women writers and singers in the formative years of the New Negro Era. What begins to take shape are rejections not against race literature goals per se but specific critiques of literacy and education as transformational. Angelina Weld Grimké's 1920 play, *Rachel*, stands as a testament against idealized notions about equality and justice in the face of mob violence and decent employment opportunities. At the same time Grimké's analysis of the limits of transformational literacy and education was emphasized in her play, Mamie Smith's 1920 record "Crazy Blues," Lucille Hegamin's 1921 "The Jazz Me Blues," and Alberta Hunter's 1922 "Down Hearted Blues" revealed a kind of literacy practice that rejects assimilationist and selfish goals of transactional literacy and instead leans on the vernacular of the folk to speak to and on behalf of a subset of the Black working class often thought in need of reclamation and transformation. As an expressive and creative apparatus, this specular literacy practice affirms the folk while illustrating yet another way Black women from the elite to the working class engaged in debates on race.

Chapter four examines the ways Black women writers extended Cooper's and Matthews's race literature goals as well as outlines the different literacy practices utilized, critiqued, and embraced by New Negro Era women writers and singers. To that end, Jessie Fauset's 1933 novel, *Comedy, American Style*, serves as my literary example. Fauset's novel highlighted the dehumanizing effects that particular kinds of literacies, including transactional literacy, and education that embrace traditional white norms over Black cultural traditions and value have on Black people's psyches. This Fauset sought to portray even as she employed her literary skills to transform the social consciousness of her readers. Additionally, I turn to blues music again to highlight the ways the classic blues singers were also engaged in critical discussions about race by way of their specular literacy practices. Ma Rainey's 1920s blues records serve as my musical example.

Chapter five completes the exploration of race, literature, music, and literacy. I conclude by noting that Zora Neale Hurston's 1934 novel, *Jonah's Gourd Vine*, and the 1920s classic blues music of Victoria Spivey illustrate the degree to which the discursive and aural texts of these women expanded deliberations about the race addressed in Cooper's and Matthews's essays. Although Hurston and Spivey employed different genres to comment on issues confronting the race, both illuminated to varying degrees the challenges Black working-class communities confronted. Hurston turned to her southern roots and training in anthropology to delight in the language and culture of the folk, and Spivey adapted the folkways of the race to tell serious and funny tales about Black people just trying to live their day-to-day lives. In doing so, Hurston and Spivey sought not to change the characters in their stories, but allowed them to live as the flawed human beings they are by relying on forms of specular literacy as their expressive mode.

LITERACY IN A LONG BLUES NOTE

Chapter One

LITERACY, THE WOMAN'S ERA, AND THE LITERARY IMAGINATION

Anna Julia Cooper and Victoria Earle Matthews

Against the backdrop of Reconstruction efforts, the establishment of Black Codes, and the late nineteenth-century period sometimes called "the Woman's Era," Anna Julia Cooper and Victoria Earle Matthews argued that race literature was a necessity for the advancement of the race. Advancement could not simply be a social enterprise. For forward movement to take place on political and economic fronts, Black people would need to be discursively responsive to public discourses that deemed them biologically inferior and cognitively deficient. Thus, Cooper and Matthews suggested that Black authors must collectively write against the tide of lies, omissions, and oppressions in hopes that life might change for the race. Subsequently, they turned to writing as a source for that change and advocated passionately for its employment by others invested in the cause of racial uplift. They believed writing had transformational power. Literacy and the literary imagination they believed were bound together in common cause. The type of literacy they utilized and advanced is encapsulated most expressly in the form of transformational literacy. Users of transformational literacy practices seek to transform the conditions of the dispossessed by turning to the discursive power of words, and they hope to transform what people believe and how people perceive themselves. Finally, users of transformational literacy practices produce new knowledge and scrutinize public discourse used to disenfranchise the oppressed. Such claims to literacy's transformational power have a long history for Black people. Writers such as Maria Stewart, Phillis Wheatley, and David Walker are a testament to its legacy and seductive and ongoing power. Although Cooper and Matthews are not the originators of transformational literacy, they are its inheritors and exemplars of its practices.

Cooper and Matthews explained their positions on the role of race literature in 1892 and 1895, respectively. Cooper's essay "The Negro As Presented in American Literature" was published in her 1892 book, *A Voice from the South: By a Black Woman of the South*. Matthews's speech "The Value of Race Literature" was delivered at the 1895 First National Conference of the Colored Women of America held in Boston, where Black clubwomen convened to defend the honor of Black women and seek solutions to the ongoing problems confronting the race. The 1890s was a difficult time, but it did provide opportunities for Black women, particularly those who authored race literature, to highlight their concerns in their own voices. The club movement, with which Cooper and Matthews were intimately connected, intersects with what some call "the Woman's Era." During this era, women stepped more boldly into public roles, demanding they be heard among the multitude. An important call to arms at that time came from May Brown (Jones 176). In 1891, Black women were called to task by Brown, who suggested "women's activism [could be deployed] as a weapon in the battle against the 'race problem'" (qtd. in Jones 176). Black women, Brown argued, "'cannot, must not, dare not be idle'" (qtd. in Jones 176). In numbers unseen before, Black women responded with words and actions.

Black women were definitely not idle. As Martha S. Jones writes, "women emerged from the rancorous debates within churches into the club movement, creating new sites for autonomy and authority, and in turn reconfiguring African American public culture into a realm of deliberation and leadership shared by male and female activists" (174). Cooper and Matthews were part of this forward movement and, as such, joined a cadre of women determined to transform the lives of Black and white alike. Each woman had dreams about the future lives of Black people, which they outlined in their writings. Both turned to the discursive possibilities offered through the conventions of middle-class literacies to present a literary vision of hope and transformation. They understood that literacy, long sought after by the enslaved and newly freed, acted as a mechanism by which words could establish the humanity of the race. Katherine Clay Bassard underscores this hope, writing that "literacy, equated with freedom and economic advancement, is an 'ideological construct' . . . and thus a product of culture and social formation" (119). Literacy helps to produce reality and, in so doing, might construct new realities in the American consciousness. Black people were indeed human and capable of the same intellectual and artistic feats as their white counterparts. Hence, Cooper's and Matthews's visions for race literature were in hopes of impacting states of freedom as well as establishing justice. Nevertheless, even as Cooper and Matthews valued reading and writing, gaining such skills remained elusive and complicated in the mid- to late nineteenth century.

LITERACY INSTRUCTION IN THE MID- TO LATE NINETEENTH CENTURY

Literacy instruction in America has varied across its history. Competing racial and ethnic and well as religious and economically advantaged groups had various uses for literacy instruction as the developing nation was taking shape. It is not the purpose of my book to trace that long history. Literacy studies scholars such as Harvey J. Graff, James Berlin, Catherine Hobbs, Shirley Wilson Logan, Jacqueline Jones Royster, Sarah Robbins, and others have done this work. Rather, I intend to revisit a period in American literacy history to chart how a desire and a need for literacy for Black people stood alongside the nation's desire to educate non-Blacks in the mid- to late nineteenth century. Graff's studies on literacy help to illuminate this point. His work on the history of nineteenth-century literacy reveals how literacy, technology, and democracy were bound together in a perpetual state of negotiation and negation. He describes how America's rapid technological growth and increasing immigrant populations were important factors in the increased focus on literacy instruction in mid- to late nineteenth-century America. Concern about too many immigrant groups clustering together within their own clans and communities and thus maintaining and cultivating values that were less widespread and more insular worried many in positions of power. Thus, Graff notes, efforts to create more stable and heterogeneous communities were necessary as the United States became a more diverse nation with respect to European immigrants. The need for literacy instruction to unify diverse communities was a major impetus as Graff suggests: "the Western faith in and commitment to education as a requirement for cohesion, stability, and progress were being translated into practice; mass public education was created and spread for the systematic and controlled transmission of literacy and the values that it accompanied" (*Legacies of Literacy* 351). A citizenry newly formed needed literacy instruction not just to provide a viable workforce but also one whose objectives and goals aligned with the formation of a nascent nation. Literacy, therefore, served as an educative necessity to produce a well-ordered populace.

The integration of specific groups assimilated into cohesive and amiable communities was a necessary factor in literacy instruction. Too much in-group solidarity could prove to be a problem in a nation that needed the masses to adapt well to a demographically and technologically changing society. Simply put, diversity of values, beliefs, traditions, and an assortment of behavioral and linguistic practices could pose a threat to the existing and evolving social order. Instruction in literacy that insisted upon the adoption of like-minded values, beliefs, and traditions could be used to stem a tide that might have turned against the evolving nation. With literacy rates growing through the educative process, Graff contends literacy would come to be used as a tool for social control (*Legacies of Literacy* 351). He also notes that "the problems of crime and poverty, increasing cultural heterogeneity, and the need to train and discipline the work force related closely to the carefully controlled, institutionalized dissemination of literacy and its moral bases" ("Nineteenth-Century Origins" 217).

Maintaining control and inculcating universal moral codes were just one side of the literacy agenda. The other side offered greater access to better jobs and increased wages if one could acquire literacy skills to enhance their professional status. Graff explains that literacy was becoming a gateway for white men to enter into the professional classes emerging in the new economies of the mid- to late nineteenth century. Rather than relying only on a class-based system that rewarded men who came from the right social class and the right families, white men could climb the ladder on thrift and hard work rather than family rank or political clout "despite their origins" (*Legacies of Literacy* 351). Rigid class systems as the only avenues to success were diminishing, at least for certain groups of white men.

As growing immigrant populations and advancing technologies compelled the nation's leaders to consider the need for mass literacy instruction, another equally important reason for educating the citizenry emerged—though here I am referring mainly to middle-class white mothers and their children. If America was seeking to function as a nation guided by principles of morality, then middle-class white mothers and authors could serve as the arbiters of that transmission. Hence, literacy instruction and American literature would go hand in hand. Sarah Robbins describes how this process worked. She explains that middle-class white mothers participated in literacy instruction by reading American literature that intentionally guided the social behaviors of their children as well as passing on values they deemed appropriate. Often, this literature typified attitudes, behaviors, and ideals that were class-based and morally stringent. Additionally, white women authors' own literary conventions advocated for a citizenry to be engaged in proper behaviors that could help lead the nation:

> The domestic literacy narrative portrayed American literature as living at the center of nineteenth-century home-based learning. That is,

in its then-familiar scenes of mothers and children discussing stories together, this genre valued literature not only as an aesthetic product but also as a source of social knowledge and improvement—for the characters successfully learning within the narratives and, by extension, for the circle of readers outside that fictive world yet presumably reenacting its values. (Robbins 3)

Thus, what middle-class white mothers read to their children mattered not just within families but also for the sake of the nation. At the same time, what white middle-class women authored mattered as well. Robbins suggests they were cognizant of the kind of material they were writing for public consumption. She cites as examples the Americans Lydia Sigourney and Sarah Josepha Hale, the English writer Anna Laetitia Barbauld, and others who intentionally authored texts that were instructive rather than fantastical. In a real sense, these mothers as literacy instructors and as literary readers and writers were in fact mothering the nation through their domesticated literacy practices. As Robbins writes, "Women's special abilities to nurture and refine meant they could have a beneficent influence on literature, both as readers and as writers; and once literature itself had been femininized, it could have a nurturing influence on social behaviors. Social interactions around consumption of literature, in turn, would shape individuals into ideal community members" (31). From the perspective of these white mothers and authors, their domestic literacy practices were active and intentional. Due to their inability to actively participate in the political process before 1920, Robbins explains how white middle-class women authors sought to deploy domesticated literacy practices in the cause for political power. She notes, "In 1789, when the adoption of the new Constitution signaled the continued exclusion of women from suffrage, alternative routes to political influence gained heightened importance and so became the focus of many middle-class women's texts" (14). This idea extended well into the nineteenth century.

White middle-class mothers and authors were not the only group concerned about the nation and its moral teachings and political process. Black mothers and authors cared too. The origins of their concerns were different, of course. They cared about the nation's refusal to educate Black people; they were deeply concerned about how American literature stereotyped Black people; and they worried about how the white press portrayed the race as criminals. Thus, their domestic literacy practice, as Robbins makes clear, was one in which Black mothers and authors made narrative choices they believed would positively influence Black and white readers alike. Their concerns, according to Robbins, are exemplified in the works of Frances Ellen

Watkins Harper: "Harper countered propaganda about the inability of former slave mothers and their children to participate in white, middle-class versions of domestic literacy by proposing an alternative model drawing upon the experiences of slavery itself as a source of knowledge and leadership" (170). Harper and other Black authors were aware of the psychic reward of constructing a literary world where Black people took command of their lives despite the history of enslavement. Consequently, she and others actively pursued participation in domestic literacy events both real and imagined that benefited the individual, the family, the extended community, and the nation.

For middle-class white mothers and authors with access to leisure and books, literacy instruction and reading together served as a time for sharing virtuous ideals with their sons and daughters, with the goals of nation-building and participating, even tangentially, in political discourse and political outcomes. But for Black mothers and authors with very little to no time to sit by the fireside and read to their children, literacy instruction and reading were about their very survival as a people. P. Gabrielle Foreman writes about those survivalist impulses using Harper's *Iola Leroy* as an example. Foreman contends that Harper's Black characters articulate a vision for an expansive definition of literacy that includes not just encoding and decoding texts but encoding and decoding people. According to Foreman, "*Iola Leroy* both argues for and illustrates the need to expand the use of literacy and interpretive skill by broadening an understanding of the freight of history" (74). The connection to literacy and the "freight of history" signals how the narrative framework of a text like *Iola Leroy* teaches readers to understand the historical impact of reading and writing on all readers. This, in turn, expands how readers perceive conventional and nonconventional literacy practices. In this way, an expansive definition of literacy makes space for the illiterate to be considered literate in the ways they "read" people and the world. For Foreman, Harper's narrative style allows some of the characters in the novel and particularly "the 'aunts' and 'uncles' to help expand [a] definition of literacy, one that emphasizes the power of interpretation" (77). In one scene, Aunt Linda decodes a face rather than a text, saying, "'I can't read . . . but ole Missus's face is newspaper nuff for me'" (qtd. in Foreman 77). In her admission, Aunt Linda underscores the basis of Foreman's claim about expansive literacy practices. One may not be able to read an alphabetic text, but can understand the world by reading people's facial expressions. Foreman's analysis here suggests that Black women authors like Harper understood that affirming a skill like reading faces is important to highlight. Reading faces is an act of survival and expands definitions of literacy.

The truth is, though, that one needs to be able to read both faces and alphabetic texts and to write to compete in the economy and politics of a nation. Harriet E. Wilson, author of the novel *Our Nig* (1859), and Harriet Jacobs, author of the narrative *Incidents in the Life of a Slave Girl* (1860), illustrated how and why Black authors should be in narrative control. Their stories described the experiences of Black women as told by Black women. The Black men and women who had been denied the right to literacy instruction knew its expansive and transformational powers, longed to access its reward, and hoped to pass on literacy to others. As Shirley Wilson Logan points out, acquiring basic or advanced literacy skills for Black women living in the nineteenth century was not really an option. Black women who desired change in their lives and hoped for a better future for the race relied on the word as their way out of literal and figurative darkness:

> It should be understood then that literacy for the nineteenth-century black woman was not an unnecessary frill to enhance the images of ideal womanhood or to make her more marriageable, as was the case for many of her white counterparts. Literacy was an essential source of power needed to address the overwhelming concerns of a people newly released from slavery and struggling to acquire what had been illegal for them to possess only a few years earlier. ("Literacy as a Tool" 181)

Although it may appear simplistic to contemporary readers that nineteenth-century Black women writers believed so fervently in the power and infinite possibilities of literacy, one must not be too dismissive. What contemporary readers take for granted, antebellum and postbellum Black writers understood to be a matter of life and death. For some, reading and writing did possess real material, cultural, and psychosocial benefits. Black writers knew that literacy could be a source of transformational power for Black people.

The long-term benefits afforded to those who learned to read and write were obvious, but Cooper and Matthews also understood the value in the spoken and written word. Scholarship on literacy history and instruction in America illustrates just how the exclusionary practices of denied literacy made its instruction more necessary. Without the linguistic proficiency to navigate the unjust laws and oppressive social customs, Black public intellectuals such as Cooper and Matthews knew the race would be left behind. Millions of white men and women, as Graff and Robbins note, were also swept up in a nation that eventually had to rely on basic and sophisticated literacy practices for its people and institutions to function in America and to help democratize the nation. The newly formed nation needed a workforce and a citizenry to be educated; otherwise, the nation could not advance as it wanted and needed to. Black women and men wanted to be equal participants alongside their white counterparts in the continued formation of the United States. Cooper is no different; she hoped her words might provide a pathway for the inclusion of Black people in American democratic life by employing and advocating transformational literacy practices to illustrate the creative genius of the race as well as to encourage future Black writers to take on the challenge.

ANNA JULIA COOPER

Cooper's educational background equipped her well to develop her theoretical work on race through a transformational lens. In so doing, writing for Cooper was enacted as a destabilizing force against racism. Her essay "The Negro As Presented in American Literature" is a tour de force arguing that American literature can never be fully American without Black people as featured subjects. Because white authors had failed to capture the essence of what it meant to be Black in America, Cooper invited future Black authors to write American literature by focusing on their peculiar position to write American stories. This sophisticated essay showcases her facility with language and knowledge of history and culture. Simply put, Cooper's highly advanced literacy skills are on full display. Vivian A. May describes her writing style this way: "Cooper structures an interplay between form and content in her writing, both to convey her social critiques and to persuade readers to think beyond the comforts of the familiar. By shifting voices, blending genres, and using interdisciplinary analysis, Cooper invites us to partake in raising our consciousness, both individually and collectively" ("Writing the Self" 18).

In this essay, long complex sentences give way to alliterative phrases and anaphoric repetitions. Her language is direct and concise, condemning when necessary and uplifting when needed. Historical allusions alongside literary ones are inserted throughout the essay, showing the audience the breadth of her knowledge. She mocked and cajoled white authors given credit for their literary efforts on the so-called Black experience. Overall, Cooper used edited American English approved by the white elite and middle classes and turned it against them. The essay is a bold denunciation of white privilege and an insightful position from which to argue for an American literature that is inclusive, expansive, and transformational. Kathy Glass notes that Cooper's philosophical approach to solving race issues included a "ethic of care and collaboration that runs counter to the capitalist philosophy urging individuals to advance at the expense of their peers" (29). Thus, at the heart of Cooper's essay on American literature and Black people is a sense of duty that she carried and expected of writers who must account for the ways their literary efforts will benefit the entire race.

If freedom means that one gets to direct one's life, imagine how that life should be lived, and find fault when expectations are not met, then Cooper's essay serves as an ideal roadmap. It is an essay that encourages future Black authors to look inward to find the inspiration to write great American stories and to use their literary talents to challenge systems of oppression. Her essay explored the relationships among fiction, reinvention, and hope in four main ways: 1) she contemplated the very definition of American literature; 2) she considered why white American authors have not been inspired to write American novels using Black people as a muse; 3) she reprimanded white authors for negative portrayals of Black people in their fiction and poetry; and 4) she urged Black people to write about their lives. She employed transformational literacy practices to frame and sustain her vision for race literature. Taken together, Cooper's observations wrestled with a number of compelling challenges facing future Black authors near the end of the nineteenth century, asking especially: how could they use their literacy skills, their lived experiences, and their imaginations in the service of Black humanity? In this essay, Cooper suggested reinvention can happen discursively. May suggests that "Cooper's self, whether the physical body or the metaphysical subject, is not fixed or isolated. Hers is a moving, thinking self, taking up the tasks at hand with a vision for freedom over the long haul" ("Writing the Self" 24). One of the ways Cooper sought full freedom for the race was to rely on her own intellectual prowess and her literary skills to offer a variety of solutions to some of the most troubling concerns Black people faced at the end of the nineteenth century.

ANNA JULIA COOPER'S LITERARY VISION

Cooper began "The Negro As Presented in American Literature" by asking what makes American literature uniquely American: Is it the people and their peculiar American situations? Perhaps it is the American landscape, or the vegetation indigenous to America? Posing these questions allowed Cooper to foreground her argument that Black people are Americans and that their peculiar situation is uniquely American; thus, it should be explored as material to be included in fiction written by American authors. Cooper pointed out that no country can create its own literature without being inspired to write about its own natural resources, which includes all its citizens. Rather than use Britain's people, customs, native animals, flowers, birds, and landscapes as inspiration, she wrote, American authors should be inspired by their "own-golden-rod and daisy" instead of "the nightingale and the skylark" (134). If America wants to stand alongside Britain as its own preeminent nation with a literature that represents its people, customs, and landscapes, ignoring or stereotyping Black Americans will only serve to make American literature irrelevant or at the very least pedestrian. Cooper argued that "no man can prophesy with another's parable. For each of us truth means merely the re-presentations and experiences of our personal environments, colored and vivified-fused into consistency and crystalized into individuality in the crucible of our own feelings and imaginations" (135). The individual experiences of its Black people could testify to the collective experiences of the American people, thereby providing American writers with authentic American stories.

Unfortunately, racism had inhibited the literary imagination of most white authors, Cooper explained in this essay; thus, they had not sought to explore the experiences of Black people to inspire them to write great American stories. This realization, though, gave Cooper pause. On the one hand, she was ambivalent about white authors using Black people's experiences as inspiration for their fictional and poetic works. On the other hand, Cooper was optimistic and believed Black people's experiences can provide great inspiration if explored honestly and with integrity. Had white Americans not reacted so viciously toward Africans and their descendants, had they felt sympathy for the people they enslaved, she wondered if perhaps they could have written great American stories about them. For all their want and need for great American literature, white authors had looked beyond the confines of home, yet what they needed for inspiration was right in front of them. Cooper concluded: "[Though they were] imported merely to be hewers of wood and drawers of water, no artist for many a generation thought them worthy of sympathetic study of a model. No Shakespeare arose to distil from their unmatched personality and unparalleled situations the exalted poesy and crude grandeur of an immortal Caliban" (135). Their conditions and place in American society had been largely ignored by some of the best American authors. Cooper opined that Britain had its Shakespeare who had examined human desires, frailties, and morals and scrutinized them to brilliant effect. Regrettably, America had yet to produce a Shakespeare who had taken what was inconsistent regarding America's ideals about justice and equality and written a masterpiece about it. Where was that great American writer who had written a Shakespearean drama that included the experiences of Black people? she asked. She considered Harriet Beecher Stowe's *Uncle Tom's Cabin* a modest attempt:

In the days of their bitterest persecution, their patient endurance and Christian manliness inspired *Uncle Tom's Cabin*, which revolutionized the thought of the world on the subject of slavery and at once placed its author in the front ranks of the writers of her country and age.... Here was a work indigenous to American soil and characteristic of the country—a work which American forces alone could have produced. (Cooper 136)

For Cooper, what made Stowe's novel valuable was its focus on American people and an American "problem." Cooper's theorizing on the literary merits of American literature demonstrated her abiding faith in the transformational power of the literary imagination. Words—not merely letters on the page but living breathing organisms—have the power to spark new ideas and to change lives. As an intellectual engaged in the business of changing lives through oratory, the written word, and teaching, Cooper imagined what good words and deeds could do to contribute to the formation of great American literature while also recognizing its transformational possibilities in the lives of Black and white alike. In writing about "nineteenth-century African American literary discourse," Carla L. Peterson describes how its writers operated under oppressive conditions, saying they "constructed a productive discourse generated from within the community that borrows the vocabulary and categories of the dominant discourse only to dislocate them from their privileged position of authority and adapt them to the local place" (13, 14). Consequently, Peterson argues, Black writers were becoming "'producers' rather than remaining 'merely, as now consumers'" (14). As a producer of new knowledge, Cooper used her writings to reveal the agency of a self-possessed Black woman writer seeking clarification, looking to inspire, and challenging the status quo.

INVOKING THE RACIAL MUSE

If the first part of Cooper's essay argued for an American literature rooted in an American ethos that includes using the lived experiences of African Americans to inspire writers to create great fiction and poetry, the second part excoriated bad literary practices—for instance, white authors' portrayals of African Americans that are divisive and exploitative. She pointed repeatedly to the hazards of being inspired by the Black race without writing about Black people justly. She warned white authors who consider using Black people as muses that they should do so with caution and sensitivity or not bother to use them at all. She wrote, "The art of 'thinking one's self imaginatively into the experiences of others' is not given to all, and it is impossible to acquire it without a background and a substratum of sympathetic knowledge. Without this power our portraits are but death heads or caricatures and no amount of cudgeling can put into them the movement and reality of life" ("The Negro" 139).

Cooper's tone here is sarcastic and gets to the matter of knowing. Imagining and knowing are two separate spheres. Given the often abusive, messy, and distant relationships between Black and white people, she argued that imagining is a short-sighted literary exercise if there is no real knowing. Thus, with conviction and scorn, Cooper reminded white authors that whiteness does not grant knowing. Vivian A. May writes that Cooper's "modes of address, including her uses of parable, analogy, derision, and humor suggests she is speaking with a 'forked tongue'" (*Anna Julia Cooper* 83). Cooper's "forked tongue" served to put white authors' literary efforts on public notice. Hence, white authors' literary efforts should be based on true knowledge rather than hyperbolic supposition, which will only cause more harm as Cooper's lived experiences had shown. In the late nineteenth century, when this essay was published, anti-Black racism was entrenched in the fabric of daily life.

CHALLENGING RACIAL TYPES

Heterogeneous not homogeneous representations of Black lives are also important. As Cooper wrote, "the colored people do not object to the adequate and truthful portrayal of types of their race in whatever degree of the scale of civilization, or of social and moral development, [if it] is consonant with actual facts or possibilities" ("The Negro" 148). With haughty truthfulness, Cooper simply wanted white authors not to use their fiction to depict behaviors they knew were neither representative nor just portrayals of Black people. For example, she accused William Dean Howells of grossly misrepresenting Black people's attitudes, bodily characteristics, and behaviors, sarcastically noting that "Mr. Howells has recently tried his hand also at painting the Negro, attempting merely a side light in half tones, on his life and manners; and I think the unanimous verdict of the subject is that, in this single department at least, Mr. Howells does not know what he is talking about" (146–47). Cooper was referring to Howells's *An Imperative Duty,* from which she quoted two phrases she found particularly disturbing: "'representing the best colored society'; and the 'bress de Lawd, Honey'" (qtd.

in Cooper, "The Negro" 147). She was pleased with neither his descriptions of Black society nor his imitation of Black vernacular. Hence, she launched a scathing rebuke so interesting that it is worth examining at length. First, Cooper argued that Howells had no business writing about a "subject of which he knew so little, or which he cared so little" ("The Negro" 147). Then she proclaimed, "to my fellow white countrymen, and especially to those who dabble in ink and affect to discuss the Negro . . . it is an insult to humanity and a sin against God to publish any such sweeping generalizations of a race on such meager and superficial information" (147). She invoked her natural right as an American citizen to speak on the same intellectual level as white men and to boldly criticize them for misrepresenting Black dialect, bodies, and identities. She also invoked her right to speak as a citizen who has the right to castigate white authors who dared to bear false witness against others, particularly Black others. May points out that Cooper also challenged Howells's representation of Black dialect and class identifications because "she clearly recognize[d] that someone like Howells holds such sway over the larger American cultural imagination that his crude depictions of so-called authentic blackness have enormous influence" ("Writing the Self" 32). For Cooper, Howells's representations cannot go unchallenged.

Cooper continued on to criticize other white authors who wrote dishonest portrayals of Black people, writing that "we meet at every turn—this obtrusive and offensive vulgarity, this gratuitous sizing up of the Negro and conclusively writing down his equation, sometimes even among his ardent friends and bravest defenders" ("The Negro" 147). Furthermore, she confessed: "Were I not afraid of falling myself into the same error that I am condemning, I would say it seems an Anglo-Saxon characteristic to have such overweening confidence in his own power of induction that there is no equation which he would acknowledge to be indeterminate, however many unknown quantities it may possess" (147–48). So often, Cooper noted, white people had mischaracterized Black people, even those who were well-meaning. They generalized the whole of the group rather than acknowledge their individual characteristics. In so doing, they had generalized so much about them that the one represented the many and they had imagined a figure that was fictive but made real. Cooper recognized singularity as dangerous; therefore, in making a case against the thing she abhorred, she generalized the characteristics of white people who, she argued, believe they have answers in the face of unknowable truths. Such generalizations had other motivations as well. May argues that Cooper's writing served multiple ends and that readers must recognize the purposes of her discursive practices, "attend[ing] to Cooper's understated points of departure, her small changes in grammar, her modulation of voice, and her uses of dry humor or pretended contrition. These varied textual strategies serve important pedagogical and political functions: to invite readers to rethink the past, reconsider the present, and envision future possibilities yet to be realized" ("Writing the Self" 32). I would add that Cooper's critique was also meant to caution Black authors not to repeat the failures of white authors.

Even though Cooper continued to condemn white authors whether their literary intentions were benevolent or malicious, she nonetheless moved forward in the essay to explain that Black people, like all other people, have complex human emotions and behaviors and that any effort to write about them must be grounded in "truth," even though she noted truth cannot be imagined if there is no real understanding of Black people's psyches. For example, Cooper provided an extended critique of Maurice Thompson, a white author who misrepresented Black interiority. In his poem "A Voodoo Prophecy," the poet imagines the voice of a "black prophet" (qtd. in Cooper, "The Negro" 152) who is seeking to avenge the enslavement of his people. In the poem, the Black prophet tells the story of his people's capture and subsequent enslavement to a white enslaver. He warns former enslavers throughout the poem that retribution is inevitable:

> You, North and South, you, East and West,
> Shall drink the cup your fathers gave me;
> My back still burns, I bare my bleeding breast,
> I set my face,
> My limbs I brace,
> To make the long, strong, fight for mastery (154)

In the poem, Thompson's prophet is not a meek man seeking to assimilate into American society. Emancipation alone did not endear him to his white "savior." Instead, he rejects his former enslaved status and embodies a kind of masculinity that Thompson infuses with savagery. Cooper found Thompson's poem at odds with what she called Black people's "accommodating" spirit. She countered that Black people will not seek to avenge their enslavement: "The Negro is utterly incapable of such vindictiveness. Such concentrated venom might be distilled in the cold Saxon, writhing and chafing under oppression and repression such as the Negro in America has suffered and is suffering. But the black man is in real life only too glad to accept the olive branch of reconciliation" ("The Negro" 154). Thompson presented the rage he believed Black people had against white people, but the representation was false. According to Cooper, he was instead representing white people's fear of reprisal for their enslavement of Black people. Since Thompson did not know what Black people really wanted, he only imagined what he thought they might want, which is revenge. Yet, in seeking to avenge his white enslavers, Thompson simply recreated a fictional character that only reinforced what white people already believed about violent Black men. Stanza eight is instructive:

> I hate you, and I live to nurse my hate,
> Remembering when you plied the slaver's trade
> In my dear land . . . How patiently I wait
> The day
> Not far away,
> When all your pride shall shrivel up and fade (qtd. in Cooper, "The Negro" 153)

Thompson imagined the formerly enslaved waiting to watch the eventual demise of the white race. Yet Cooper was not convinced by Thompson's representations. The content of this poem did not reflect the kind of literary and literacy efforts Cooper utilized and supported. It did, however, according to her, illustrate that Thompson had no idea what Black people really desire as freedmen and -women. Rather than seek revenge against their white oppressors, Cooper believed Black people want to move on and participate in American democratic life without any restrictions on this activity.

Cooper was loath to give Thompson credit for his attempt to write about a Black man, yet his specious portrayal of the Black prophet gave Cooper an opportunity to juxtapose the ethos and behaviors of Black people against white people who had enslaved them and then treated them like second-class citizens when they became free. However, she may, in fact, have been engaging in rhetorical play. Perhaps Cooper was emphasizing the lack of vindictiveness of Black people to illustrate the cruelty of southern whites and the indifference of northern whites who maintained their positions of authority. She offered a thesis that suggests all people ought to be judged on an individual basis and not on the behaviors and actions of an entire race, writing, "The [white] Southerner is not a cold-bloodied villain. Those of us who have studied the genius in its native habitat can testify that his impulses are generous and kindly, and that while the South presents a solid phalanx of iron resistance to the Negro's advancement, still as individuals to individuals they are warm-hearted and often even tender" ("The Negro" 155). Cooper was careful to acknowledge the individual behaviors of some whites, though she acknowledged southern resistance to Black advancement was real. Lest she not adequately challenge racial oppression from northerners, Cooper criticized white northerners who she said believe in justice but not equality. This northerner, she wrote, "thinks it better for the country, better for him that justice be done. But he doesn't care to have the blacks, in the concrete, too near him" (155). This subordinate but important commentary on white attitudes in the South and the North seemed to motivate Cooper's real intent in this section, which was to explain that relationships among white and Black people in the United States were complex and any intentions to believe or imagine otherwise were misguided. Consequently, she encouraged Black authors to do the job white writers had been unable to do: to write about the emotional and psychic complexities of Black people and their relationships to the world and to portray Black people as individuals.

This section in the essay about white authors who failed at writing about the lived and imagined experiences of Black people allowed Cooper to criticize their efforts and their racism. Howells and even more Thompson had tried to enter into the psychological impulses of Black people. In verse, according to Cooper, Thompson sketched out what he believed to be the anger that lives in the breast of the Black prophet who speaks on behalf of the Africans forced into slavery. Thompson described the African prophet as remembering his former homeland as the vast "wild" land he once roamed. The imagery is replete with untamed desire, childlike innocence, and unfettered violence. Thompson, Cooper surmised, hoped to adequately portray emotions he believed to be innately true. In seeking justice for a people denied justice, however, Thompson reinscribed injustice. Justice, it seems, cannot be called upon to be examined imaginatively by white authors who have no concept of the meaning of bondage and no understanding of the will to be free. To Cooper, Howells's and Thompson's attempts at trying to reconcile what it ultimately means to be Black were sorely lacking. This made her unwavering in her critique of their failures and their inherently racist beliefs. To be Black is to be a complex human being, which Cooper said their literary treatments failed to honor. Thus, white authors cannot be trusted to write insightfully about a people they do not know. Therefore, Black authors must take on the task of representing the psychic lives, educational outcomes, and material conditions of Black people.

THE ROLE OF THE BLACK WRITER

Since nineteenth-century white authors, for the most part, were thus, Cooper noted in her essay, not equipped or unwilling to write about the lived experiences of Black people fairly and justly, in the third and final section of her essay she encouraged future Black authors to contribute to the making of great American literature. The challenge, as Cooper so eloquently and directly outlined near the end of this essay, is that Black authors had explored the pain of enslavement and limited freedom in oratory rather than literature (158). She did not criticize oratory but rather suggested that fiction can capture the pain and the beauty just as well, even while acknowledging that time and "freedom of mind" (158) have proven to be hindrances. She wrote, "a bird cannot warble out his fullest and most joyous notes while the wires of his cage are pricking and cramping him at every heart beat [sic]" (158). Yet Cooper did not give in to former hindrances. She honored the contributions of Black folklore and folk songs (158) and maintained that they are a gift from Black people to America. Such gifts are suggestive of what could be if Black authors were inspired not by didacticism alone but by observation and imagination:

> I am brought to the conclusion that an authentic portrait, at once aesthetic and true to life, presenting the black man as a free American citizen, not the humble slave of Uncle Tom's Cabin—but the man, divinely struggling and aspiring yet tragically warped and distorted by the adverse winds of circumstance, has not yet been painted. It is my opinion that the canvas awaits the brush of the colored man himself. (158)

Cooper concluded that only Black authors can write human stories about what it means to live as a Black person in America. Without Black people's consent, they have been written about so ineffectively by white authors that she believed it is only those who had experienced slavery and were living in its aftermath who could write great American stories.

In the end, Cooper made it clear in this essay that reading and writing are valuable not just for the individual but also for the community. Hence, transformational literacy as practiced and embraced by Cooper and her contemporaries is action oriented. Her critiques of white authors such as Stowe, Howells, and Thompson, who have left an indelible imprint on white and Black readers alike, are reminders of just how precarious it can be to allow white authors to write stories about Black people even if they claim benevolence. Hers is a cautionary tale: she said, "there is an old proverb 'the devil is always painted black—by white painters'" (159). For the late nineteenth-century Black writer, it was time to paint the "devil" as it was perceived by a Black hand. Cooper thus illustrated and advanced in her essay that the transformational nature of literacy, which extends beyond the writer to the reader, must always be engaged through a process of regeneration and rejuvenation.

COOPER'S TRANSFORMATIONAL LITERACY PRACTICES

The objectives Cooper outlined for Black authors will be a burden they carry beyond the late nineteenth into the twentieth centuries. Cooper realized, as did her contemporary Matthews, that words have psychosocial and political impact. As Jacqueline Jones Royster makes clear, "the very act of writing, especially for people who do not occupy positions of status and privilege in the general society, is a bold and courageous enterprise rather than simply a demonstration of the ability to express oneself" (*Traces of a Stream* 104). To write and to write oneself into the American enterprise are revolutionary acts. Thus, it is imperative that Black people who had the time, resources, and talent take writing seriously. Cooper believed in the creative abilities and transformative power of Black authors. She was herself an example of the possibilities that literacy could wield against racism and sexism. Hence, Cooper's own activity system enhanced by her practice in and advocacy of transformational literacy practices served her well and could help others achieve the just ends they deserved. The literary imagination could do just as it intended: help Black people imagine a world where the descendants of enslaved Africans can make sense of the world around them and the world of the past, and perhaps dissect the contradictions and the beauty that made America both a land of freedom and a land beset by carnage and bondage. These imaginings can transform the way Black people see themselves and perhaps even how white readers see them as well.

Cooper wanted, as she mentioned at the end of this essay, a Black Chaucer: a great Black writer who can turn what is viewed as lowly about Black people into a masterpiece. Of Chaucer's brilliance, she wrote, "it was the glory of Chaucer that he justified the English language to itself—that he took the homely and hitherto despised Saxon elements and ideas, and lovingly wove them into an artistic product which even Norman conceit and uppishness might be glad to acknowledge and imitate" ("The Negro" 224). Black people, she argued, had already given the world music and fables. By her account, it would only be natural that they produce great American stories, take the fabric of their lives and weave stories about their American experiences as no others could, and in doing so, their own Black Chaucer can give voice to an expansive literary imagination.

Cooper was a product of her time and place but also a visionary who could see beyond that. Educated, self-assertive, and imaginative, she articulated a vision for freedom and justice that belongs in the hands of Black authors. As a Black woman, Cooper understood the momentous effort it would take to overturn decades of misinformation. Roadblocks were already in place—those that were legal and those that were a function of custom. Race and gender were inhibitors to success but should not diminish one's advocacy, which she knew all too well. Brittney C. Cooper explains how Cooper dealt with race and gender challenges: "Cooper's use of embodied discourse as a disruptive textual practice ultimately locates black female bodies within the project of racial knowledge production and the reorganization of place or public space" (8). Although Black women such as Cooper and others experienced the embodied tensions of Black womanhood and race, they were still knowledge producers. Thus, despite those tensions, Black women and men had to engage deeply in uplift and transformational work. Cooper is an exemplar of that engagement.

In practical terms, however, the Black writers Cooper imagined who would provide new and honest assessments of Black life would be no ordinary Black authors. They had to be articulate and visionary risk-takers; they had to be familiar with the master's language to make sense of Black people's place in the world. Writing about nineteenth-century Black writers, and specifically Frederick Douglass, Valerie Babb notes that Douglass and others had to know the discursive conventions of standard English if they wanted to participate in an already-established literary tradition: "it is hard to dispute that for an enslaved African American to become part of the nineteenth-century European American literary establishment required mastery of the American and English written prose, a mastery denied him or her by lack of formal education and/or literacy laws" (366). Cooper knew this as well, and her own work reflects her understanding of the belletristic conventions of American letters. Not understanding would have come at an enormous cost. Furthermore, Cooper understood that Black authors could not capitulate to the basest desires of white readers who might enjoy reading fiction that reinforced their racist opinions about Black people; thus, it was incumbent on Black authors to imagine fictive worlds where their words could reveal the humanity of a people whose humanity had never been acknowledged by the broader white world.

Underlying Cooper's vision for race literature was a commitment to the ways freedom and justice should be actualized within and outside the discursive texts of Black authors. This means that identifying race as a problem was as important as providing solutions. When Cooper concluded, "With this platform to stand on we can with clear eye weigh what is written and estimate what is done and ourselves paint what is true with the calm spirit of those who know their cause is right and who believe there is a God who judgeth the nations" ("The Negro" 160), she meant that no idealized mythos would work, but vision and a clear ethics could provide a sufficient starting point. Cooper wrote this vision in the sophisticated language of an intellectually gifted thinker and writer who had adapted the standard writing conventions of the white elite and middle classes. May writes that these linguistic identifiers should not be taken as mere complicity but rather discursive necessity (*Anna Julia Cooper* 58). She says that Cooper recognized the value of acquiring and producing knowledge as well as adapting the standard written conventions of English valued and practiced by the white majority in order to use those same conventions to overturn ideas that forced Black people to the margins. In obtaining those technical, educational, and cultural accoutrements, Cooper had a linguistic foundation she could deploy against racism for herself and on behalf of Black people.

VICTORIA EARLE MATTHEWS: VISIONARY LITERALIST

Victoria Earle Matthews, Cooper's contemporary, also theorized about why literature has a role in uplift efforts. As a journalist, creative writer, and public intellectual, she valued the transformational power of literacy too. Her 1895 speech, "The Value of Race Literature," is a testament to this belief. "The Value" is a formidable denunciation that challenges the white gaze on the Black body and mind. In the sophisticated language of the elite and middle classes, Matthews politicized her words and placed Black humanity at the center of discussions of justice and fairness. Like Cooper, Matthews turned to the word to transform and inspire race women to take their literacy skills and use them in service to their communities. Royster explains the value of literacy in the lives of Black women: "They sought to learn, to better themselves, to change their worlds. In their hands, literacy became a tool for inserting themselves directly and indirectly into arenas for action and for doing whatever they could to mediate and manage the critical process of change. To their credit, they consistently used their language abilities and their intellectual powers to change hearts, minds, and conditions" (*Traces of a Stream* 110).

Matthews's "The Value" is an example of literacy at its transformational best. The address, delivered at the First National Congress of the Colored Women of America, held in Boston, is an amalgamation of five interwoven themes: history, literary bibliography, literary criticism, Black nationalism, and racial uplift. She linked these themes to inspire the attendees to take up the pen and write, and, in so doing, she called forth a political and social ultimatum: to transform their lives. For her, the race needed to be proactive rather than reactive. Black people with the literacy skills to match their passion for change needed to write race literature that highlights the successes of the race as well as to hold white authors accountable when their literary and journalistic representations were wrong. Relying on the literacy conventions of the white middle class, Matthews's speech illustrates her facility with language, her ease with form, her complete confidence in authorial knowledge, and the transformational possibilities for literacy.

DEFINING RACE LITERATURE

Matthews defined race literature at the outset of her speech. Rather than use traditional definitions that might only include works of fiction, race literature for her encompassed a broad range of genres including "Histories, Biographies, Scientific Treaties, Sermons, Addresses, Novels, Poems, Books of Travel, miscellaneous essays and the contributions to magazines and newspapers" ("Value" 170). She also defined race literature not only by a Black writer's focus on racial issues but to include any texts written by a member of the race. In the early part of her speech, Matthews wondered if race literature is necessary "in a country like ours apart from American Literature" (170). She answered in the affirmative: given the history of Black people in America and their current conditions, the literature they write necessitates a separate category called race literature. Such a debased institution as slavery required radical racial reformation. Matthews asserted: "All this impious wrong has made a Race Literature a possibility, even a necessity to dissipate the odium conjured up by the term 'colored' persons, not originally perhaps designed to humiliate, but unfortunately still used to express not only an inferior order, but to accentuate and call unfavorable attention to the most eradicable difference between the races" (171).

Matthews suggested as well that race literature is necessary because it can provide insight into the ways Africans and their descendants survived enslavement. In other words, she was confident there would come a time when someone wanted to know what allowed the enslaved to endure with their bodies and minds bruised but intact. Such a study as this, she believed, could produce race literature. Matthews's hope was that race literature, when consistently published, would eventually be considered "universal literature" (173). As well, Matthews recognized that race literature might finally prove that Africans and their descendants were not intellectually inferior as had been suggested by race science. Henry Louis Gates Jr. explains why Black women like Matthews argued so vehemently for the creation of race literature:

> Writing, many Europeans argued, stood alone among the fine arts as the most salient repository of "genius," the visible sign of reason itself. . . . We *know* reason by its writing, by its representations. . . . most Europeans privileged *writing*—in their writings about Africans, at least—as the principal measure of the Africans' humanity, their capacity for progress, their very place in the great chain of being. ("Writing 'Race'" 9; emphasis in original)

Matthews was not unaware of the racialized assessments concerning the discursive abilities of Africans during and after the Enlightenment. Matthews also understood how the discursive arts can be infinite. Thus, she was determined in "The Value" to emphasize why it is imperative that Black authors use transformational writing as a form of uplift and counterprotest.

Race literature, in Matthews's words, need not be solely focused on "race or creed" ("Value" 173) as mere abstractions to be analyzed dispassionately; rather, race and creed should be examined and written about to explore the psychological damage of enslavement. Matthews observed, "our history and individuality as a people, not only provides material for masterly treatment; but would seem to make a Race Literature a necessity as an outlet for the unnaturally suppressed inner lives which our people have been compelled to lead" (173). Her declaration was not a simple one. She wanted Black authors to use race literature to take a deeper exploration into the psyches of people who had once been forcibly owned by other humans over centuries. Voicing what enslavement and limited freedom meant had proven difficult even for Black authors, so the depth of that pain was often treated with objectivity rather than raw emotion. Matthews suggested, therefore, that a healing transformation of the psyche might be possible when Black authors tapped into these most troubling and loathsome realms. Matthews's 1893 story "Aunt Lindy" attempted to reveal the inner lives of the formerly enslaved. The narrator describes how the married couple in "Aunt Lindy" were unable to outwardly mourn for the children taken from them during their enslavement: "Lindy and Joel, who years before had seen babes torn from their breasts and sold—[were] powerless to utter a complaint or appeal, whipped for the tears they shed" (3). Later, the narrator reveals yet another tragedy borne out of the strictures of enslavement and freedom. Even in their freedom, Lindy and Joel are not able to outwardly grieve the loss of stolen children: "But in the busy life that freedom gave them, off, when work was done and the night of life threw its waning shadows around them, their tears would fall for the scattered voices—they would mourn o'er their past oppression. Yet they hid their grief from an unsympathizing generation, and the memory of their oppressors awoke but to the call of fitful retrospection" (3). In the quiet space of their home, Lindy and Joel can express grief. However, any public expression of it is not allowed. Such constraining of emotions fails to acknowledge the harm and sorrow experienced by the enslaved and the newly freed. Thus, Matthews articulated a literary vision in which acknowledgment of these traumas is transmitted from writer to reader.

The pain associated with enslavement was so acute that even some Black authors who had sophisticated literacy skills had trouble describing it. This Matthews did not acknowledge in her speech, but later writers have. In his 2013 book, *Word by Word: Emancipation and the Act of Writing*, Christopher Hager describes the process whereby the enslaved after emancipation negotiated linguistically the trauma experienced due to enslavement. He turns to Adam Plummer, an enslaved Black man who kept an "eccentric diary" (79), to explore the difficulty of using words to describe the trauma of enslavement. Plummer's diary provided a snapshot of an enslaved man's life on the cusp of impending freedom. In it, Plummer "recorded the births, marriages, and deaths of members of his family, his owner, and Abraham Lincoln . . . as well as copied down parts of letters he exchanged with his wife, Emily" (79). He also wrote down two titles in his diary: "'The Life of Adam Plummer and Emily Plummer' and 'This is the History of Adam Francis Plummer'" (79)—presumably, the titles of his unfinished and unpublished autobiography. In addition to the diary's record of dates and events, Hager describes moments when Plummer tried to record his "suffering" as a slave (80). This occurred when Plummer recorded the dates when his wife and children were due to be sold:

> "'1849 the 24 of March Emily and 4 Children for Sale' and 'November 25 Day 1851 Emily Plummer and five Childrens who whous sold publick' . . . 'The said woman was bought by Mrs. M A Thomson in the Washington City 16 street North to the plac Meaderen Hill. There she loeh for a short time about four years and banished form my Eyes. 1855 if thn wrote shorte letters to See or hear forme her, but I hear form not.'" (qtd. in Hager 80)

Plummer recorded facts about his wife and children's pending sale and actual sale dates and his attempts to communicate with his wife. Familiarity with written language provided him the words to do this. The facts are devastating, and they convey much of his heartache. Yet words do not provide him the language to fill in the psychic gaps. Did he feel physical pain when he learned about the sale of his wife and children? Did he shed tears? Was he enraged? Surely, Plummer was upset that he was separated from his wife and children. Recording the dates of their impending and actual sale dates provided evidence of his suffering. Nevertheless, what was his mental state? One has to surmise his mental condition because Plummer did not express the full weight of his loss.

Plummer also copied letters into his diary from his wife, which had been written by someone else since she was illiterate (Hager 80). In one instance, his wife admitted that she was "'unhappy,'" and in another instance she "'hope[s] [he] is better than [her]'" (qtd. in Hager 80). Both were obviously upset about their separation, yet neither seemed able to directly address just how painful their separation was. "Unhappy" described her state of being, but not the enormity of her loss. Perhaps the gaps do, indeed, tell the story. Plummer and his wife were eventually reunited after Emancipation and the Civil War (81). Matthews suggested that the story of people of African descent in America is a story rife with drama and intrigue. Stories like Plummer's are one among many that could help tell the story of bondage and freedom. Unfortunately, Matthews surmised, no Black author had yet to capture the story of enslavement and freedom. That Plummer's diary and correspondence with his wife illustrate the difficulty of expressing what it means to deal with ongoing tragedy even when one is literate is evidence of the difficult job ahead for Black authors. For instance, in the section where he recorded the tentative and actual dates of sale of his wife and children, Plummer did not rage against slavery or white people, nor did his wife in the correspondence Plummer recorded in his diary. Between the lines and omissions, the couple must have felt anger and despair. Plummer and his wife's difficulty in expressing their most private emotions does not negate the fact that, as Matthews suggested, Black writers need to explore the interior lives of Black people, which includes how they lived through enslavement and how they were living through restricted freedom after Emancipation.

Matthews attempted to explore the inner lives of Black characters in her short fiction, including in "Aunt Lindy" when it is revealed that the man who took Lindy and Joel's children away is "Marse Jim," whom she has been asked to care for after a devastating fire ravaged the town where they lived. Once Lindy recognizes her old master's face, the narrator describes her reactions as full of rage and turmoil: "Her blood was afire, her tall frame swayed, her long, bony hands trembled like an animal at bay; she stepped back as if to spring upon him" (7). Lindy does not act on her rage, but Matthews allowed her to have feelings that were typically suppressed. The scenes in which Lindy is given permission to experience pain are the places where Matthews's vision for race literature to unveil the "suppressed inner lives of Black people" appear at the intersection of literacy, performance, and transformation. Kerstin Rudolph suggests that "The depiction of Aunt Lindy . . . represent[s] strong incentives to take the folksy slave representations out of the hands of white authors. Looking to unappreciated heroes and fictionalizing common black people in dignified ways emerge, then, as a pressing task for black writers, and asserting the right to represent antebellum slave experiences stirred them to write as activists" (114). The narrator of the story reveals that, even as Aunt Lindy deals with her trauma, she remains constrained by the customs of the dominant society to mask those feelings of anger and resentment quickly. However, Rudolph is right to argue that Matthews as a Black woman author provided Aunt Lindy with depth that white authors had not given to their Black characters. Thus, "Aunt Lindy" becomes one manifestation of Matthews's vision for race literature. Elizabeth McHenry writes that Matthews was "inspired by the literary accomplishments of women such as those behind the Woman's Era" and "believed that other black women, whose attendance at the Congress underscored their readiness to act and desire for direction, would inspire and sustain a literary movement that would alter the consciousness of the nation" (197). One way to influence the "consciousness of the nation" was for future Black authors to dismantle the old Black types that were part of the white imagination.

CHALLENGING "NEGRO TYPES"

Matthews like Cooper wanted literature to reject what were then called "Negro types." The portrayal of Black people as slovenly, unintelligible, criminal, lustful, or violent bothered Matthews. Thus, she argued for race literature that was not only representative of Black people like French literature was of the French and Chinese literature of the Chinese, but also literature that could forevermore confer respect on Black people:

> When the foundations of such a literature shall have been properly laid, the benefit to be derived will be at once apparent. There will be a revelation to our people, and it will enlarge our scope, make us better

known wherever real lasting culture exists, will undermine and utterly drive out the traditional Negro in dialect—the subordinate, the servant as the type representing a race whose numbers are now far into the millions. ("Value" 173–74)

Matthews believed, as European and American whites had made clear that a people who had not written "great" literature would never be respected or considered civilized, a distinctively Black literature was needed. Her call for writing race literature was similar to what Henry Louis Gates Jr. explains as the need for authentic Black voices: "The recording of an authentic black voice—a voice of deliverance from the deafening discursive silence which an enlightened Europe cited to prove the absence of the African's humanity—was the millennial instrument of transformation through which the African would become the European, the slave become the ex-slave, brute animal become human being" ("Writing 'Race'" 11–12). As Gates highlights, the outward expression of humanity is a discursive activity, and it is one that Black writers like Cooper embraced and advanced. Matthews also believed that the continual creation of race literature would someday erase in the white imagination the image of the ignorant vernacular-speaking Black person, although some of her successors would come to embrace forms of Black vernacular and reject such notions about linguistic inferiority.

In her section of the speech on "Negro types," Matthews mocked white American authors such as Mark Twain, Harriet Beecher Stowe, and William Dean Howells, who had produced acclaimed literature and whose caricatures of Black people were therefore granted authority even though those portrayals were poorly conceived and lacked a basis in actual Black life. She critiqued Twain's *Pudd'nhead Wilson*, Stowe's *Uncle Tom's Cabin*, and Howells's *An Imperative Duty* as failed attempts at capturing the spirit and lived experiences of Black people. Furthermore, in a scathing rebuke of Francis C. Phillips's "A Question of Color," Matthews rejected the story's premise in which a refined Black Englishman is married to a white prostitute who ultimately rejects him because he is Black. His reply to her rejection is to "say his prayers at her feet at night and morning notwithstanding" (qtd. in Matthews, "Value" 176). Matthews called the description of their union and his reaction nonsense. Later, she asked the audience for patience while she described one more example of a white author's failed attempt at Black representation. This example was of a white woman who wrote about the condition of women in America but failed to give adequate space to Black women. When this writer gave some attention to Black women, the representation was so horrible as to leave Matthews appalled. Her response: "All this is the outcome in the nineteenth-century of the highest expressions of Anglo-Saxon acumen, criticism, and understanding of the powers of Negroes of America!" ("Value" 176). Since white authors did not know enough about Black people to write about them fairly and adequately, she felt free to mock their literary efforts and call on Black writers to write more informed and imaginative works that feature Black people. In doing so, Matthews called for a race literature that might, in Kerstin Rudolph's words, "heal the battered psychology of a recently emancipated people" (112).

"THE PREJUDICE OF COLOR"

While Matthews rebuked white authors for their depictions of the Black race and its dialects, she also reprimanded white people for evaluating the color of Black people's skin rather than their moral character. Matthews recognized that a racial caste system is implemented by white people to distinguish themselves from Black people and to justify enslavement and the establishment of the Black Codes. Caste and color defined intelligence, manners, speech, style, and beauty by gradations of skin color with white skin color being the most prized and dark brown skin color the most degraded. She asked the audience to consider how color prejudice operates in the public sphere:

> The prejudice of color! Not condition, not character, not capacity for artistic development, not the possibility of emerging from savagery into Christianity, not these, but the "Prejudice of Color." . . . Since our reception on the continent, men have cried out against this inhuman prejudice; granting that, a man may improve his condition, accumulate wealth, become wise and upright, merciful and just as an infidel or Christian, but they despair because he can not change his color, as if it were possible for the oppressor to change his wicked heart. ("Value" 171)

Matthews scoffed at the idea that color should determine one's fate in life. If she and other Black people were to believe that color determines character, then one drop of Black blood would condemn Black people to the shadows forever, which meant Black people will never really be an enlightened *people*. To be Black is to be marked forever. Yet Matthews knew color is not a determining factor as it relates to intelligence and good moral character. What is elective and determinative is how one chooses to treat others. She made the point that one is not born racist; one is made a racist and chooses to remain so in the face of competing knowledge. Therefore, evaluating an external characteristic that is fixed is absurd, but Matthews remained hopeful. As a skilled orator, she appealed to her audience's sense of righteous indignation. She spoke to the audience in a language they could understand. By the nineteenth century, race and racism were constructs meant to keep Black people under the control of the white majority. To express her frustration but also to reveal the continual motivations for the dichotomization of the races, Matthews turned to Black rhetorical traditions to connect to her audience, particularly the practice of "signifying." She "signified" in this section and throughout the speech to expose the hypocrisy of racism and its utter ridiculousness. Keith Gilyard and Adam Banks describe the ethos of signifying: "To signify is to make meaning within a Black rhetorical world that exists alongside and in relation to a white one" (56). When Matthews declared the futility in the argument that skin color determines hierarchy but that wickedness is not endemic to whiteness, she offered the penultimate signifier undercutting such racist bunk.

RACIAL RESPONSIBILITY: AN APPEAL TO EMOTIONS

Despite the racial climate at the time Matthews was speaking, she still believed Black authors were poised to take control of their literary lives, which in turn could positively impact their lives and the lives of all Black people. Throughout her speech, she encouraged Black authors to produce great and authentic stories by sometimes cajoling or scolding them. She asked the conference attendees to consider how they were building on the literary legacies of their predecessors. She challenged her audience and appealed to their communal obligations to prod them into participating actively in reconstructing a viable and valuable history for the preservation of Black life. Matthews sought to persuade the audience to be knowledge producers rather than information consumers. As a skilled rhetor, she was participating in rhetorical acts that are centuries-old by appealing to emotions that link the individual to his and her community in hopes of effecting real change. Catherine Hobbs calls this process "effective literacy," meaning a level of literacy that enables a user to effect change in her own life and in society, writing that "'The power to act in society,' a phrase suggesting both empowerment and transformation, encompasses many of the functions we mean by the term effective literacy" (1–2). To be an effective orator or writer, Aristotle recognized a rhetor must employ persuasive appeals around character, emotions, and logic. At pivotal moments in her speech on race literature,

Matthews appealed to emotions she hoped would elicit action. As Aristotle suggested, rhetors had to use language effectively to produce in their audience the right kind of mood, which in turn can help strengthen an orator's persuasive appeals. According to Aristotle, "persuasion may come from the hearers, when the speech so stirs their emotions. Our judgments when we are pleased and friendly are not the same as when we are pained and hostile. It is towards producing these effects, as we maintain, that present-day writers on rhetoric direct the whole of their efforts" (1356a). Skilled rhetors must know how to evoke the right kinds of emotions from their audiences to have the most impact. In other words, a rhetor must decide which words might stimulate political action, social change, or creativity.

Matthews, it seems, decided the right kind of persuasive appeal was to link advocacy to her audience's sense of duty to themselves and their communities. Rather than allow her listeners to remain passive, Matthews required them to be active listeners whom she entreated to write race literature. She already knew that some of the women attending the convention had contributed to race literature, and she wanted others to write as well. She also wanted them to write literature that can activate tangible results, so that the social and economic conditions for the race will change. Words that affirm their conditions but illustrate their resolve can help solve the race problem confronting them at the end of the nineteenth century and on into the twentieth century. Intentional practices such as these locate transformational literacy at the heart of Matthews's rhetorical impulses. Matthews's speech embodies Lauren Heap and Kate Vieira's statement that "critical discourse . . . [can] help writers and readers develop empowered identities, social visons, and social change" (38).

To help the convention attendees make sense of Matthews's question and to appeal to their sense of duty, she cited a number of Black authors who had already contributed to race literature. She then spent a considerable amount of time explaining the significance of the journalistic contributions of Black authors. Matthews believed the efforts of members of the Black press and the Black owners of periodicals ought to be better supported by members of their race ("Value" 181). She mused over the juxtaposition between progress and regression if the members of the race did not support their own press. Matthews understood that actual commitment to racial uplift must also derive from financial not merely verbal support. As a journalist, Matthews was aware of the need for financial support of the Black press. She wrote for Black-owned periodicals, including *The Woman's Era*, which had "begun in 1894 . . . [and] became the official organ of the National Association of Colored Women in 1896" (McHenry 190). Elizabeth McHenry believes "*The Woman's Era* is representative of the ways that black women created through their literary work a collaborative space in which to represent themselves and expand their identities" (190). In the late nineteenth century, *The Woman's Era* was a unique publication, being written both by and for Black women. In white periodicals, Black women were often described as loose and sexually uninhibited, which was a direct result of a racist system justifying its brutal treatment of Black women. *The Woman's Era* was one small way that Black women writers could take ownership of their narratives and present positive depictions of Black female identity. When Black women had the ability to control whom they interacted with and how they would be perceived by members inside and outside their communities, they did so with a zeal that is apparent in *The Woman's Era*. One method by which these women did so was by banding together in women's clubs, so that the periodical's editors and publishers, Josephine St. Pierre Ruffin and Florida R. Ridley, described it in an early issue as "the only paper in America published in the interest of women's clubs" (7).

Trying to attract advertisers, Ruffin and Ridley described their readers as being "particularly among women of the refined and educated classes" (7). The two were among a group of "refined" Black women who were dedicated to uplifting the race. Their hope was *The Woman's Era* would act as site of contact between writers and readers who could all be transformed by the work of each other. Matthews's contributions to *The Woman's Era*'s Eminent Women Series is an example of the transformational possibilities inherent in literacy. Her 1896 profile of Harriet Tubman is both information and inspiration. About Tubman, she wrote, "let us all meet in the benign presence of this great leader, in days and actions that caused strong men to quail, this almost unknown, almost unsung, 'Black Joan of Arc.' . . . We owe it to our children to uncover from partial oblivion and unconscious indifference the great characters within our own ranks" ("Harriet Tubman" paragraphs 3–4). This form of transformational literacy acted as a reminder to Black people that their history included great women and men among them. There are many reasons for them to be proud of the race.

Since Matthews was a contributor to *The Woman's Era*, she most likely believed in its informational and transformational potential. This likely explains the turn toward chastisement in the speech when she scolded the audience for not financially supporting the Black press. She exclaimed, "our struggling journalists not only find themselves on the losing side, but as if to add to their thankless labor, they oftentimes receive the contemptuous regard of the people who should enthusiastically rally to their support" ("Value" 181). One assumes that the audience members were concerned about racial uplift, but Matthews recognized she needed to prod them to become more active in their uplift efforts. By supporting newspapers and periodicals owned and authored by Black people, they could better harness their intellectual and economic resources. Hence, Matthews demanded that attendees examine their communal responsibilities. Her request was twofold. First, the admonishment allowed her to indirectly ask the attendees to continue to support *The Woman's Era*, and second, it allowed her to directly request they support other Black-owned newspapers and magazines lest they be willing to continue to give the white white-owned newspapers and magazines their money even though those editors rarely hired Black journalists. The following sums up Matthews's responses to apathetic support: "If our newspapers and magazines do not amount to anything," she emphasized, "it is because our people do not demand anything of better quality from their own. It is because they strain their purses supporting those white papers that are and always will be independent of any income derived from us. Our contributions to such journals are spasmodic and uncertain" (181). She recognized that financial and communal support was necessary if Black people ever wanted to produce quality work but also to sustain their work over time, writing, "It is hard for the bulk of our people to see this; it is even hard to prove to them that in supporting such journals, published by the dominant class, we often pay for what are not only vehicles of insult to our manhood and womanhood, but we assist in propagating or supporting false impressions of ourselves or our less fortunate brothers" (181). Matthews attempted to appeal to the attendees rationally. Why support a white press that demeans them, she asked, and then complain when those periodicals publish false stories or highly inflammatory ones? Such behavior, it seemed to Matthews, was not logical especially since Black people could use their dollars to support their own efforts to uplift the race.

This may have been a risky move as some of the attendees might have been implicated in her critique, but she may have felt that speaking judiciously and logically about the role of Black people in participating in a mythology surrounding Black inferiority was necessary. According to Aristotle, "persuasion is effected through the speech itself when we have proved a truth or an apparent truth by means of the persuasive arguments suitable to the case in question" (1356a). The conference attendees would have been keenly aware how the white press criminalized and demonized Black people. Matthews used reason to try to prove that indifference, apathy, and economic support of white newspapers were causing Black people to work against their own social, economic, and political interests. After listening to her speech, if her audience saw that white editors who refused to hire Black writers or to publish articles in the service of Black people were doing all members of the Black community harm, then perhaps they would more vigorously support the Black press. Such reasoning, Matthews hoped, would influence the attendees to support their own, and in doing so, it might change how Black people were represented in the popular (white) press. Shirley Wilson Logan defines the audience as "those Matthews wanted to reach because of their potential as agents for change" (140). To make her appeal more tangible, she praised Black editors and writers such as T. Thomas Fortune, E. Bruce, and Ida B. Wells-Barnett as exemplars of great talent working to uplift the race discursively and in practice. Everyone had a role to play; they could support writers, become authors, and/or continue to write to uplift the race.

THE ROLE OF WOMEN

The last section of Matthews's speech focused on the role of Black women in supporting and contributing to race literature. It is not a long section, but the sentiment expressed is an important one. Matthews declared "woman's part in Race Literature, as in Race building, is the most important part and has been so in all ages" ("Value" 184). Black progress, for Matthews, could never exist without the aid of Black women as they alone bore the future of the race; it was their bodies and their nurturing where Black existence begins and where it must continue. Black women were thus duty-bound to use their intellects and literacies to change the nation. Brittney C. Cooper sums up this process of transformation, writing that "Race women took it at as their political and intellectual work to give shape and meaning to the Black body in social and political terms, to make it legible as an entity with infinite value and social worth. In doing so, they hoped to create livable terms upon which black women could live and engage socially" (21). As a writer focused on using her literacy skills to produce new knowledge and to contest racist ideas about Black people, Matthews also looked beyond the self to encourage other Black women to engage their energies in this work as well. As she repeatedly made clear in the speech, Black people could not rely on white authors to write objectively and humanely about Black experiences. Hence, Black women writers must lead the charge. Matthews emphasized her point by returning to an earlier thesis regarding the failures of white authors. She noted how easy it was for them to "caricature the Negro" and how difficult it was for them to depict the best of Black people ("Value" 184). It was incumbent then upon Black women to do that work, either by writing it themselves or by giving birth to a generation of authors who can be the creators of race literature that will honor the race. In that setting, as Shirley Wilson Logan notes, Matthews "faced an audience of peers, certainly roused and ready to respond and already responding in a variety of ways" (141).

LITERACY AS TRANSFORMATIONAL

Matthews's speech was multifaceted. It was part condemnation and part call to arms. It highlighted her oratorical skills and her intellectual acumen. It illustrated her understanding of the power of literacy to effect change. Reading her transcribed speech gives a clear indication of her purpose. She intended to stir the crowd to influence them to act on her participatory call for action. As a woman who was keenly aware of the dangers of inaction, Matthews warned the audience that inaction would delay their hopes for change just as supporting the white press would continue to work against their own interests. Thus, with conviction and cajoling, Matthews explained how writing about the best of Black people and revealing their "suppressed inner lives" could be transformational. No people could emerge out of enslavement by relying on white authors to author their recovery from such a traumatic time. It would take the literacy skills of Matthews and others with the intent to transform lives to have real impact. As Royster notes, "literacy has enabled African American women to create whirlpools in the pond of public discourse.... This image suggests, that, with the acquisition of literacy, African American women were able to amass energy and concentrate it—deliberately and with persuasive intent—in support of sociopolitical action" (*Traces of a Stream* 42).

Matthews is emblematic of a continuing spirit demanding change for Black people in the late nineteenth century. Her literacy practices reflected an abiding faith in the power of the word, and she used this knowledge to her advantage. At a time when many women, both Black and white, were expected to stay in the domestic sphere, Matthews recognized that home and civic duties were not mutually exclusive. For Black women intellectuals like Matthews, trying to locate spaces where education, family, and community responsibilities were combined as powerful triads, and she and other Black women writers proved that Black women could be dutiful wives, social activists, and civic-minded. Matthews was part of a small cadre of Black women engaged in discussions about the race who considered themselves of high moral character and thus prepared to show the newly freed that full freedom and justice might be earned by the pen and in their daily efforts. Matthews spoke her truth, adapting the linguistic practices of the white middle class as her mode of communication, though she utilized that communicative style to fight injustice. Literacy for Matthews was an active mediation between writer and audience meant to spur individual action with communal outcomes. In adopting this point of view, Matthews like Cooper recognized the transformational value inherent in the literacy process. The knowledge they and other Black women acquired by learning to read and write was returned to the communities they served, hoping their individual investments would provide long-term outcomes. This form of transformational literacy was one they hoped would be taken up by other members of the race who sought to use words to inspire change and action.

By the end of the nineteenth century, Cooper and Matthews had witnessed a remarkable transformation: the end of slavery and the dawn of freedom. Freedom had been granted, but many of the newly freed were unprepared for life as freedwomen and -men. Their unpreparedness had nothing to do with their intellectual abilities. It had everything to do with the denial of education and the lack of literacy instruction while they were enslaved. Their initial inability to transition to a comfortable life devoid of forced servitude was exacerbated by a number of economic, social, and political factors. Cooper and Matthews knew life was not going to be easy for Black people after the Civil War. Even though literacy rates were increasing and the Freedmen's Bureau had established colleges for Black women and men, the majority of the masses were just looking for their place among other free women and men in America. Knowing the difficulties that were behind them and recognizing the difficulties that lay ahead, Cooper and Matthews wrote about the ways that the literary imagination could help the masses form new identities and embody values and morals that were truer to life than had been previously represented in the literature and mythology of the white imagination. In their discourse practices, they sought to employ their middle-class and transformational literacies to motivate their peers to act and to inspire members of the race to improve and transform their lives. Cultivating a literary imagination among the learned and the creative was their method for helping to cultivate identities that were neither servile nor savage. Reacting against the failures of some white authors who were unwilling to write honestly about Black people and their own experiences as women on the racial margins gave them the impetus to encourage their own to go out and write great American stories.

Chapter Two

LITERACY AND EDUCATION

Katherine D. C. Tillman and Pauline E. Hopkins

Like their contemporaries Anna Julia Cooper and Victoria Earle Matthews, Katherine D. C. Tillman and Pauline E. Hopkins seriously considered how writing race literature might shape the consciousness of the nation. Recognizing that the world around them remained fraught for Black people, Tillman and Hopkins used their literary imaginations to help the race negotiate a time when lynchings were used to terrorize Black communities and the US Supreme Court's *Plessy v. Ferguson* decision gave national legal weight to the separate but equal doctrine. In effect, the 1890s gave white citizens the right to discriminate against their fellow Black citizens by legal means and through social custom. The promises of Reconstruction and the Thirteenth, Fourteenth, and Fifteenth amendments to the US Constitution—known as the Civil War Amendments—were rendered null by white northern apathy and southern bitterness. Yet Tillman and Hopkins were not cowed by the political landscape confronting them in the 1890s and early 1900s. Their vision for an America that was truly democratic remained part of their hope for a brighter future, so they answered the call of their Woman's Era peers. In 1892, Cooper had expressed how the Black race's peculiar position as formerly enslaved just might help America reconcile its democratic ideals, on the one hand, and confront its hypocrisy, on the other hand. Such introspection from a literary perspective would center African Americans' humanity and simultaneously give America its own literary masters. In 1895, Matthews had outlined a vision for race literature designed to give Black people agency. Race literature, broadly conceived, could give the race opportunities to refute and revise histories written by white authors that were harmful to the collective consciousness of Black and white alike.

Accepting the premise that writing could have transformational results, Tillman and Hopkins turned to it as one way to uplift the race and contest racial oppression. Tillman wrote poems, essays, and short fiction in service to racial uplift. Hopkins was even more prolific, writing in many genres as well. In this chapter, I analyze two of Tillman's novellas: *Beryl Weston's Ambition: The Story of an Afro-American Girl's Life*, published in two installments in 1893, and *Clancy Street*, published in serial form in 1898 and 1899. Both were published by the *A.M.E. Church Review*, the African Methodist Episcopal Church's official journal. Each of these novellas is centered around literacy activities occurring at home and in school, all of which encourage middle-class values in the pursuit of self-knowledge with communal aims. Also in this chapter, I examine Hopkins's novel *Of One Blood*, published in serialized form in 1902 and 1903 in the *Colored American Magazine*. *Of One Blood* is a diasporic novel linking Africa-descended people back to their ancestral homeland in Ethiopia to reveal the intellectual prowess of both Africans and Black Americans. Central to the thematic concerns in Tillman's novellas and Hopkins's novel are the revelatory outgrowths of literate minds at work and the transformational possibilities of literacy and education in the right situational contexts. In many ways, their fiction operates as the physical manifestation of Cooper's and Matthews's race and literary aims.

KATHERINE D. C. TILLMAN'S *BERYL WESTON'S AMBITION*

In *Beryl Weston's Ambition*, Tillman presented an idealized picture of an industrious, smart, and proud Black family, particularly the Weston and Warren families. For the most part, the characters who inhabit the novella strive to be decent people and are religious-minded. The tiny few who falter are given grace and time for reclamation. Literacy and education propel the characters forward, and knowledge seekers are rewarded. The first scene in *Beryl Weston's Ambition* occurs "at one of the leading Afro-American Colleges in the United States" (207). Beryl Weston, the sixteen-year-old protagonist, has just learned that her mother has died. Unfortunately, she will have to leave college and go home to help take care of her father and young siblings. She learns about her fate after reading a letter written by her mother prior to her death. In the letter, Beryl's mother asks "a hard thing" of her daughter: "to give up College, and study at home, where you can look after the comfort of your father and the children" (222). Beryl is initially heartbroken. She does not want to stop attending college, but she eventually accepts her fate. Once home, she continues her studies, remains focused on learning, and expands her knowledge with the aid of Dr. Warren, a local doctor who helps Beryl continue her education and whom she eventually marries. During her morning routine at home, she "recited lessons in geometry and Greek to

Dr. Warren between the hours of 10 and 12" (223). At night, she continues to participate in literacy activities for both herself and the family domestic, Binie, by "read[ing] aloud from some interesting book" and "help[ing] Binie with her English studies" (230). Beryl fulfills her mother's wishes to help with the family by educating her siblings: "she heard the children's lessons from 9 to 10 o'clock in the morning" (230). By doing so, she guides their literacy learning. She becomes their surrogate mother, actively influencing the literacy practices of her siblings (Robbins 56–57). Beryl is transformed by literacy and transmits the benefits of that literacy transformation to her siblings.

Beryl's character is a curious one. At sixteen years of age, she is very studious, so much so that at one point when she is asked by one of her good friends to attend a revival, she turns her friend down so she can study more, saying, "'no thank you, I have my Caesar to learn'" (Tillman, *Beryl Weston* 214). At that moment, Beryl wants to learn more than she wants a religious experience. She is known at the college to be the "smartest girl in the whole school" (208). Her goal "was to become an instructress in the modern languages and higher mathematics" (217). She is inspired to teach by the principal of her college, Miss Hand, a woman she deeply admires. Even after she leaves college, Beryl is invested in learning. She is guided by Dr. Warren's instruction, and, for a time, she is an educator outside the physical boundaries of the classroom by educating her siblings and Binie at home in Tennessee. Eventually, Beryl will become a teacher at her former school.

By the end of the novella, Beryl embodies all that is right about a young Black woman as defined by race literature. The death of her mother transforms her strong desire to achieve and leads her to familial acts of instruction and a communal desire to help uplift the race. Through the challenges she faces, she illustrates how young Black women can develop intellectually, spiritually, and communally. Her intellectual maturation occurs with the aid of Dr. Warren, who "conducted his talented pupil safely through the most difficult theorems found in her geometry, and taught her to wrestle successfully with Greek and German verbs" (232). The narrator reveals that Beryl reads classic literature with Dr. Warren, noting, "together they read all the best modern poets; sighed over the hapless Elaine and her hopeless passion for Sir Lancelot; held up to scorn his friendship with the beautiful Queen Guinevere; admired to the highest extent that exquisite poem known as 'Aurora Leigh'" (232). For Tillman, they are reading the right kind of literature written by some of the most respected British writers. Dr. Warren guides her education in a similar way Robbins describes middle-class white mothers doing for their children, though Beryl is not a child. Middle-class white mothers were concerned not only that their children learn how to read and write, but also that what they were reading had an impact on their morals and behaviors (Robbins 15). As a Black woman writing in the 1890s, Tillman too recognized that modeling learning processes and behaviors and alluding to specific texts served literary and material ends. Thus, Tillman shows her awareness of the transformational possibilities of literacy. For instance, Dr. Warren and Beryl were reading classical books and great poetry, meaning Beryl's intellectual development will be enhanced by reading classical texts. All of the educational instruction Beryl receives from her college days to her life back in Westland is intended to shape her into a representative Black woman, one whom other Black youths reading the novella could admire and imitate.

Beryl is guided by her instructors at college, Dr. Warren, and other community members; she also acts as a guide. Readers are told she instructs her brother and sister, Joseph and Ellen, and can assume she chooses only texts that will enhance their knowledge and improve their character. In fact, readers at least know she discusses classic children's tales with them such as *Cinderella, Little Red Riding Hood*, and *Jack and the Beanstalk*. These are moral tales that teach children that wrongdoing never wins in the end. Good and respectable behavior will be rewarded. She also guides Binie's education. Beryl is a good person who is instructing others by guiding their literacy practices. Because she is so consumed by education, Beryl dedicates her life to the pursuit and distribution of knowledge. At one point in the novella when a prominent Black preacher, Harold Griswold, proposes to her, Beryl tells him she cannot marry him, saying, "'I never intended to be a minister's wife; I am too ambitious. It is now my pet dream to enter the literary world'" (Tillman, *Beryl Weston* 240). Beryl wants to be a published writer and becomes one when it is revealed that "some of her poetry found its way into one or two popular magazines. One poem entitled 'Flowers of Memory' found its way into the heart of the public" (244). Beryl understands if she wants to influence more than the members of her local community, she will need to broaden her reach, thus extending the beneficiaries of her literacy skills beyond the confines of her community in Westland, Tennessee.

THE RIGHT KIND OF SPEECH AND THE RIGHT KIND OF EDUCATION

Throughout *Beryl Weston's Ambition*, the narrator reiterates the importance of a proper education. In one of the early scenes, Cora, a close friend of Beryl's, is admonished for not using proper grammar. The narrator remarks,

"Cora, who paid little regard to the rules of English grammar . . . rather prided herself upon the large amount of slang that she had at her command" (208). "Proper grammar" was then and is now used to delineate class and intellect. It is not clear in this scene what slang Cora uses; however, readers know the narrator disapproves of it. Linguistically, Cora is behaving out of turn. In the later twentieth century, speech attitudes became more inclusive, as in Geneva Smitherman's explanation of the nuances of Black speech: "Black English . . . is a language mixture, adapted to the conditions of slavery and discrimination, a combination of language and style interwoven with and inextricable from Afro-American culture" (3). The narrator of this novella is speaking as a late nineteenth-century advocate of race literature, however, so the signal in this scene is that readers should not speak in the local vernacular as Cora does. It is obvious that Cora, at least at the beginning, does not quite have the right attitude about education, but other characters do. For example, Beryl's father, Jim Weston, is illiterate when he first meets the woman who will become her mother. Though initially enslaved, her mother had learned to read and write "by stealth" (Tillman, *Beryl Weston* 213). After being freed, her mother "had spent much time in study . . . and was teaching in the log schoolhouse, at Westland, when Jim first met and loved her" (213). By teaching him to read, she passes on her literacy skills and knowledge to her husband, who refines his speech and continues to improve his literacy skills:

> In Jim Weston's speech there was abundant proof that seventeen years of association with a woman of refined speech like Beryl's mother was, had not been wholly lost upon her uneducated husband. She had not only taught him how to read, write, and cipher, but had persuaded him to take *The Yankee Blade* and a popular magazine known as *The Arena*, so that he might be well informed of the vital topics of the hour. (221)

Jim's evolving speech patterns and reading material demonstrate Tillman's abiding faith in the transformational value of literacy. Proximity to his wife and her direct instruction transform Jim from a hard-working though illiterate man to a literate and informed person. Jim's transformation signals that race is not an impediment to learning. Not only does he learn to read, but he also learns how to comprehend what he is reading and to build a foundation of what Jenny Cook-Gumperz calls "socially approvable knowledge" (1).

Reading newspapers and magazines ensures that Jim learns about the most current political and social matters, which informs how he interacts with his family and community. Henry Giroux explains the social and political value of literacy and its concomitant critical literacy: "in the broadest sense, literacy is a myriad of discursive forms of cultural competencies that construct and make available the various relations and experiences that exist between learners and the world. In a more specific sense, critical literacy is both a narrative for agency as well as a referent for critique" (155). Although Jim is a successful provider for the family, Beryl's mother wants her husband to also be a knowledgeable person who is politically and socially aware. For late nineteenth-century Black families, learning should be a communal endeavor, with one eye toward uplift and the other eye on acquiring knowledge and where appropriate producing knowledge.

There are additional places in the novella where literacy activities are highlighted. When Beryl leaves college, Miss Hand, the principal, gives her a volume of poetry (Tillman, *Beryl Weston* 209). When Beryl is asked to attend a revival but refuses her friend's invitation, she feels guilty, and when she can no longer read Caesar, she "took up a half-finished essay, which she was preparing to read before the Alcott Literary Society, of which she was a member" (215). Elizabeth McHenry writes about the historical significance of literary societies for Black people:

> In the late 1820s and early 1830s, free blacks in the urban North formed literary societies as a place in which to read and experiment with rhetorical strategies. Embracing the Enlightenment stress on the importance of the life of the mind, they turned to reading as an invaluable method of acquiring knowledge, and to writing as a means of asserting identity, recording information, and communicating with a black public that ranged from literate to the semiliterate to the illiterate. (24)

Although *Beryl Weston's Ambition* takes place during and after Reconstruction, literary societies were still then a vital part of Black communities especially for educated elite and middle-class Black women. McHenry adds that "the dates of the greatest activity of . . . the Boston Literary society coincided with the black women's club movement, which began in the last decade of the nineteenth century and remained vibrant into the first decade of the twentieth century" (184). Among the activities that McHenry says occurred in the literary societies, lecturing and delivering papers were essential parts of the intellectual development of their members. In the novella, Beryl is working on a paper she will deliver to members of the Alcott Literary society. In school and in her social life, her transformational literacy activities coalesce around self-improvement with communal aims.

WRITING AND READING THE RIGHT AUTHORS

Earlier in Beryl's life, when she was home on a summer break from school, she had convinced her mother, who was showing signs of illness, to leave the house and go out into the orchard to be with Beryl and her siblings. There, Beryl "would read aloud passages from her favorite authors" (Tillman, *Beryl Weston* 218). Beryl offers Binie, who is disfigured from a "horse accident, something to read to take her mind off her troubles. She gives her the *Ladies Home Journal*" (225). When Beryl comes to the realization that she will have to stay home instead of returning to college, she writes letters to "Miss Hand, Cora Grey, Eva Ross, and other friends" (226). When she confides to a family friend, Nurse Warren, how her life has been turned upside down, Nurse Warren gives her a book—*Ben Hur*—sent by her son, Norman. All of these acts involve reading and writing, and all of the writing and reading are class appropriate.

An exchange between Harold Griswold—the new minister in town from Oberlin College—and Dr. Warren—the intelligent and handsome physician—seems to embody Tillman's faith in literacy and education as well. Near the end of the novella, Harold and Dr. Warren discuss the "race problem," and Dr. Warren suggests that Black Americans should "emigrate to places where prejudice does not exist" (233). He makes this suggestion, presumably, because he had been educated in Europe and had found success there. His former enslaver, whom the narrator describes as thinking of him like one of her children, first tried to educate him in America, but animosity against him due to his race forced her to remove him from school in America and educate him in England with her own two children. Harold, however, suggests that Black Americans should stay in the United States since they helped build the young nation. Given the progress Black people have gained since Emancipation, Harold argues their successes illustrate growth rather than stagnation, saying, "'In every Southern State we have Afro-American colleges, taught and controlled usually by competent colored men and women. We have magnificent churches, banks, stores, several publishing houses, and over two hundred newspapers'" (235). Time has even allowed Black people, he says, to "'command ... the English language'" (235). Dr. Warren responds to Harold's list of successes by asking to "examine some of the race literature" (235). Harold gladly gives him the title of three "representative papers—the *Indianapolis Freeman*, the *Detroit Plaindealer*, and the *A.M.E. Review*" (235). Later, Dr. Warren subscribes to "several race papers, and orders copies of Simmon's 'Men of Mark' and Williams's 'History of the Negro Race'" (235). Dr. Warren was not up-to-date with the progress of African Americans because he had lived in England for fifteen years; however, Harold's knowledge is evidence enough for him to reconsider his position. As a Black woman writer, Tillman wanted the fictive world in *Beryl Weston's Ambition* and her other creative works to have impact beyond the printed page. Her hope, it seems, was for readers to recognize the successes of the characters in her fiction and to then model their own lives after those good and respectable characters. Moreover, such hope extended beyond the race and invited whites to see Black people as strivers living as peaceful and honorable human beings. If their interactions were limited and hierarchal, perhaps words can transform attitudes. Tillman modeled personal transformations throughout this novella. For instance, Dr. Warren is persuaded to change based on his interactions with Harold Griswold and the additions to his reading list. He uses his literacy skills to transform his thinking, attitude, and behavior.

In *Beryl Weston's Ambition*, readers are introduced to an ambitious and intelligent young woman attending a Black college. They meet her family and learn she comes from proud and industrious people who value family and community as well as education. The Westland community in Tennessee, where they reside, is a stable one full of good though mostly illiterate people. Within the fictionalized world that Tillman creates are Black men in leadership positions who care about the race. For them, access to race literature is an important part of their experiential learning. Thus, they support the Black press and engage in debates about Black progress. The debates around racial progress were not abstract; indeed, Reconstruction had not come near to solving the problem of race in the United States. Poverty, racial violence, education, and civic participation were all issues on the minds of everyday Black people, and they were concerns Harold and Dr. Warren consider as race men. Harold suggests to Dr. Warren that the fight for racial progress must continue in the face of opposition: "I know we have fearful odds against which to contend, and that the race between the two races is an unequal one, but I believe that we ought to remain in America, and 'push the battle to the gates'" (234). Dr. Warren is encouraged by Harold's optimism and determination, and I suspect that Tillman here hopes their optimism might influence her readers and encourage them that transformations, including those that are personal and political, are slow but worth the fight.

LOOKING BACK: CONTEXT AND HISTORY

Forty-eight years had passed between the official end of slavery and the publication of *Beryl Weston's Ambition*. Though slavery had ended, white people were not ready to accept Black people as their equals. Reaction against the war amendments and Reconstruction efforts showed that white southerners in particular wanted to retain power over the lives of Black women, men, and children. One need look no further than the Black Codes, laws that imposed a kind of neoslavery, to see the reality of white southerners' attempts to control the lives of African Americans. In one instance, Saidiya V. Hartman describes how the Black Codes operated in Mississippi: "if 'the laborer shall quit the service of his employer before the expiration of his term of service without good cause, he shall forfeit his wages for that year up to the time of quitting.' Any white person or civil officer was entitled to arrest a black laborer who quit the service of his employer without good cause" (145). After Black Codes were passed throughout the South in the late nineteenth century, Black activists and writers such as Cooper, Matthews, and Tillman waged campaigns to counter their second-class citizenship in a number of ways, as racist rhetoric that demonized Black people grew ever more insistent and uglier. One of those voices was that of Ben Tillman, governor of South Carolina from 1890 to 1895 and US senator from 1895 to 1918, a virulent racist who disparaged Black people while governor and on the Senate floor. As Francis Butler Simkins wrote in 1937, "Tillman's belief in the innate weakness of Negro character led to an extremely pessimistic view regarding the future of the race despite the opportunities extended by the abolition of slavery. In the face of the optimism of hopeful Southerners he pointedly claimed that the race had retrograded, not progressed, since emancipation" (166).

Retrogression theories around race suggested that Black people, and Black men in particular, had been well behaved while they were enslaved, but once free would return to what Tillman called their "naturally bestial selves." In these theories, the supposed savage impulses they retained from their African ancestors would run wild if given too much freedom. The belief among some whites like Ben Tillman was that Black people would do to whites what whites had done to Africans and their descendants, a claim made in Maurice Thompson's poem "A Voodoo Prophecy" (which Anna Julia Cooper had questioned). According to Simkins, Tillman believed Black men would attack white men, "marry white women, and use white children as servants" (166). Furthermore, because Black men could not control their sexual desires, they would rape white women. Black people could thus not be trusted with full freedom, only limited freedom. Tillman suggested that one way to gain control over Black bodies was to repeal the Fourteenth and Fifteenth Amendments. That, of course, did not happen, though those amendments were nullified by white rule at the time and for years thereafter.

Ben Tillman's racist rhetoric, though shunned on the Senate floor, was not challenged by his colleagues as Simkins makes clear: "Tillman's Southern colleagues signified their disapproval by withdrawing from the floor of the Senate during his anti-Negro tirades. But no Southern senator dared reply; no Southern politician dared make the Negro question a campaign issue against the South Carolina leader. They knew his words made him popular at home" (172). Unfortunately, other white people had similar feelings and expressed them openly during this time. Beyond the retrogression theory was another theory at the time, southern paternalism as explained by Guion Griffis Johnson, which maintained Black people belonged to a permanently inferior race and thus were inherently unable to assimilate (497). Edgar Gardner Murphy, "an Episcopal clergyman of Montgomery, Alabama," suggested that if Black people lived among the better class of whites, they could learn to imitate whites and make progress but only among their own people; overall, Murphy believed that white people were responsible for any economic progress made by Black people, saying, "the white man is largely the market for his labor and the opportunity for his progress" (qtd. in Johnson 497).

In this context, the literary mountain that Katherine D. C. Tillman had to climb started long before Cooper and Matthews issued their goals for race literature, detailing the failures of white authors whose literary efforts undermined Black life and Black achievement and calling on Black writers to explore all the complexities associated with African American life in bondage and freedom. I cannot say with certainty if Tillman read Cooper's essay or heard Matthews's speech, but I can say with near certainty that Tillman must have felt the sting of the racist rhetoric used by many white people at the time and felt compelled to respond. Perhaps feeling the weight of the community or wanting to express her own personal desire, Tillman deployed her own transformational literacy skills in service to her community. In line with her contemporaries' visions for race literature, Tillman created characters who were motivated by an individual spirit to better themselves and by a communal responsibility to uplift the race. In Tillman's *Beryl Weston's Ambition*, Beryl epitomizes what a respectable young woman of her time was supposed to do for the self and the community. She believes in education, "speaks correctly," respects her parents, loves her siblings, and is an active community member. Beryl's mother, with the aid of intelligence and cunning, had educated herself and eventually taught her husband how to read. Literacy instruction is thus bound together with love and family obligation. The father owns land and is able to provide for his family. Beryl marries a handsome young doctor, and they enter into a relationship that fulfills their individual desires. After marriage, the narrator tells readers this newlywed couple "returned and resumed their lifework at Westland" (245). In every way, the Weston and Warren families are ideal Black families. They work, read, and participate in community life. Tillman has created characters who exist within Black communities who thrive on hard work and epitomize middle-class values. These model citizens are so good that their values and behaviors should be adapted by readers of Tillman's novella. Claudia Tate suggests that Tillman's fictional works "dramatize the formation of a black middle-class cultural ethos. Largely set in an interracial context and cast within a domestic milieu, these works depict the development of personal identity, racial pride, and ambition as an individuated model for the collective advancement of black people in general" ("Introduction" 55). That story of individual ambition and communal obligation mediated through reading, writing, and literacy instruction is Tillman's response to believers in retrogression and southern paternalism who were unwilling to share power with the newly freed. Although Tillman's response was a fictional one, the very act of her writing stories about good and respectable Black people and families contested what many were saying publicly and writing in the white press. The Weston family, along with the newly formed Warren family, and the Westland community were repudiations of the racist theories and themes circulating in the white press and in American literature.

TRANSFORMATIONAL LITERACY ACTIVITIES IN *BERYL WESTON'S AMBITION*

Equally important in the novella is Tillman's focus on the literacy activities of both the major and minor characters. In many ways, the literacy activities drive the novella forward. John T. Guthrie and Vincent Greaney explain literacy activities include "what people read and how much time they spend doing it" and consider such questions as "what are the uses and purposes of literacy acts" and to "what extent that literacy is utilized to acquire knowledge . . . [and] reaffirm a sense of worth" (68). The opening scene of *Beryl Weston's Ambition* describes a young woman receiving a telegram while attending "one of the leading Afro-American colleges" (207). The news, of course, is not pleasant, but readers are immediately immersed in a world where reading and writing are central aspects of one's identity. When Beryl learns she must go home because her mother has passed away, she is on the train reading a book of poetry given to her by Miss Hand (209). When the narrator explains the family history, readers learn that her father was once illiterate but learned to read when his wife instructed him. Though once a slave, she had learned how to read and write and was once a teacher (213). All these literacy activities describe forward movement and, in so doing, articulate just how important reading and writing can be for a people whose economic and political power is limited but whose literacy learning and transformational possibilities are boundless.

Beryl, the oldest of the Weston children, had received lessons in "algebra and French, under the guidance of a young white woman" (213) before heading off to college. Once home with her family after her mother's death, Beryl instructs her siblings and receives instruction herself. Her friends who remained in college write letters to Beryl, and she writes back. When the day's work is completed on the farm, Mr. Weston reads by the fireside surrounded by his children: "when the tea-table had been cleared, and the dishes washed and put away, the farm hands retired to their respective homes, and the family adjourned to the sitting room, where Jim Weston soon became lost in the columns of his favorite newspaper" (224). There are many more scenes where literacy is a focal point. These activities are designed to showcase the Westland community members as active learners even though some are not educated in school settings. Their literacy activities illustrate how reading provides them with a sense of community and knowledge of current events and builds self-worth. As well, characters like Beryl, Dr. Warren, and Harold, who have acquired sophisticated literacy skills, take what they learn, process it, and then participate in transformational activities to improve the lives of members of their racial communities.

KATHERINE D. C. TILLMAN'S *CLANCY STREET*: FREEDOM AND THE WRONG KIND OF EDUCATION

Most of the story in Tillman's *Beryl Weston's Ambition* takes place in Westland, Tennessee, a small community in the South. The main characters in that story never fret about money, nor do they concern themselves too much with racism. In many ways, the characters exist in a community without fear and reprisal from white people, though the expectations and standards to live a respectable life are imposed by the majority group even though white characters are absent. Family, religion, and education are important institutions to the inhabitants of Westland, and social mobility occurs and sociocultural capital is earned when they adopt forms of literacy that are respected by the majority group. The Westons and Warrens represent ideal Black families who are good, honest, respectable, and economically independent. The setting, however, of *Clancy Street*, Tillman's later novella, is "Clancy Street in Louisville, Kentucky's populous metropolis" (251). In it, Tillman describes the inhabitants of the streets surrounding Clancy as "disreputable" (251). The novella is centered on the Waters family, a working-poor Black family trying to survive by respectable means in an urban and ethnically diverse community. Unlike the Westons, the members of the Waters family are always concerned about money, and they do not live in a homogeneous Black community and racism does not seem to impact their day-to-day lives. In Louisville, they live next to and nearby poor white and Black people who are all struggling financially. Initially, Zeke Waters, the father, is employed by a white man who owns factories in Louisville, and his wife and children are hired by white families who need help with some domestic duties. Despite the economic differences between the Black families in these two novellas, the importance of literacy learning is the same. To transform perceptions of the self, the race, and the broader white community, the characters must go through a process of reclamation. In so doing, the transformation serves the greater good.

Clancy Street is different from *Beryl Weston's Ambition* in many ways. Each novella highlights the value of literacy instruction and education, but *Clancy Street* describes the pitfalls of life for Black characters who do not receive the benefit of literacy instruction and education. In fact, Tillman spends as much time describing the negative effects of a lack of literacy instruction and education as she does its successes. In *Clancy Street*, the Waters family is described as a humble family struggling to make ends meet. When finances are low, hard work and providence ameliorate their suffering. But other characters in the novella struggle because of bad choices. This illustrates that literacy learning and education are not simply about gaining knowledge, but for teaching individuals and families how to conduct themselves publicly and privately. In other words, there are social dimensions to literacy that inform behaviors. Literacy offers transformation of the mind, body, and spirit. In the opening paragraphs of *Clancy Street*, the narrator notes the degree to which enslavement prevented the development of civic knowledge and civic participation of those formerly in bondage and newly freed. In fact, the narrator suggests that, in many ways, the newly freed were underprepared for citizenship. Lack of education caused many of them to rely on information and behaviors that were detrimental to their intellectual, spiritual, moral, and communal development. As such, the narrator accuses some of the "ex-slaves" of justifying unethical behavior such as stealing from "white men" as their right since their wages had been stolen from them when they were enslaved (252). The narrator admonishes the formerly enslaved for not staying true to their marriage vows. This behavior, the narrator notes, is a consequence of the nonbinding marital relationships slave masters encouraged among enslaved men and women.

Lack of literacy instruction and education also impacted their temperance choices and religious practices, which in turn made some underprepared for freedom. For instance, the narrator comments on the perils of freedom. Freedom had given Black men opportunities to drink alcohol, which was sometimes encouraged by former "overseers and owners" (252). Without the ire of their former masters chastising them for drinking at inopportune times of the day, the narrator suggests Black men drank with impunity. Such behaviors impacted individual Black men, but it also negatively impacted their families. The narrator describes the impact in this way: "Drink transformed the ignorant Negro workman into a brute. He who had cowed beneath the overseer's stinging lash under the influence of liquor, became the terror of his wife and children" (252). The narrator disparages alcohol and the white enslavers who encouraged Black men to drink; the narrator also chides Black men for tormenting their wives and children but not reacting against the white men who brutalized them.

The narratorial voice is a strong one that also criticizes immodest behaviors and the financial habits of the newly freed. Complaints against them include failing to save for the future, though there is some recognition that enslavement had been so restrictive as to negatively influence their financial choices in freedom. Further critiques include "uncivilized" religious practices: "in Israel's God they had strong confidence and their hope was expressed in many fervent, if ofttimes, ludicrous prayers and plaintive songs" (251). With the right educational training and religious instruction, past religious practices deemed uncivilized and therefore inappropriate could be moderated, the narrator implies. Consequently, characters embracing what the narrator suggests are the right kinds of religious practices—Caroline Waters, for instance—are acceptable, while characters supporting a debased form of religious practice—Granny Ball, for example—are not. Criticisms against lack of prudent financial choices and ostentatious religious practices underscored by the narrator in *Clancy Street* highlight the class tensions among Black people described by Evelyn Brooks Higginbotham in her work on the faith beliefs, practices, and organizations of Black women: "The effort to forge a community that would command whites' respect revealed class tensions among blacks themselves. The zealous efforts of black women's religious organizations to transform certain behavioral patterns of their people disavowed and opposed the culture of the 'folk'—the expressive culture of many poor, uneducated, and 'unassimilated' black men and women dispersed throughout the rural South or the newly huddled in urban centers" (*Righteous Discontent* 15).

Although Higginbotham is writing specifically about Black Baptist women, her thesis is instructive for my purposes here. In *Clancy Street*, the narrator does not mention a denominational affiliation, but expresses similar sentiments regarding appropriate and inappropriate worship practices. The disapproval described by Higginbotham and expressed by the narrator is based on class-based tensions and criticisms. The narrator strongly suggests that demonstrative worship practices, as an observable phenomenon that can be witnessed by Black and white alike, further expose Black people to white derision and Black middle-class censure.

THE RIGHT KIND OF EDUCATION

Despite the narrator's admonishments regarding non-socially approved behavioral practices in the first few chapters of the novella, all is not lost on Clancy Street. There are some "good" and "honorable" Black people trying to make their way (Tillman, *Clancy Street* 251, 268). The juxtaposition of those who mismanage their freedom with those who strive to do well is evidence of the good work that literacy instruction and education can do for those who capitalize on its benefits. The heroine, Caroline Waters, is born into a poor family, but what her family members lack in money they make up for in thrift and hard work. The Waters family is not the perfect family when introduced at the beginning of the story. Its members are, however, capable of real change, and Tillman uses them to exemplify the importance of personal and familial transformation. Although Caroline wants an education, financial constraints on the family will force her to stop attending school for a short time: "For the first time in three years, Caroline had been compelled to stay home and she regarded it as a great trial" (268). When this happens, Caroline is twelve years old. Her father, Zeke, formerly had a steady job, but the factory where he was employed shut down, Anne, her mother, who had been employed sometimes as a domestic or seamstress, is now too ill to work and, although sick, is taking care of her newborn girl. In the meantime, the Waters children, Caroline and her oldest brother, Abe, work to help the family. Even though she is forced to stop attending school, Caroline remains optimistic about her future. Like Beryl, she wants to be a teacher. She will soon get an opportunity to fulfill her wish to attend school again when she sees a white woman, Mrs. Langdon, looking forlorn on the street. When Caroline asks if she is "'looking for some one,'" Mrs. Langdon replies 'yes; for a girl who wants to work and go to school'" (274). Fortuitously, this is just what Caroline wants, so she asks Mrs. Langdon, "'would I do? I want to go to school so bad'" (274). With permission from her parents, Caroline is hired to work in Mrs. Langdon's home. From there, their futures are intertwined. Like Beryl before her, Caroline's desire to go to school is palpable.

Once Caroline is in the home of the Langdons, her maturation as a student, her religious conversion, and the influence she will have on family and friends are noteworthy. Caroline is the transformational exemplar. At her new school, Caroline is seated next to the "brightest girl in the class, an effort that greatly stimulated our little heroine's efforts" (279). She also decides to perform well in school because she wants to impress Otto Lewis, a boy she likes and admires. The narrator reveals that Otto is the smartest student in the school. Throughout her time in the Langdon household, Caroline thrives in school, and her religious devotion grows. When she seeks a church that will enhance her spiritual knowledge, she finds she can learn best from "Rev. Hall, the young pastor, a graduate of a noted Negro college, and a New England theological school as well" (280). At this juncture in the story, all is going well for Caroline and the rest of the Waters family. Readers learn that Caroline is the "valedictorian of her class" (283). In her valedictory speech titled 'Wilberforce, the champion of Negro Liberty'" (284), she pays homage to William Wilberforce, the English abolitionist who fought to end the slave trade. It is revealed too that Caroline has been considerably influenced and cultured by "books and schools" (284). By the end of the novella, Caroline's education has moved her beyond her poor and working-class roots—at least socially and culturally—by improving her literacy skills and enhancing her education not only in school but under the guidance of the Langdon household. Accordingly, Caroline's literacy skills have been transformational. She has moved from one social class to another and did so because she values learning and the principles of good behavior, devotion to parents, and love of Christ. Caroline is the model citizen. Claudia Tate describes the purposes of Tillman's fiction as a form of didactic fiction: "Didactic fiction, in general, became a principal medium for disseminating new notions among African Americans about what constituted the laudable black self, family, and community. Inculcating new ambitions through inventive role models for African-American women and men as well as revising understandings about individual and group perfectibility are precisely the tasks to which black women authors of post-reconstruction domestic novels directed their works" (*Domestic Allegories* 172). Caroline is the exemplar in this context. She values education, models good behavior, and grows in her faith. She is so good and her faith so devoted to Christ that she convinces her parents to become active Christians.

The catalyst that changes the fortunes of the Waters family is when Caroline meets Mrs. Langdon. Before that, the family had been struggling financially and spiritually. However, Mrs. Langdon's offer to hire Caroline and allow her to attend school sparks a spiritual change. While working at the Langdon home and with time to worship on Sundays, Caroline decides to find a place to fellowship. She eventually finds a chapel pastored by Rev. Hall and later gives her life over to Christ. Her testimony follows: "'I thought of his goodness and purity; I thought of his kindness to sick and sad, I thought of his death on the cross and then I thought of his goodness and purity; I thought of his death on the cross and then I thought of my sins and I wanted so much to get rid of them and be near him, that I just gave myself to him fully and my burden left me and since then I have been so happy'" (Tillman, *Clancy Street* 281). Caroline's parents are inspired by her devotion to church and Christ; they eventually become devoted to Christ's teachings and seek to encourage others to become active in the church. The narrator describes the conversion experience of Hettie, Caroline's best friend, who, unlike Caroline, had fallen victim to temptation after being pursued by a charming white man. Anne, Caroline's mother, had warned Hettie to stay away from him by explaining the history of miscegenation, but Hettie did not listen and is described as "embark[ing] on a life of sin" (282). Yet Caroline and Anne are able to convince Hettie to repent and become a Christian (282). Caroline's father is so enamored with Christ's teachings that he becomes a minister and helps Rev. Hall: "dear old Zeke kept on growing in grace until the Lord chose him as a mouthpiece and he became a local preacher and Rev. Hall's efficient helper" (282). Many of the characters in *Clancy Street* mature socially and religiously because they have been instructed in what Cook-Gumperz calls "socially approvable knowledge" (1). Based on her description near the beginning of *Clancy Street*, Tillman seems to disapprove of religious practices based too much on expressive emotions; rather, she approves of religious practices that are instructive and void of exoticism. Anne, Zeke, and Caroline demonstrate the right kind of attitudes about faith and practice it accordingly. Caroline's parents develop more conscientious religious outreach practices, which give them respect among their fellow community members. They are held up as exemplars.

TRANSFORMATIONAL LITERACY ACTIVITIES

Good things happen to the characters in *Clancy Street* when literacy instruction and education are at the forefront. This is not to suggest that those who are educated either formally or informally see immediate benefits. The absence of any literacy and educational instruction, however, does not bode well for the uneducated and the irreligious. Without education, the narrator suggests time and again that Black people are prone to believe in hidden forces that are disreputable, such as the belief in and practice of Voodoo. The novella has two chapters on "Negro Superstition," one of which focuses on characters who seek love and retribution on the advice of a voodoo priestess, Granny Ball, and the other in which Caroline and Hettie reveal a rather simplistic version of Christian faith. Neither the outcomes nor the belief systems benefit the individual or the community. The narrator thus does not hide frustration regarding ill-conceived beliefs concerning religion, but is willing to praise sanctioned behaviors and approve certain kinds of spiritual beliefs and practices.

There are numerous scenes in Tillman's *Clancy Street* in which literacy activities are praised implicitly and explicitly. Anne, for example, even though she is from a poor family, learns to read because her father "had been a minister" (255), which afforded her access to learning she might not have otherwise received. Because Anne can read and "took both the leading Sunday papers," she reads them aloud to Zeke and the neighbors (255). Anne teaches her husband how to read and is described as being an "omnivorous reader ... [who] had access to the library of an old employer" (255). She owns a small library, and among her books are the Bible, "a translation of 'William Tell,'" and others (255). The names of prominent authors and titles of books are mentioned. Caroline reads as much as her mother does and is scolded sometimes as a child because she chooses books over her household chores. Anne tells Caroline she would have named her Harriet Beecher Stowe but for the love she has for her own grandmother, who was named Caroline. Anne also tells her daughter that Stowe's novel *Uncle Tom's Cabin* "helped to free us" (257). Taken together, these literacy activities serve to encourage reading to gain knowledge to better the self, the family, and the community. All of these activities are transformational. The literacy activities throughout *Clancy Street* serve as a sociological good and afford the characters economic advancement. According to Claudia Tate, Tillman "repeatedly dramatized the home, school, and church as proponents of literacy. The activity of appropriate reading accordingly became a sanctioned vehicle for controlling the population's leisure time, social and spiritual values, and ultimately their general behavior" (*Domestic Allegories* 173). Moreover, writing, an activity not much utilized by the characters in this novella, is no less powerful as Tillman makes clear when she praises Stowe's *Uncle Tom's Cabin* for helping to bring an end to slavery. Writing such an impactful novel, according to Tillman, directly changed the lives of the enslaved. Tillman's assertion about Stowe may not be fully correct, but her core sentiment is well taken. Writing can empower the marginalized and change consciousness.

Near the end of Tillman's *Clancy Street*, all is well with the Waters family, or so it seems. Caroline is performing well in school and due to graduate as the valedictorian of her class. In one of the final scenes, she is practicing her valedictory speech when she learns that Mrs. Langdon is ill. This foreshadows what might appear to be a terrible ending to a story that highlights the possibilities of literacy and education. Caroline forgoes giving the valedictory speech, so she can help take care of Mrs. Langdon, who has typhoid fever. Sadly, Caroline eventually dies from typhoid fever she contracted in nursing Mrs. Langdon back to health. Yet her death is not divine punishment from God; rather, it signifies Caroline's goodness and the continued need for literacy instruction and education for the race. Her death will ensure that many other Black youths will be educated due to the benevolence of the Langdon family. To honor Caroline, Mrs. Langdon and her husband commit themselves to the education of Black youths, including Otto Lewis, Caroline's beau, and her brother, Abe. Eventually, Otto and Abe become ministers who will spread the gospel and become exemplarily men in their communities. Her parents become more committed Christians and continue their community outreach with fervor. Within the scope of the novella, Caroline's intelligence, hard work, and loyalty prove to the Langdons that Black people are not an inferior people. This is revealed when Mr. Langdon admits that Caroline had taught him a lesson and he could "no longer doubt the capabilities of [her] race" (285). Langdon's response as a white businessman initially indifferent to the plight of the newly freed helps to reinforce Caroline's already pristine character. Simply put, it took just one relationship with an exemplarily Black person to convince Langdon that his previous suppositions were ill-founded. Theoretically, this is how transformational literacy practices function. The writer, Tillman in this instance, deploys her literacy skills for the advancement of the race. In her fictional account, Caroline, the smart, good, and religious Black character, transforms the beliefs of a staid and wealthy white character. Such transformation might also change the minds and hearts of white readers too, thereby rebuking theories that assert the inherent inferiority of the race.

MATERIAL FORMATIONS

In *Beryl Weston's Ambition* and *Clancy Street*, the values embraced are situated within literacy and educational practices linked to the white middle classes but adapted for uplift purposes for the community members in Westland, Tennessee, and Louisville, Kentucky, and for readers of these novellas. The good characters realize that reading and writing lead to greater understanding of the world and the self, and most of the not-so-good characters eventually learn that lesson too. If they want to be accepted in their communities and in the broader society, adherence to certain kinds of middle-class values and lifestyle practices causes fewer problems. To demonstrate what happens when literacy and education are not at the center of one's life, Tillman juxtaposes the good and the seemingly bad characters as symbolic examples to be imitated or not by her real-world readers. Thus, her novellas are not an appeal to aesthetics per se, but an appeal to personal and communal actualization. This is one form of critical literacy. Ira Shor explains the legacy of critical literacy to which Tillman appeals as a Black woman writer: "We are what we say and do. The ways we speak and are spoken to help shape us into the people we become. Through speech and other actions, we build ourselves in a world that is building us. We can remake ourselves and society, if we choose, through alternative words and dissident projects. This is where critical literacy begins—words that question a world not yet finished or humane" (1). Black women writers with access to a broad range of readers could ill afford to write literature for strictly artistic purposes. As McHenry notes, "rather than direct political or economic protest, middle-class black Americans saw their literary work as a means of instilling pride in their own community; stressing the importance of racial solidarity and self-help, they struggled to turn the pejorative designation of race into a source of dignity and self-affirmation" (149). That struggle to turn the word to action did not stop Tillman from believing in its transformational import.

Racist theories such as retrogression and southern paternalism were contested, even if indirectly, by women like Tillman. As a Black woman writing in the late nineteenth century, Tillman aimed, on the one hand, to foster curiosity and admiration for the Black family and, on the other hand, to write its positive existence into the consciousness of her readers. In so doing, Tillman had, for all practical purposes, met Matthews's goals for race literature. She had not, though, written the great American novel that Cooper suggested should be the objective of the Black writer. Tillman's attempts were modest, yet they encapsulated the basis of both Cooper's and Matthews's basic claims. Justice and full freedom can be acquired through an engagement with ideas about race, using the literary imagination that is critical of the current racial system while also offering suggestions for individual and communal improvement and advancement.

Tillman's own adoption of the standard idiom of the white middle class, along with her characters' adoption of it, illustrates the degree to which she recognized that certain kinds of written communication might be more persuasive than others. Perhaps by showing that Black characters from working poor families can speak and write "properly", these families can by degrees learn to be good citizens. Hence, participating in literacy activities that yield positive results such as the ones described in *Beryl Weston's Ambition* and *Clancy Street* can help Tillman reject post-Emancipation race-based theories that argued against such transformations. Tillman's novellas demonstrate a writer undeterred by the fraught environment around her and the race. She set out to dispel myths about lack of thrift and intelligence. Her literary form of sentimental or domestic fiction was not radical. There was little deviation from traditional form, content, and character development. There is no creative risk-taking in her writing, and no sense in which differences between Black and white people were laid bare. Rather, she suggests that Black people can and are like their white counterparts if given opportunities to succeed. Tillman's contemporary Pauline E. Hopkins will add other-worldly dimensions to her fiction that will expand notions about literacy and race.

PAULINE E. HOPKINS

Hopkins is another Black woman writer who used the pen to rebuke racist theories and express her mission and values. She was a prolific writer whose writings addressed such topics as African diasporic concerns, Black history, and women's issues. In her literary biography of Hopkins, Hannah Wallinger notes that Hopkins was most prolific between 1900 and 1904 (59). Although much has been written about *Contending Forces*, which is probably the best known of her four novels, I have chosen to analyze one of her lesser-known works, *Of One Blood: Or, the Hidden Self*. In this novel, Hopkins deploys her sophisticated literacy skills in multidimensional ways. The novel captures the imaginative spirit of Hopkins's creativity as it bridges the gaps between history and knowledge, past and present, and the real and the imagined. It is a novel about race that realizes the possibilities and limitations of literacy even for the educated elite. In this diasporic novel that juxtaposes ancient African history with the foundations of Western civilization and late nineteenth-century life, Hopkins hopes to use history to link African excellence to Black Americans' hidden potential. According to Daphne A. Brooks, "'the hidden self' of *One Blood* . . . is both a geographical territory and a spiritually diasporic terrain" (291). These objectives coalesce around achievement and possibility. It is at the intersection of achievement and possibility where Hopkins wrestles with key aspects of literacy as a transformational enterprise.

Of the fiction analyzed in this book thus far, *Of One Blood* is the most ambitious and complicated as it includes mysticism, myth, mystery, rape, incest, and racial politics all together in one meandering novel. Transformation of the self is based on the revelation of African and American history intertwined with the dynamic possibilities of literacy and education. Recent scholarship on Hopkins has focused less on these literary qualities and more on her unattributed use of others' work in her texts. Geffrey Sanborn, for instance, identifies in *Of One Blood* "at least seventy-two passages, amounting to 18 percent of the novel as a whole, [that] are more or less transcribed, without attribution, from other texts" (68), while JoAnne Pavletich notes, in Hopkins's novel *Winona* her proclivity for "appropriating—or conquering—others' words and giving them new meanings" (116). My concern, however, is not with whether Hopkins was plagiarizing others' work or commenting on it for literary effect, but rather with how she understood literacy as a persuasive force that could transform attitudes and behaviors.

OF ONE BLOOD: REUEL'S EDUCATION

Readers might imagine Hopkins's *Of One Blood* as a Venn diagram. In the first circle, from top to bottom, are the words "race," "literacy," and "education"; in the second circle, from top to bottom, are the words "Africa," "science," and "history"; and in the final circle, from top to bottom, are the words "mystery," "miscegenation," and "mysticism." Despite their position within each circle, all the words there have equal value and meaning. The novel's main character, Reuel Briggs, links the words, and the other characters help their meanings come to life. Reuel is a Harvard medical student who, although Black, is passing as white. The narrator's description of Reuel notes the characteristics that allow him to pass: "the nose was the aristocratic feature, although nearly spoiled by the broad nostrils, of this remarkable young man; his skin was white, but of a tint suggesting olive, an almost sallow color" (443–44). Reuel is a brilliant student: his peers "all voted him a genius in his scientific studies, and much was expected of him at graduation" (444). He had even written articles that "had produced a profound impression" (444). In every way, Reuel is the quintessential student.

Reuel is given an opportunity to showcase his supreme intellect when a beautiful young woman, Dianthe Lusk (the name of John Brown's first wife), is brought to the hospital where he is training. She is presumed dead, but Reuel believes he can bring her back to life. Dianthe is a Fisk Jubilee singer whom Reuel and his friends had seen perform the night before she arrived at the hospital. Reuel is in awe of her voice and realizes he has seen a vision of her in his dreams. While she is in the hospital, the other doctors, including Reuel's best friend, Aubrey Livingston, believe she is dead, and there is no possibility of her resurrection. However, Reuel is a brain specialist and a mystic and knows he is capable of bringing the seemingly dead back to life. He reveals his mystical capabilities to the other doctors after they have concluded nothing more can be done to save Dianthe. He admits to them, "'I have numberless times in the past six months restored consciousness to dogs and cats after rigor mortis set in'" (467). He believes he can do the same for Dianthe, but the other doctors remain skeptical until he proves them wrong. He gives Dianthe his "life-giving powder" (470), and she comes back to life. His colleagues are astonished by his abilities. He is knowledgeable in the sciences approved by members of the white race, and he is also knowledgeable in the supernatural, which is belittled by the same group. Reuel explains the supernatural to the other doctors, saying, "'The supernatural presides over man's formation always'" and "'Life is that evidence of supernatural endowment which originally entered nature during the formation of the units for the evolution of man. Perhaps the superstitious masses came nearer to solving the mysteries of the creation than the favored elect will ever come'" (469). Reuel suggests to all who are against science that is yet unknown or practiced by the few that they should suspend disbelief.

His response to the other doctors' disbelief in the supernatural is linked to Hopkins's inclusion of some of William James's ideas expressed in his essay "The Hidden Self," appropriated for use in *Of One Blood*. "The Hidden Self," published in 1890, was a response to the work of M. Pierre Janet and M. Binet, two Frenchmen who studied and wrote about conscious and unconscious states. Their findings, James admitted, had brought on "quite a commotion" (para 3), yet he argued their work should not be dismissed. He suggested that academics and scientists ought not shun what cannot be scientifically verifiable or what is scientifically fantastic. There are unknowns, he said, that will be revealed to some but not to others; perhaps in due time and with the right amount of research, the truth might be uncovered. In James's words, "if there is anything which human history demonstrates, it is the extreme slowness with which the ordinary academic and critical mind acknowledges facts to exist which present themselves as wild facts with no stall or pigeon-hold, or as facts which threaten to break up the accepted system" (para 2). Janet and Binet's work had challenged the accepted system as it related to hypnotic states, and so does Reuel. More to the point, Reuel is an amalgamation of the two men's scientific ideas and practices in that they seem to believe they can cure what seems incurable and know what is unknowable. In fact, Reuel is so taken with Binet's theories specifically that he believes more scientific experiments can be conducted on the "mysteries of existence" (Hopkins 448) that Binet promoted in his work.

In Reuel, Hopkins gave a Black character extraordinary powers, both commensurate and incommensurate with those usually associated with his race. On the one hand, Reuel is a learned young man well on his way to healing the sick with scientific knowledge he has gained in medical school. He can transform the dead into the living realm. His education has equipped him to do so. This kind of education and ability is rarely associated with someone of his race, yet he dabbles in the supernatural and is successful in that as well. Reuel's scientific abilities in the supernatural are for all intents and purposes an anomaly and a contradiction. Martin Japtok reacts to Hopkins's rendering of Reuel's scientific gifts in this way: "Hopkins validates here what has been seen, in the tradition of hoodoo and conjuring, as a specifically African (American) mode of knowing" (407). Hopkins does not, like Tillman, scoff at practices unacceptable to the majority group, at least in Reuel's case.

Because Reuel learns formally and independently, his education helps him save Dianthe. In many ways, he has received the best that literacy and education offer. He is a student who synthesizes vast amounts of knowledge, tests his hypotheses, and applies what he has learned from trial and error. Yet Reuel's education will extend well beyond Harvard and his living quarters, and he will receive a different kind of education, one that he will be taught in Ethiopia. While Reuel is taking care of Dianthe, he falls in love with her, and she falls in love with him. Once she is well, Reuel asks Dianthe to marry him, and she says yes. They marry soon after, but Reuel realizes his small apartment is no place for his wife. He is still a poor student and cannot sufficiently provide for Dianthe. He seeks the counsel of Aubrey, his best friend, who tells him about a lucrative job opportunity on an expedition to Africa to "the site of ancient Ethiopian cities; its object to unearth buried cities and treasure" (Hopkins 494). It requires a two-year commitment, which Reuel accepts and leaves the care of Dianthe to Aubrey. Much happens once the expedition arrives in Africa, but two incidents stand out. One occurs when Professor Stone, a white anthropologist spearheading the expedition, reveals that humankind originated in Africa; the other is when Reuel learns his true identity. These profound revelations coalesce around literacy, knowing, and the past and change Reuel's life.

During a discussion with the men on the expedition, Professor Stone discusses the race and origin question. He places Africa—specifically, Ethiopia—at the center of the "arts [and] sciences" (521). The great civilizations of Egypt, he declares, learned from the Ethiopians. All humankind, he asserts, came from Ethiopia, "'but of this we are sure—all records of history, sacred and profane, unite in placing the Ethiopian as the primal race'" (521). Reuel listens intently but is at that time unwilling to engage Stone in additional race discussions after Stone reveals his beliefs about the origins of man. Indeed, Reuel has more to learn from Stone, which includes learning about Ethiopia's connection to biblical figures and history. Stone explains that Ethiopia predated Egypt's glory, based on what he learned from a "cameldriver who accompanied [him] to Thebes" (534) on an earlier expedition. Equally important, Reuel learns from Stone that a king will return to Ethiopia to restore it to its former glory. Stone says that "'An offspring of that Ergamenes who lived in the reign of the second Ptolemy—[will] return and restore the former glory of the race. The preservation of this hidden city is for his reception'" (535). Unbeknownst to Reuel, he is the offspring who will reign over Ethiopia again. Before he takes the throne, he will be educated in ancient Ethiopian rituals that rival any scientific knowledge he has gained in America. This is the power of oral and written literacies.

On a walk by himself, Reuel unintentionally finds the hidden city of Telassar, which the men on the expedition were looking for. The hidden treasures they seek are there. While he is in Telassar, through a series of strange twists and turns, he learns his true identity and is invited into the community he will eventually lead back to glory. His guides, Ababdis and Ai, provide the necessary details. They tell him, "'Thou art Ergamenes—the long-looked-for king of Ethiopia, for whose reception this city was built'" (554). Moreover, in a recitation he learns that he has come from a chosen people: "'Son of a fallen dynasty, outcast of a sunken people, upon your breast is a lotus lily, God's mark to prove your race and descent. You, Ergamenes, shall begin the restoration of Ethiopia. Blessed be the name of God for ever and ever, for wisdom, and might are His, and He changeth the times and the seasons. He removeth kings and countries, and setteth them up again'" (555). The clues about Reuel's royal background that he had seen in visions in his childhood begin to emerge while he listens to the musicians recite his past and his future. It is a revelation that shames and inspires him. He is shamed because he is passing as white, but he is inspired because his destiny hinted at through visions he saw as a child is confirmed. This experience has transformed Reuel. The returned king needs a queen, and Reuel is introduced to queen Candace, whom he will eventually marry. The consummation of their marriage will bring forth a "dynasty of kings" (561).

This marvelous and improbable tale uncovers Reuel's hidden self. The re-education of the newly revealed self is a fascinating one. In his new life in the hidden city of Telassar, Ai teaches Reuel how life is governed there. Ai teaches him about the culture's supreme being and worship practices and how the sages, the educated elite, learn the "secrets of [the] kingdom" (561). Ai has the knowledge Reuel needs to take his rightful place as King Ergamenes. As a diligent and willing student, Reuel asks Ai to "'teach me what thou knowest'" (572). Ai gives Reuel a book that will teach his soul what it needs to know (573). He even teaches Reuel how to see into the future and the past. Doing so helps Reuel see the fate of his wife and best friend back home. He ultimately learns about Aubrey's treachery and the forced marriage between his wife and Aubrey. His expedition to Africa and the knowledge gained are the catalyst that triggers Hopkins's criticism of Western educational practice. Such practices have denied the existence of Black excellence and a foundational history for Black people. Hazel Carby points out that Reuel's "archeological expedition to Africa was the journey into Hopkins'[s] vision of black history and her challenge to the mythology of the superiority of European civilization" (*Reconstructing Womanhood* 156). There is more to learn and more to appreciate about Africa's hidden treasures and knowledge that have been hidden not just to Reuel but to the race. Reuel has acquired knowledge in science, medicine, and the occult, and in Africa he learned Arabic and understood the ancient language of prophecy spoken by his ancestors. His education in the United States and Africa has transformed him in more complete ways. His education in America was incomplete because it did not include histories of Africa and the significant contributions Africans have made to the world.

RACE, *THE HIDDEN SELF*, AND THE LIMITS OF LITERACY AND EDUCATION

From the start of Hopkins's novel, education is of supreme value. The protagonist attends Harvard medical school, and he is the best student in his class. Additionally, Reuel is not just any medical student; he is one who has published articles and is recognized as a scholar outside his medical school education. In every way, Reuel epitomizes all that is good about mastering sophisticated literacies and obtaining an education. Yet, based on how the novel is written, it seems Hopkins is not yet sold on the value of sophisticated literacies and an elite education that *only* uplifts Western accomplishments while ignoring African achievements. Hence, Reuel only really becomes educated when he learns about his hidden self. When his true identity is revealed, his literacies coalesce to enrich his education and his life, demonstrating that literacy is most valuable when it teaches the self about the self. He can only truly be transformed and use his literacies in service to his new community when he learns the full truth. Keith Gilyard writes about the importance of literacy and identity formation in his academic memoir, which provides a helpful backdrop for understanding Reuel's transformations. Gilyard describes why pedagogies of instruction matter to him as one who is teaching basic writing to underprepared Black students. He writes, "my interest is not merely in the ways Black students can learn; I am also concerned about the psychic costs they pay. A pedagogy is successful only if it makes knowledge or skill achievable while at the same time allowing students to maintain their own sense of identity" (11). Hopkins too understood the relationship among literacy instruction, education, and identity formation. Her character Reuel is transformed when the instruction he receives from Ai and the other sages includes history and language that affirm his ancestry and place in the world. This learning helps to shape an identity he subconsciously knew belonged to him.

The early chapters in Hopkins's *Of One Blood* focus on Reuel's education and intelligence as well as tangentially on the education of Aubrey. Readers are first introduced to Reuel when he is alone in his sparsely decorated room surrounded by "books and the apparatus for experiments" (441). The narrator explains that Reuel has recently read *The Unclassified Residuum* (443) and that he has published articles and earned some recognition for his work (444). Reuel is serious about his education. His best friend, Aubrey, is also in medical school at Harvard, but Aubrey's focus is not as singular as Reuel's and he is not as studious. Dianthe is a Fisk Jubilee singer, part of a choral group raising money for Fisk University, a Black college founded during Reconstruction. While these characters are all privileged in some way, sophisticated literacy skills do not protect them from the evils of slavery's legacy. The institutions that sanctioned the enslavement of Africans and their descendants bring forth destruction to Aubrey and Dianthe. It is a sordid tale that Hopkins weaves to expose the hypocrisy of slavery and the relentless drive to categorize races from superior to inferior to justify a racial caste system to devastating effect. Moreover, it tells the story of the limits of literacy and education that are reductive rather than expansive and transformational.

Dianthe is the classic damsel in distress. She is a beautiful mulatto lost in the unconscious for most of the novel. In stages, her unconscious is made conscious by the brilliant and handsome Reuel, himself a biracial person. He falls in love with her while he nurses her back to health. She falls in love with him, and they eventually marry. All the while, Aubrey, Reuel's best friend, is in love with her as well, even though he is engaged to someone else. Using selfish machinations, Aubrey finds a way to force Dianthe to marry him while Reuel is away on his expedition. In an outing organized by Aubrey for Molly, his bride-to-be, and Dianthe, the woman he truly desires, Aubrey's intentions are revealed. He engineers a drowning for Molly and a rescue from drowning for Dianthe. While Dianthe is recovering from nearly drowning, Aubrey shows her a letter stating Reuel has died on his African expedition. All the while, Aubrey is pleading with Dianthe to marry him; she resists but eventually agrees. Readers soon learn that Dianthe should not have married either Reuel or Aubrey. After Dianthe has married Reuel, been supposedly widowed, and then coerced into matrimony with Aubrey, the narrator reveals that Reuel, Aubrey, and Dianthe are siblings. They were born to a biracial mother, Mira, and her master's son, Dr. Livingston, who is father of all three. Unknown to any of them at the time, but later revealed to Reuel and Dianthe, is that they have committed one of the gravest sins: incest. Consummation of Dianthe's marriages to her brothers has broken divine and secular laws. Dianthe is horrified, and Reuel is dumbfounded and then incensed. This twisted tale of sex and incest is described at one point in the novel by the siblings' grandmother, Hannah, to Dianthe as "'dese things jes' got to happen in slavery'" (605). Her matter-of-fact acceptance of the situation is painful for Dianthe to hear. The revelation of the siblings' relationship is a testament to the dangers of hidden knowledge and histories.

Despite the enormous value placed on literacy by scholars and laypeople alike, literacy as a technology apart from its social, cultural, and economic dimensions can have less impact, particularly for those on the margins like the characters in *Of One Blood*. Gilyard explains the sometimes-contradictory outcomes of literacy by suggesting "literacy has no monopoly on profundity but unmistakably contributes to it" (23). The enslavement of Africans and their descendants was designed to keep them debased and ignorant. Families were torn apart, literacy was denied, and women were forced into sexual liaisons with their masters or relationships with men whom they did not choose. Thus, family histories are not always tightly woven stories passed down from generation to generation. Reuel's family history is a result of dangerous lies and omissions. Carby describes the familial disruption in *Of One Blood*, writing that "the double nature of this incestuous relationship between two brothers and their sister was Hopkins's vision of a hell in which 'the laws of changeless justice [bound] Oppressor and oppressed' in the most literal way possible" (*Reconstructing Womanhood* 160). Thus, Reuel, Dianthe, and Aubrey are victims of that slave system that wielded its hands in multiple directions. Reuel chose to pass, which forced him to deny his very existence as a Black man. Aubrey is a selfish and cruel man seeking to fulfil his lustful desires at any cost to his morals and to the ultimate demise of Dianthe, his sister. Dianthe has no real agency. She is simply a beautiful woman caught between two men who love her but who are, in fact, her brothers. If literacy is to be an empowering and transformational agent, then truth cannot be extracted from instruction.

Hopkins's *Of One Blood* thus illustrates the complexities linked to certain kinds of literacy practices. It is true that some literacy instruction outweighs no literacy instruction; however, there are social costs to the self and the community if the learning is one-dimensional. Transformational literacy practices must aim to challenge, transform, and advance; otherwise, individuals, families, and nations suffer. Reuel, his siblings, and the minor characters demonstrate that learning without self-actualization as part of literacy learning can be spiritually and psychically corrosive. Timothy Barnett explains this difficulty with literacy, taking Frederick Douglass and Richard Wright as examples. Both men, Barnett argues, wrote painfully regarding the psychic costs of literacy. Learning to read and write provided them with an awareness of their conditions as Black men. At various points in their lives, Barnett argues this was devastating. "Douglass's experiences," Barnett writes, "suggest that critical literacy brings us closer, maybe too close, to some of the core themes of our lives" (361), while "Richard Wright's story suggests many of the same themes: the seemingly magical connection between literacy and material change as well as the need to consider critical literacies as potentially destructive—not in and of themselves, but because they help us see with more clarity and feel with more depth a world that is often brutal and complex" (361–62). The Livingston children are not denied access to literacy and its material rewards per se; they are, however, denied familial information that could have saved them from heartache and trauma. Thus, an oral tradition steeped in a literacy that connects families from one generation to the next obscures realities that could have been revealed before death and destruction. Perhaps had they been given an education that linked a kind of critical literacy with the academic and the familial, then maybe some of the issues confronting them might have been avoided.

With reasons best understood in a nineteenth-century context, Reuel devalues the Black part of his racial ancestry while in America. Yet a transformation occurs, and he gains confidence, learns about his history, and acquires a new sense of his self-worth when Ababdis, Ai, and the musicians tell him about his royal lineage and Egyptian and Ethiopian history. They help him to decode a familial history that had been mostly hidden to him. Reuel epitomizes what changes can occur once one learns through oral or textual histories about the true nature of their existence. James Paul Gee describes how what one says, does, writes, behaves, and believes helps to form an individual's identity. Gee defines this formational process that takes place during the transmission and exchange of discourse among individuals as a discourse practice. For Gee, literacy is a discourse: "Discourses are the ways of being in the world; they are forms of life which integrate words, acts, values, beliefs, attitudes, and social identities" (527). The discourses (scholarly, medical, societal) that Reuel learns to value do not inhibit his cognitive abilities, but they do inhibit his desire for love, self, family, and African ancestry. To be phenotypically identified as Black was then to be denied entry into medical school, so Reuel had decided to pass as white. On the one hand, personal advancement compels him to pass; on the other hand, there is shame. The discourses or literacies he wants to gain give him access to opportunities afforded to white people, however distressing it may be for him. Unfortunately, this kind of transformation of self, one that accepts his racial inferiority, is problematic, which Hopkins highlights. Reuel knows he is Black, but he does not really know his familial and ancestral history, which means he has little to be proud of based on his perception of Africa. In America, he is not sure what he can be proud of as a Black man, but eventually he learns he can be proud to be King Ergamenes in Ethiopia.

Reuel's elite education fails to educate him properly about African nations that have as glorious a history as any European ones. This same education also impacts how white people perceive Black achievement or lack thereof. His friend Charlie Vance exemplifies this problem. While on the expedition, Charlie is confronted by Ai, who asks him to explain white people's treatment of Black people, saying, "'I have heard of your people ... they are the people who count it a disgrace to bear my color, is it not so?'" (Hopkins 584). Charlie replies, immaturely, that someone who looks like Ai could pass without problems. Ai, of course, is not satisfied with Charlie's answer. He demands to know why Black people with dark skin and "crisp of hair" such as Jim, the Black servant who accompanies the men on the expedition (585), are treated so unjustly. Charlie, ever the fool, is unable to give a satisfactory answer to Ai. In fact, Charlie is annoyed by the questions, even though he conceals it from Ai.

Notwithstanding Charlie's annoyance, his lack of an adequate response is helpful because it reveals the extent to which literacy and education are tied to values and beliefs. Charlie is convinced that he comes from a superior race even in the face of the magnificence he sees in Telassar and its dark-skinned inhabitants. His white skin, family money, and education cause blind spots. Although Hopkins does not report Charlie's academic credentials, presumably he has as good an education as Reuel and Aubrey. Even if this is not the case, it is obvious he comes from a financially secure family because his father is a lawyer whose home is described as existing on "grounds [that] were extensive and well kept telling of the opulence of its owner" (455). Thus, whatever his educational background, it is highly likely that it is elite and/or middle class in its instruction and practice. Therefore, arguably, his literacy practices and his education as well as the institutions that supported slavery and the Black Codes have reinforced his beliefs about his so-called innate superiority. Lynn Z. Bloom writes about how middle-class educational practices function in the service of citizenship and, I would argue, identity politics. Although she is referring to composition instruction, her analysis is instructive here. "When students learn to write, or are reminded once again of how to write," she says, "they also absorb a vast subtext of related folkways, the whys and hows of good citizenship in their college world, and by extrapolation, in the workaday world for which their educations are designed to prepare them" (656). Although Bloom is writing mostly about a late twentieth-century phenomenon, it is not a leap to suggest that Charlie and others like him as impressionable students embraced and adopted the teachings and beliefs of their elite and/or middle-class instructors such as Bloom describes. The values they espouse, as he expresses in his conversations with Ai, are a result of the educational content taught and valued by a group of white people that had and continued to devalue the historical, cultural, and linguistic contributions of Africans and their descendants.

LOOKING FORWARD

In the second half of *Of One Blood*, Hopkins created an ideal paradise where men and women with Black and bronze skin rule over themselves. They have vast knowledge and wealth. They have autonomy over their lives. Such financial independence and high self-worth can be replicated in America, Hopkins hoped. The hidden self that is ostracized in America can be remade with the right kind of knowledge. Literacy and education can be reconstituted and reformulated to transform the race with an eye toward Black consciousness rooted in African and American sensibilities. Melissa Asher Daniels writes that *Of One Blood* "is more interested in promoting black consciousness and cultural distinctiveness than in advocating actual repatriation" (159). Whatever one thinks of Hopkins's paradise, she was, for the most part, invested in creating a space both literally and figuratively that could provide Black people with hope. Her attempt was a radical departure from Katherine D. C. Tillman, her contemporary, who relied on respectability politics and Christian faith as avenues for acceptance and redemption in the post-Reconstruction era in *Beryl Weston's Ambition* and *Clancy Street*. Hopkins, though, challenged institutions that failed to acknowledge Africa's greatness (even though her ideas about Africa were somewhat flawed). For Hopkins, Africa was not a dark nation without scientific or artistic traditions; it was a place where other great nations sought guidance. Thomas J. Otten suggests, however, that Hopkins's "attempt to reevaluate Africa's historical role is characteristic of much black writing of the time; in arguing African contributions to Western culture, Hopkins extends a project begun by writers like William Wells Brown . . . and Alexander Crummell" (241). Otten is right, but he too easily dismisses the uniqueness of Hopkins's *Of One Blood*, specifically in relationship to Tillman, whose fictional works made no reference to the contributions of Africans to Western civilization. I would suggest that Otten misses the point entirely: it is not simply about Hopkins adopting the rhetorical strategies of her male contemporaries to enlighten readers about the glory of Africa, but rather demonstrating the extent to which transformational literacy practices offer possibilities for engagement and transformations when a more complete education is offered to both Black and white people.

Did Hopkins write the great American novel that Cooper hoped would come from the pen of the Black writer? Did she write great race literature that examined the interior lives of Black people as Matthews suggested had not been done yet? Did her novel begin to illustrate the ideological shift taking place among Black women writing about the lives and experiences of more heterogeneous and transitory communities that were forming in the aftermath of Reconstruction? I am not wholly convinced that *Of One Blood* is the masterpiece that Cooper desired. It is, however, a complicated novel interspersed with flawed characters who embody states of being that are reflected in a slave system that wielded its influence on the newly freed as well as the white beneficiaries of that slave system. It is a novel that uplifts Ethiopia for the benefit of Black people who need to view themselves as tied to and existing beyond their former slave status. It is a novel that warns against valuing literacy practices and education that demean the worth of Africa, Africans, and their descendants, though some of Hopkins's ideas about Ethiopia as described in the novel are too narrow and even nativist. It is not a novel that explores the interior lives of its Black or white characters at a substantive level, though it explains how racial hierarchies, which are fictive abstractions created by humans, have real consequences for the newly freed. This is why, on the one hand, three siblings are unknowingly involved in incestuous relationships with each another and why, on the other hand, the death and destruction of two of the three are a result of the mystery of their parental lineage. These acts are reminders of both the futility and the dangers of racial hierarchies and racial hatred, as well as the limits of some forms of literacies taught and practiced.

Although literacy activities take place in both Tillman's novellas and Hopkins's *Of One Blood*, the issues and people explored in these works are very different for the two writers. The settings in Tillman's novellas are rural and urban. The Black families and individuals who help move the plots along strive to be good and respectable. Basic, academic, and religious literacies are the invisible and visible forces that decide whether success or communal alienation is an outcome for individuals considered both good and not so good. Religious practices that are not in line with more modest practices expressed by Black and white Christians are criticized in *Clancy Street*. For instance, hoodoo and voodoo practices linked back to Africa are outright shunned in that novella. Members of the Black underclass in *Beryl Weston's Ambition* and *Clancy Street* are expected to engage in personal transformations whereby their literacies and religious practices meet standards of approval by the white majority and the nascent Black middle class. There is a real desire in *Beryl Weston's Ambition* and *Clancy Street* to prove the worthiness of the race. Literacy, indeed, leads one down the path to hope and redemption in Tillman's novellas.

Conversely, intact Black families are not at the center of *Of One Blood*. Instead, there are sets of individuals existing at times independently and communally. Bad acts are committed knowingly and unknowingly by the educated elite. The settings shift between the United States and Africa. Whereas African occult practices are criticized in *Clancy Street*, they are embraced in *Of One Blood*. Good and evil in Hopkins's novel are not delineated by a simple black and white binary but are revealed by a multiplicity of historical forces that have led to detrimental results in the lives of the characters. Hopkins's experimentation in *Of One Blood* reflects, I believe, a novelist playing with form and time but also one teasing out character and morality. Thus, the characters force readers to reconcile spatial boundaries as well as racial affiliations. What does it mean to be Black in America and in Africa? What does it mean to be white? What does it mean to be African? What makes one American? What makes one African? As Hopkins makes clear in *Of One Blood*, "caste prejudice, race pride, boundless wealth, scintillating intellects refined by all the arts of the intellectual world, are but puppets in His hand, for His promises stand, and He will prove His words, 'Of One blood have I made all races of men'" (621). For her, we are the same; no one is above the other.

Although Hopkins's *Of One Blood* is a more complex novel than Tillman's *Beryl Weston's Ambition* and *Clancy Street*, each of these women articulated her hopes for more expansive freedom and ascribed humanity to Black people employing the literacy practices and values of the white middle class and the small but growing Black middle class. Each woman argued against racist theories such as retrogression and southern paternalism, though they did not outright name them in their novels. They did, however, challenge and compose stories in which Black women and men are responsible citizens, while those who are not are ostracized—not because they are racial others per se but because they fail to adhere to principles that align with uplift efforts. Young Black adults seek to gain sophisticated literacy skills and higher education to better the self and the community, especially in Tillman's novellas.

The tasks that confronted Tillman and Hopkins and the newly emerging artists of the early twentieth century were difficult. The transformational aspects of literacy that were touted as one way to humanize the Black masses were confronted by a country unwilling to grant rights to or share power with the newly freed. Reconstruction efforts had come to a grinding halt by the late 1870s. Educational pursuits were on the rise but remained difficult to obtain for the masses of Black people. White supremacists' theories remained intact and permeated every aspect of Black life. Race-based theories that demeaned and harmed Black progress continued to be a part of white American consciousness. Race ideology and practice were bound together in the twentieth century as much as in the eighteenth and nineteenth centuries. The emerging Black elite and middle classes hoped to gain advantages due to their own advanced literacy practices and education, but their progress was often muted by southern white rage and northern white apathy. Black migration from the South to the North and Midwest challenged not only social relationships among Black and white; it radically altered the ways Black progress and respectability were actualized in the physical spaces occupied by the newly arrived and in the literature and music of the New Negro Era. In the wake of these challenges, Black women writers and singers took new paths by employing the literacy practices of the white middle class, critiqued forms of transactional literacy practices and also embraced and utilized the vernacular traditions of a subset of the Black working class employing specular literacy practices to great lengths. In the end, Black women writers and singers in the early decades of the twentieth century exemplified a dynamic shift beginning to take shape as their discourses reflected a people with different ideas about the race.

LITERACY IN THE NEW NEGRO ERA

Angelina Weld Grimké and the Classic Blues Pioneers
Mamie Smith, Lucille Hegamin, and Alberta Hunter

Pauline E. Hopkins's novel *Of One Blood*, released in installments in 1902 and 1903, envisioned a world where Africa-descended people are connected to their African ancestry. This connection provided Black Americans a foundation that predated their enslavement in America and hopefully gave them the psychic tools they needed to build strong families and institutions in the United States. Among the chief mechanisms for reconstructing their confidence was knowledge of the past, which, in turn, helped to provide knowledge of the self. In so doing, sociological and psychological transformations can take place. In *Of One Blood*, knowledge of the past and the self was disseminated in the oral tradition as well as discursively. Thus, literacy was enacted at both the spoken and discursive levels by Hopkins to transform the lives of the characters in her novel, but also in the material world to transform perceptions of the race by Black and white readers. Specific kinds of literacies and knowledge matter, as Hopkins emphasized in *Of One Blood*. That an African intellectual tradition can stand alongside a Western one ensures that Africa-descended people in America have a history they can be proud to claim. While Hopkins was critical of the United States' position on Black people and Africa in *Of One Blood*, there was some semblance of hope when she argued we are all of one blood. Superficial differences in skin color amount to false and dangerous dichotomies. Thus, it is unnecessary for whites to continue to oppress Black people.

Hopkins's hope for a better future was set against a country moving quickly into technological innovations that changed the lives of Americans in ways previously unimagined. Advancements in visual arts like silent films and the phonograph, transnational mobility, and the mass production of household goods and services altered the ways Americans engaged with families and communities. Access to school and college resulting from Reconstruction efforts gave Black people opportunities for educational advancement unavailable before the Civil War. Nevertheless, tighter restrictions placed on Black Americans' ability to move about safely within their towns and cities shifted racial dynamics in ways designed to halt the political and economic progression of Black people. Lynchings, which Ida B. Wells in the late nineteenth century had reported being used as a tool for social and political control of Black people, continued to be deployed to terrorize Black communities in the early decades of the twentieth century. This and other factors caused a mass exodus of Black people from the South to the North to seek more freedom, higher wages, and the possibility of achieving their dreams. Isabel Wilkerson describes this exodus, when Black people "set out for cities they had whispered of among themselves or had seen in a mail-order catalogue. Some came straight from the field with their King James Bibles and old twelve-string guitars. Still more were townspeople looking to be their fuller selves, tradesmen following their customers, pastors trailing their flocks" (9).

These changes were reflected in a period then known as the New Negro Era or Movement (now better known as the Harlem Renaissance), the intellectual and cultural flourishing of a new generation of Black writers, musicians, singers, and artists. The date that the Harlem Renaissance began is debated: A. Yemish Jimoh notes that Nathan Irvin Huggins, David Levering Lewis, and E. Franklin Frazier recognize this movement as "beginning . . . in 1919 with the parade of the 369th Infantry Regiment from downtown to uptown Manhattan," while Venetria Patton and Maureen Honey "have revised the New Negro literary movement's beginnings to 1916 and the production of Angelina Weld Grimké's play *Rachel* that year" (489). What is not debatable is that those with the literacy skills to expand on the old worlds or imagine new ones used their talents to expand notions of Black selves in the public imagination.

The most familiar writers of the period are probably W. E. B. Du Bois, Alain Locke, Langston Hughes, Zora Neale Hurston, and Jessie Fauset. The movement was also characterized by its middle-class conservative sensibilities tied to Locke's vision of the movement in his anthology *The New Negro*. Paraphrasing Henry Louis Gates Jr. and Arnold Rampersad, Barbara Foley emphasizes this point:

> Locke's anthology signifies less a recognition of the New Negro's arrival as interpreter of black modernity than an attempt—and a politically conservative one at that—to bring a certain version of that modernity into being. In their readings, Harlem Renaissance culturalism is the inverse of New Negro radicalism; the suppression of the

latter by the former involves not a dialectic of transmutation but a process of takeover, eradication, and obliteration. (5)

The classic blues singers as writers and performers subverted Locke's takeover even as he ignored the radicalism of the New Negro Era artistic contributors. According to Foley, Gates and Rampersad accuse Locke of a discursive reimagining of the New Negro Movement as a cultural movement rather than a radical and politicized one. Such acknowledgments by Gates and Rampersad are important and underscore my reading of the New Negro Era, particularly as it begins to take shape in the 1920s among Black women writers and entertainers. In many ways, I see these writers' and entertainers' cultural expressions moving away from domesticity and sentimentalism and into despair and realism. The 1920 print publication of Grimké's play *Rachel* and Smith's 1920 record "Crazy Blues" offer versions of cultural politics that are at once radical and enigmatic. Despite the differences between the two, their cultural expressions point to a transitory time in American life that offered a subversive exploration into Black lives that rendered the domestic and sentimental fiction of the late nineteenth century uninteresting. Grimké's and Smith's predecessors had deployed their literacy skills in a fight for the very survival of the race, believing the pen might wield a mighty power. In other words, they believed in literacy's transformational possibilities. Grimké, Smith, and other women writers and classic blues singers were poised to launch distinctive perspectives utilizing different literacy practices. The often-linear narrative of the New Negro Era suggests there was a single unifying theme on how the race should exist and solve the race problem, but these women coming from different social classes and using various literacy practices illustrate a diversity of opinions emerging in the early decades of the twentieth century.

Grimké seemed ambivalent about the kind of outcomes literacy produces: she saw both the limitations of and possibilities for literacy to transform the lives of Black people, particularly the Black middle class. The characters in *Rachel* exist in both physical and psychic spaces where their dreams turn into nightmares because white gatekeepers do not really value the literacy skills they profess to value. Conversely, the classic blues singers valued a literacy practice anathema to the more modest of the race. This literacy practice, specular in tone and form, asked not for transformation of the self to gain acceptance from white gatekeepers and Black moderates, but for acceptance and affirmation of the authentic self. Consequently, in the hands of Grimké and the classic blues singers, ideas about literacy and the race were reimagined. Even before the New Negro Era formed into a recognizable movement and the Harlem Renaissance took shape, the concept of a "New

Negro" emerged at the dawn of the twentieth century with literary musings and cultural products and sensibilities that were more rebellious. According to Erin D. Chapman, "through their art and activism and their commitment to self-determination, the New Negroes meant to assert themselves as agents and subjects—no longer mere objects—in these new racial discourses; they meant to affect the hegemonic understanding of racial character and racial politics" (9). Rather than commit themselves to singular ideas about the race, these New Negroes considered themselves inheritors of a new and expansive world where they could construct new attitudes and ways of being unmoored from their people's enslaved origins. This change has been attributed, in part, to time, geographical relocations, new technologies, musical innovation, and World War I. Black women's creative expressions were at the forefront of capturing these changes. New Negro women seized opportunities as writers and singers hoping to inform and change the fortunes of the race in the struggle for autonomy and equality. In their literary works and blues lyrics, these women actualized the limitations and possibilities for the way literacy might inform democratic processes and how conservative constructions of Black womanhood could be a barrier to a fully realized self. Black women writers and singers of the time were thus still heeding the call of Anna Julia Cooper and Victoria Earle Matthews to produce race literature, though with new interpretations of what that meant.

ANGELINA WELD GRIMKÉ'S *RACHEL: A PLAY IN THREE ACTS*

Grimké was a teacher, journalist, playwright, and poet, but her name is probably more recognizable as the daughter of Archibald Grimké, lawyer, community leader, and consul to the Dominican Republic, and the niece of the Presbyterian minister Francis Grimké and of Sarah and Angelina Grimké, both of whom were prominent abolitionists. Angelina Weld Grimké, however, carved out a literary life she hoped would be impactful. As life began to take shape for Black Americans in the first two decades of the twentieth century, Grimké realized the promises offered by her predecessors were unrealizable. Issues of race, freedom, and justice would not be resolved by acquiring sophisticated literacy skills since white gatekeepers refused to open the doors to equal employment and equal treatment. Deborah Brandt describes how literacy is linked to institutions that withhold and grant power, writing that literacy is

> primarily a resource—economic, political, intellectual, spiritual—which, like wealth or education, or trade skill or social connections, is pursued

for the opportunities and protections that it potentially grants its seekers. To treat literacy in this way is to understand not only why individuals labor to attain literacy but also to appreciate why, as with any resource of value, organized economic and political interests work so persistently to conscript and ration the powers of literacy for their own competitive advantage. (*Literacy in American Lives* 5)

Set in the early 1900s, *Rachel* reveals these promises and perils outlined by Brandt. Grimké's three-act play opens on the remaining members of the Loving family: Mrs. Mary Loving, the mother; Rachel, the daughter; Tom, the son; and Jimmy, Rachel's adopted son. They live in a northern city somewhere in the United States at the start of the twentieth century. At the beginning of the play, the Loving family is an ideal family with middle-class values and aspirations. Indicators of their middle-class values include art that hangs on the wall, a "full bookcase," and "an upright piano" (*Rachel: A Play* 1–2). Readers, however, quickly learn that the family members' middle-class status symbols mask the reality of their lives. Grimké's play quickly becomes a psychological thriller meant to disrupt middle-class notions about fairness and equity. Through Rachel's story, the truth about Black middle-class existence is revealed. In the early part of Act I, intimations of Mrs. Loving's somewhat irritable disposition indicate a kind of discomfiture that has less to do with worry over her children and more to do with racial disharmony. This is revealed later in Act I when she explains to Rachel and Tom that their father had not abandoned the family as they had assumed but was not present because he had been lynched along with their brother, George, by "Christian people—in a Christian land" (23). In Act II, the tension builds as it is revealed that Rachel, Tom, and Rachel's suitor, John Strong, are underemployed because of racial discrimination. In Act III, Rachel decides not to marry because doing so might produce Black children she cannot protect from racial insults and attacks. Lynching, employment discrimination, motherhood, and religious hypocrisy are the evils in this play, and all are linked to literacy and education. The early optimism Rachel expresses for motherhood in Act I is slowly and painfully crushed, and a sense of hopelessness permeates much of the play. All the rewards that were articulated as avenues for social and economic advancement show themselves to be useless against systems of racial oppression. Literacy, learning, and education neither improve the characters' economic status nor protect them from racial discrimination. Literacy, thus, is not transformational in ways the Loving family had hoped. Marriage and children do not ameliorate Black suffering. Religion does not soothe their souls. The realities that undermine Black people's education, employment, marriage, children, and religion bring on despair and disillusionment, especially for Rachel, in a direct challenge to the benefits of literacy anticipated by earlier writers.

LITERACY, RACE, AND EMPLOYMENT DISCRIMINATION

All the young adult characters in *Rachel* have earned degrees but are unable to find work in their fields of study. John Strong, Rachel's suitor, is educated but unable to find work commensurate with his skills. He is eventually forced to work as a waiter to help take care of his mother. Rachel learns this fact from her mother and responds sarcastically by castigating American democracy. She tells her mother, "we sing a song at school, I believe, about 'the land of the free and the home of the brave.' What an amusing nation it is" (9). Although her mother does not respond to Rachel's criticism, it is apparent that Grimké intends to deploy Mrs. Loving's silence and Rachel's statement as an indictment against a nation that preaches one ideal for all but does not apply the principle to its Black citizens. Hence, Rachel's reaction to John's employment situation is not just fictional but representative of the challenges confronting the new professional class of educated and trained Black specialists who are underemployed. Rachel and Tom are educated too. Tom earned a degree as an electrical engineer, and Rachel earned a degree in the domestic sciences. Unfortunately, neither can find employment in the fields for which they were trained. Tom is eventually forced to wait tables like John, and Rachel takes in sewing to help the family. The employment situations described in *Rachel* are not fictional problems that arise only in the play. These were real problems affecting an emerging Black professional class. Employment discrimination was not only a white southern problem; northern manufacturing companies and public school administrators were unwilling to hire Black people even when they had the educational background and intellectual acumen to work alongside comparably qualified whites.

Both Rachel and Tom lament their lack of job choices. In Act II, Tom expresses this outrage to his mother, suggesting, "we are destined to failure—they, success. Their children shall grow up in hope; ours, in despair" (42). Tom knows Black children's opportunities for success are bleak. At this point in the play, Grimké reveals the sense of dread and hopelessness that has confronted not only members of the Loving and Strong families, but other educated Black people in American society. What has literacy learning and education to offer Black people if the political systems and employment infrastructures that keep them in second-class status remain in place? How transformational can literacy and education be in their lives? *Rachel* reveals that race continued to determine employment outcomes for Black people, specifically for the Black professional class who were better positioned educationally to reap the rewards of the literacies and educations they had acquired only to be left behind by white gatekeepers or killed by white lynch mobs. Although Cooper and Matthews argued that literature written by Black writers might work to strengthen community bonds and break down racial barriers, Grimké recognized its failure to do so even as she hoped her own writing would have an influence. She believed that to be learned was to be socialized in the language of the dominant group. Deborah Brandt and Kate Clinton point out that literacy learning can be "understood . . . principally as a form of socialization" (344). Literacy as "a form of socialization" has its limits, which the characters in *Rachel* reveal. Yes, the characters are educationally transformed; they have acquired specific skill sets and literacies, but their economic, political, and social conditions have not improved in any meaningful way. They have earned degrees. Unfortunately, the society in which they live has yet to be transformed enough to accept them as equals.

An aspect of literacy learning that Cooper and Matthews understood is that learning the right kind of literacies could teach Black people the cultural traditions and social customs most valued by the dominant group, which perhaps could then provide them with opportunities to better their social status and economic condition as well as adopt the stylistic conventions of standard American English to challenge their oppressive conditions. This means that Cooper and Matthews also recognized literacy's revolutionary import. If Black people could learn the literary and prose conventions well, they could take those literacy competencies and write race literature that would illustrate Black people's humanity but also assimilate them into the broader American society. Cooper and Matthews knew they could not rely on white authors to create positive representations of Black people. They therefore called on their own people to do that work. The literary works by Tillman and Hopkins examined in the previous chapter revealed what literacy skills, time, and imagination could do to help elevate Black people. In contrast, Grimké's *Rachel* begins to point out the social and economic limits of literacy. To be of practical value, the acquisition of basic or even advanced competencies in different kinds of literacies must have political will and support from outside Black communities. This is to ensure that the acquisition of literacy, at least in *Rachel*, will have beneficial results for those skilled to perform jobs for which they will be hired despite their race.

If, as Elaine Richardson writes, African American literacy traditions are "dynamic and fluid cultural matrixes from which revolutionary life and culture-sustaining ideas can be fashioned" (679), it is also true that Grimké recognized that even revolutions need words linked to political will. They need the will of the people who act on their beliefs; they need white employers to give them a fair chance at employment opportunities, which John, Tom, and Rachel are not afforded. It can be surmised that, before their troubles with underemployment, John, Tom, and Rachel embraced the ideals of literacy learning; but they suffered because, even though they were educated, white northern employers had not yet accepted Black people as worthy employees. While all three are eventually employed, Tom more than the others expresses his rage at not being allowed to work in his field of expertise. This he does in Act II by noting his powerlessness to change the fate of his future children and other Black children:

> TOM. In the South, they make it impossible as they can for us to get an education. We're hemmed in on all sides. . . . In the North, they make a pretense of liberality: they give us the ballot and a good education, and then—snuff us out. Each year, the problem just to live, gets more difficult to solve. How about these children—if we're fools enough to have any. (Grimké, *Rachel: A Play* 49)

Tom understands that rearing children not only requires money but also institutions that recognize their humanity. Because he cannot provide these to his future children, Tom declares it foolish to have them. Like his sister, Rachel, who later decides not to have children, Tom intimates having children might not be prudent. With less rage than her brother, Rachel also acknowledges her own employment troubles. Unable to secure a teaching job, Rachel admits to John she will never be an educator: "there's no more chance for me than there is for Tom,—or than there was for you—or for any of us with dark skins. It's lucky for me that I love to keep house, and cook, and sew. I'll never get anything else" (50). Consigned to this reality, Rachel decides to make the best of her employment situation. The exchanges between Tom, Rachel, and John expose how the acquisition of sophisticated literacies gained through formal education may be fruitless, not because of individuals' own ineptitude but due to racial discrimination. These three characters want to work in their chosen professions, but their race is a barrier to equal employment opportunities and ultimately to personal and familial success. Grimké's acknowledgment of the difficulties the rising Black professional class suffered due to racism is a consequence of the false ideals of freedom, which suggest that freedom is its own reward, whereas for true freedom to exist white gatekeepers must stop denying the rights of African Americans. Unfortunately, the measuring stick for entry into white spaces of inclusion was often transitory. It was the classic moving goal post metaphor at work in the fictive and real lives of Black people.

Grimké's didacticism in *Rachel* regarding the false hopes of literacy and education goes further. A minor character in the play, Mrs. Lane, considers the limits of literacy and education more broadly. Mrs. Lane's daughter, Ethel, is being mistreated at school by her white teacher and white schoolmates. Alarmed at the psychological damage inflicted on her daughter, Mrs. Lane decides to find another school for her child to attend. To do so, she first has a conversation with Rachel about a school in her neighborhood. Rachel tells her she believes the school will treat Ethel well, given that Jimmy, her adopted son, is presently being treated well there. But, unbeknownst to Rachel, Jimmy is being taunted and assaulted at the very school she is praising. Ultimately, Mrs. Lane decides to move Ethel to the school Jimmy attends, but she is not sure changing schools will matter in the long run. She explains to Rachel, "'I'm going to have Ethel educated. Although, when you think of it,—it's all rather useless—this education! What are our children going to do with it, when they get it? We strive and save and sacrifice to educate them—down underneath, we know—they'll have no chance'" (58). Mrs. Lane recognizes that acquiring literacy for its transformational possibilities is not enough. Black people should reap financial rewards. Yet Mrs. Lane sees the futility of it and is all but hopeless. In *Rachel*, the politics of race determines economic outcomes despite qualifications, and it also impacts self-worth. In *Beryl Weston's Ambition* and *Clancy Street*, literacy and education are sacrosanct and transformational. Even in *Of One Blood*, literacy learning and education that integrate African and Western worldviews can be positive, life-affirming, and transformational. Conversely, in *Rachel* because the characters realize that education in specialized fields does not provide access to decent jobs and protection from racial oppression, literacy is at best a social accoutrement and at worse pointless.

The sense of hopelessness that permeates the action in the play contests much of the hopefulness present in the prose and fiction of the women writers I examined in chapters 1 and 2. The high regard for reading and writing is apparent throughout Cooper's and Matthews's declarations about race literature. The characters in Tillman's novellas embrace literacy acquisition and education. The most intelligent character in Hopkins's *Of One Blood* is a young Black doctor attending Harvard medical school. Informal and formal instruction is held in high regard in that novel. There is, however, reason for the cynicism expressed about education in *Rachel*. If the play begins in 1900, that means all the characters are thirty-five years removed from the official end of slavery in the United States, which should have been enough time for the Black professional class to reap the rewards of formal education. Put simply, freedom from bondage had given Black people hope that life would be different for them. Unfortunately, at the turn of the twentieth century, segregation became etched in law, lynching was pervasive, and Black underemployment was widespread. Grimké highlighted these systemic racial problems in *Rachel*.

THE PAIN OF BLACK MOTHERHOOD

Rachel's multidimensionality links literacy and education to the pain of Black motherhood by illustrating how barriers to financial stability harm families and communities. Rachel wants desperately to mother Black and brown babies and to create a loving home for them. Yet nothing she or the other characters in the play have done to fashion themselves into model citizens works to protect them from racial violence and employment discrimination, not even adopting the literacy practice and, by extension, the social customs of the dominant white group. Painstakingly, Grimké highlighted these problems. Literally and metaphorically, literacy lets them peek inside the door but not enter the building. Rachel's obsession with motherhood illustrates this dichotomy. She loves to play with the children in her building, especially Jimmy, with whom she has developed a strong attachment. Early in Act I, Rachel tells her mother, "I pray God every night to give me, when I grow up, little black and brown babies—to protect and guard" (13). Children make Rachel happy although her happiness is shattered when she learns the truth about her father's absence: that her father and brother were lynched when the family lived in the South. Their father "edited and owned, for several years, a small Negro paper" (24). Mrs. Loving explains to Rachel and Tom that Mr. Loving was a fearless man who criticized white mob rule in his newspaper. His fearlessness resulted in the death of both himself and their oldest son, George. Upset about Mr. Loving's public criticisms, a local lynch mob forced its way into the family's home, which Mr. Loving tried to protect but was eventually "dragged . . . out" (25) with his teenaged son, who tried to protect his father. Literacy activities in this case brought on devastating consequences. Mr. Loving's critique of injustice is seen as a rebellious act, which is not a right extended to Black citizens. While Mr. Loving's purpose was to use his literacy skills to inform the public and to stop barbaric acts from happening to his fellow African Americans, his own transformational literacy skills were devalued by white gatekeepers who wanted to mute any further critiques.

Mrs. Loving, Rachel, and Tom are in the house when Mr. Loving and George are taken away by the lynch mob. Their lynching force a devastated Mrs. Loving and her remaining children to flee the South. Although Mrs. Loving does not describe the lynching scene, Rachel and Tom instinctively understand what happened and are horrified to learn how their father and brother died. Tom is filled with despair and rage and emphatically utters, "when I think—when I think—of those devils with white skins—living somewhere today—living and happy—I—see—red" (26). Rachel is filled with dread and hopelessness, saying to her mother:

> RACHEL. Then, everywhere, everywhere, throughout the South, there are hundreds of dark mothers who live in fear, terrible, suffocating fear, whose rest by night is broken, and whose joy by day in their babies on their hearts is three parts—pain. . . . Why—it would be more merciful—to strangle the little things at birth. And so this white nation—this white Christian nation—has deliberately set its curse upon the most beautiful—the most holy thing in life—motherhood! Why—it—makes—you—doubt—God! (28)

Rachel learns the world is a cruel place and that Black fathers cannot speak and write without suffering consequences and Black mothers cannot protect their children. This is one stain of white rule. She also learns to distrust God because God does not protect the innocent and the good. Tom's and Rachel's reactions to the lynching of their father and brother reveal the torment that white mob violence imposes on survivors. Although they did not witness the actual violence, Tom and Rachel do not escape its reach. Once Mrs. Loving reveals the truth about the deaths of their father and brother, the psychological damage is done, and the rest of the drama becomes a series of testimonies to the trauma of lynching for Black families. As Koritha Mitchell writes, this play "depicts lynching survivors in ways that acknowledge that their identities are shaped by mob violence" (54). The Loving family cannot escape the reach of mob violence even though they move away from the original site of the terror.

Rachel's disposition moves from childlike effervescence early in Act I to confusion and despair in Act II and madness in Act III as the weight of the lynching takes its toll on her. Despite what she learns about her father's and brother's deaths, she willingly becomes Jimmy's adopted mother because she wants to care for this orphan boy after his mother and father died from smallpox. Rachel also cares for the other children in her apartment building, but she fawns over Jimmy, and he radiates in her presence. She coos, "Jimmy, you're sweet and clean enough to eat. (*Kisses him; he tries to strangle her with hugs*)" (Grimké, *Rachel: A Play* 33). The love they have for each other will be tested not by their own moral failings but by external forces that remind them of their race. For instance, Jimmy is called a "n----r" (61) as he leaves school one day and is then physically assaulted by the same boys. Jimmy is physically as well as emotionally hurt and asks Rachel to tell him what the word means, but she is unable to explain it to him; she pretends the boys meant no real harm. Since Rachel is unable to make sense of the trauma Jimmy experiences and her own experiences at hearing that word come out of his mouth, she begins to descend into madness. Her vulnerability makes the racial insults and racial attacks he suffers almost unbearable and unspeakable. She is, though, able to call the racial hatred Jimmy and other Black and brown children experience a "blight" and calls it "terrible" (62). Rachel's descriptions of racial tyranny are apt, yet she is still unable to utter what race hatred really is to Jimmy or to herself. She does not have the language to describe her sense of powerlessness because the literacy she has acquired has not equipped her with mastery over her feelings on race. Rachel is learned in the social discourses of fairness but not those of sustained racial critique. James Paul Gee's theories about literacy as acquisition and learning apply here: acquisition means one acquires information but does not necessarily learn how to analyze the information, whereas learning means one can question received information. For Gee, learning "inherently involves attaining, along with the matter being taught, some degree of meta-knowledge about the matter" (539). Rachel seems to lack that "learning" form of literacy: she experiences her race but does not have the language to contest and dismantle racism.

    Now as then, naming and describing what race is and how race-based traumas impact the body and the mind are difficult for the victims. Writing in 1989 about the literary canon and its relationship to race, Toni Morrison argued that race is often "unspeakable," an illusory object that is floating in the air but is also weighty, concluding, "thus, in spite of its implicit and explicit acknowledgment, 'race' is still a virtually unspeakable thing" (3). To speak race into existence at that moment with Jimmy is to confront it, which Rachel is not ready to do. It is hanging in the air as an "unspeakable" thing she cannot utter but feels its weight. She has no immediate plans to challenge the boys who harmed Jimmy or even to confront racial oppression head-on. She therefore lashes out at God, whom she had identified in Act

I as placing her on earth to be a mother: "And the loveliest thing—almost, that ever happened to me, that beautiful voice, in my dream, those beautiful words: 'Rachel, you are to be the mother, to little children.' . . . Why, God, you were making a mock of me; you were laughing at me, I didn't believe God could laugh at our sufferings, but He can. We are accursed, accursed! We have nothing, absolutely nothing" (Grimké, *Rachel: A Play* 62–63). The loving and spirited Rachel is gone and has been replaced by an accusatory and eventually psychologically damaged one. Rachel cannot understand why racism is impacting her good and respectable family. She cannot understand these traumatic moments, given the family's social and educational position in society. However, she learns that school is not safe and that literacy and learning do not shield. This predicament, it seems, is one that Grimké wants her readers to reconcile because *Rachel* is rife with confusion and contradictions. Language and sophisticated literacy skills do not equip Rachel with the ability to name the unspeakable. That which she cannot name cannot be challenged or undone. This inability to name the pain, in turn, helps to make Rachel mute. Literacy, as conceived by her Black writer predecessors, does not provide the kind of social capital imagined by Grimké in *Rachel*. There are too many institutional barriers for transformations to take place.

The world is troubling for and to Black people even when they are free, especially for members of the rising Black middle class who were acquiring the accoutrements of the white professional class but were unable to enjoy its benefits. As Claudia Tate points out:

> The ethic of hard work and frugality that had been a central doctrine in the post-Reconstruction texts is found to be deficient by Grimké's early modern black characters because they find working hard for success invites severe racial strife. Their fictive lives reflect real ones, as black people of Grimké's epoch reluctantly realized that Booker T. Washington's agenda of black economic self-sufficiency, deferred enfranchisement, and conciliation were failed strategies of racial advancement. (*Domestic Allegories* 227)

Grimké's play with its shadow of lynching reflects the horror of mob violence as well as the frustration with denied access for those who have worked so hard for success. Anne Mai Yee Jensen argues that Grimké and other playwrights wrote lynching plays to contest white people's rationales for lynchings, which were often perpetrated under the pretense that aggressive and hypersexual Black men needed to be controlled. Jensen notes, "Those who wrote lynching plays used the genre to counteract mainstream images of African Americans, especially as they portrayed black families, and to rethink popular representations of black men and women" (392). I argue that Grimké's play *Rachel* is doing something more. It is also a critique of education writ large and literacy specifically. Rachel comes from what was defined as a "good" family. Her father could read and write; he owned a newspaper. Her mother uses sewing skills to provide for the family. Rachel and Tom are educated. The children in the play are among the most innocent, and the young men work hard to help care for their families. They epitomize goodness. If Jensen is right that the lynching plays were an attempt to rewrite Black womanhood and Black manhood, then Grimké's Loving and Strong families succeed as representations of strong and proud Black families who are mirror images of good and respectable white families. Even their last names are indicators of their goodness, but sadly for them and other middle-class Black families, race trumps sophisticated literacies and goodness. For the Loving and Strong families, literacy gives them no economic or political power. Thus, in a real sense, literacy gives them a casual look into middle-class life, but not real access to it. J. Elspeth Stuckey writes about how systems of oppression penalize and reward literate learners by creating what she calls a "bottleneck," which she describes this way: "to be literate is to be legitimate; not to be literate is to beg the question. The question is whether literacy possesses powers unlike other technologies. The only way to address the question is to be literate. What more effective form of abuse than to offer clandestine services" (18). This is precisely what happens to the Loving and Strong characters. They become literate in specialized fields only to be told both explicitly and implicitly by white gatekeepers that their race precludes them from benefitting from their literacies. However, had they not acquired sophisticated literacies, they would have been described as incapable of higher learning.

Hopelessness abounds in *Rachel*—in contrast to Cooper's, Matthews's, Tillman's, and Hopkins's texts that I examined earlier in this book, which were hopeful about the future for Black people. As theorists, public intellectuals, and creative writers, these four women imagined worlds where Black people were rewarded for their acumen and work ethic. In Tillman's novellas *Beryl Weston's Ambition* and *Clancy Street*, the main characters remain hopeful even in the face of racial caste systems. The two lead female characters, Beryl and Caroline, thrive because they work hard and believe they have every right to live, learn, love, and work as their white peers. Learning to read and write has both intrinsic and extrinsic value for them. Literacy is transformational in their lives. In Hopkins's *Of One Blood*, hope is resurrected because an amalgamation of American and African traditions offers possibilities for individual and collective success. Moreover, in *Beryl Weston's Ambition* and *Clancy Street*, to mother is not to carry a burden, even though life brings its own set of trials to some characters. Conversely, in Grimké's play, Rachel is devasted by the racial caste system that takes away her power to love and to protect Jimmy and any biological children she might have. Her brother is distraught about his place in the world. Powerlessness in the face of rampant racial discrimination is an agonizing reality that Rachel and Tom have difficulty accepting. Acquisition of sophisticated literacies in their fields has not helped them.

Because of her frustration with racial oppression, Rachel lashes out in a fit of rage. She tells God "If I kill, You Mighty God, I kill at once—I do not torture" (Grimké, *Rachel: A Play* 63). Rachel suggests God tortures because God watches as his Black and brown people suffer unspeakable harm while nothing is done to stop their pain. God does not protect the innocent or the educated striving to be decent and to form stable families. In killing the roses she has been given by her suitor, Rachel thus kills immediately, so that the roses, her metaphorical children, do not have to suffer. Rachel is merciful; God is not. Craig Prentiss suggests Grimké's *Rachel* is "part of a theme that prefers the death of a child over a child's suffering" (180). Moreover, he writes that theme was used "not only to protest white mob violence but also to highlight the dissonance between common religious beliefs and lived experience. [Grimké's play] not only challenges God's justice directly but also measures implicitly the value of life itself against the circumstances in which life is lived" (180). God's refusal to intervene on behalf of the dispossessed was not explored in *Beryl Weston's Ambition*, *Clancy Street*, or *Of One Blood*. Grimké therefore provides an important and divergent voice here—one that I believe points the finger directly at white people for their ongoing racism that harms Black families. Black suffering has real consequences, as Grimké shows, and white people cannot absolve themselves as the actors inflicting that suffering. In *Beryl Weston's Ambition* and *Clancy Street*, Black characters suffer, but Tillman does not directly point the finger at white people. In Hopkins's *Of One Blood*, the Black, African, and white characters suffer, but their suffering is caused by a number of factors, one of which is race-based hatred. However, in *Rachel*, there is sadness and hopelessness that cannot be remedied until white people stop their racist practices.

CHILDLESSNESS AS RACIAL SELF-PRESERVATION

Literacy and education, which should provide upward mobility for the educated characters in Grimké's *Rachel: A Play in Three Acts*, are upended when race trumps fairness. Literacy is not, in fact, transformational for these characters. By the end of the play, love and domesticity are challenged when Rachel ultimately rejects marriage and motherhood. John, her suitor, wants to marry, but Rachel decides she cannot in good conscience bring children into the world to suffer because she will be unable to protect them from racial insults, attacks, and discrimination. All that Rachel had hoped for at the beginning of the play is slipping away; thus, it is better to choose celibacy over marriage even though this decision is a difficult one as she reveals in her lamentation: "I shall never—see—you—now. Your little, brown, beautiful bodies—I shall never see.—Your dimples—everywhere—your laughter—your tears—the beautiful, lovely feel of you here. Never—never—to be" (96). The decision not to have children causes her to weep inconsolably, and this decision along with others ultimately leads to her mental breakdown. As Craig Prentiss notes, "Rachel can arrive at no coherent sense of selfhood that allows for God, sexual desire, and motherhood—and racial prejudice. The equation will not work, no matter how she configures it. Her response to prejudice is at first confusion, then a suppressed hysteria, and finally an image of the self that borders on megalomania" (470).

All of those reactions underscore just how traumatic racial hatred is for the psyches of Black people. Grimké illustrates that race hatred leaves psychological as well as physical and other imprints and that a perpetual state of racial marginalization can have long-lasting effects not just on individuals but communities. On the one hand, Rachel may present as a weak, hysterical woman unable to deal with life's hardships. On the other hand, her inability to accept racial hatred as a normal facet of life suggests that Grimké wants to illustrate the profound trauma that racial caste and mob violence impose on Black people. Rather than construct a homeplace where Black people rise above race hatred, Grimké creates scenarios where race and injustice impact the very heart of life itself: the regeneration of a people. In her own words, Grimké explained the impetus for *Rachel*:

> From morning until night, week in and week out, year in and year out, until death ends all, they never know what it means to draw one clean, deep breath free from the contamination of the poison of the enveloping force which we call race prejudice. Of necessity they react to it.... Now the purpose was to show how a refined, sensitive, highly strung girl, a dreamer and an idealist, the strongest instinct in whose nature is a love for children and a desire to some day to be a mother herself—how this girl would react to this force. ("Reason and Synopsis" 51–52)

Grimké shows the force is so strong that Rachel decides not to marry and procreate, given that racial hatred might one day kill her children. This fictive character's choice not to marry should demonstrate to white women readers just how insidious racial violence is for Black women. Home, love, and family form the triad that links many Black and white women, but Grimké writes about a character who chooses a nontraditional path. Black and white worlds collide for a disastrous outcome in *Rachel*, in contrast to the more hopeful Black life portrayed in *Beryl Weston's Ambition*, *Clancy Street*, and *Of One Blood*.

1920s: SHIFTS AND TRANSFORMATIONS

Grimké's *Rachel* explored the dichotomy between an American ideal of a good family and the democratic practices that fail to intervene in racist behaviors both legal and extralegal. Ultimately, readers are left to ponder whether literacy, education, marriage, and motherhood will lead Black women and their families toward full citizenship. For Grimké's Woman's Era predecessors, domesticity was an answer; that was not so for some New Negro women writers like Grimké who found the distance between ideal and reality too far to cross. Writing about the role of domesticity in Grimké's texts, Claudia Tate stresses, "Grimké's writings mark a place where the domestic plots of social optimism become outmoded, and explicit depictions of social alienation and racial protest commence to satisfy the expectations of twentieth-century black readers" (*Domestic Allegories* 210). Optimism gives way to hopelessness, and the belief that God does not protect Black women, men, and children from racial hatred is uttered throughout much of *Rachel*. Sophisticated literacy skills acquired in formal educational settings do not lead to gainful and satisfactory employment. Racial harmony will not be won because Black people become more like their white counterparts. Literacy is not transformational in this play in any tangible way.

This departure from the racial uplift rhetoric of the late nineteenth and early twentieth centuries reveals a shifting tide in the literary works of Black women writers such as Grimké, whose *Rachel* called attention to the hypocrisy of a nation that demands Black people's acquiescence but fails to reward that acquiescence. Grimké was willing to indict white people, particularly white women whose indifference causes bodily and psychic harm. She wrote that white women "are about the worst enemies with which the colored race has to contend" ("Reason and Synopsis" 52). Yet, in writing this play, Grimké hoped white women might identify with a character like Rachel, as a woman longing for motherhood, family, and stability. She envisioned that such links might appeal to their shared desires, writing, "If, then, the white women of this country could see, feel, understand just what effect their prejudice and the prejudice of their fathers, brothers, husbands, sons were having on the souls of the colored mothers everywhere, and upon the mothers that are to be, a great power to affect public opinion would be set free and the battle would be half won" (52). By communicating with the white men in their lives, perhaps white women could spare Black women the pain suffered by the indignities of racial discrimination.

Rachel's departure from the themes of earlier Black women writers is important because the play openly indicted white people for their violent treatment of Black people. It named the problem and recognized the hypocrisies that underlie democratic ideals that maintain power with white gatekeepers. Moreover, *Rachel*'s departure is significant because, in it, Grimké revealed that racial discrimination has both economic outcomes and psychic consequences. No one wins in *Rachel*. Grimké lashed out at both ideological and structural issues in the play. Progress is not possible if barriers to success are not removed. Literacy alone will not end Black suffering. Goodness and righteousness do not end Black suffering. Unlike the plot in *Rachel*, in which the destructive forces of race hatred permeate all aspects of the characters' lives, Tillman's plots in *Beryl Weston's Ambition* and *Clancy Street* do not illustrate the destructive nature of race hatred. Rather, Tillman created plots in which confident characters succeed based on their work ethic and Christian faith. Moreover, because Tillman's work was published by the "A. M. E. church . . . we can safely assume that she directed her works primarily to a black audience" (Tate, *Domestic Allegories* 18). For Black readers of Tillman's fiction, real life could be informed by fictional models in which goodness and hard work could supersede racism. In Tillman's *Clancy Street*, for example, Mr. Langdon, whose wife employed Caroline, finally recognizes her goodness and the possible goodness of other Black people based on her good and noble deeds. Caroline sacrifices her own health to care for Mrs. Langdon when her employer has typhoid fever; she is so dedicated to Mrs. Langdon that she misses giving her valedictory speech. Caroline eventually dies because she contracts typhoid fever after caring for Mrs. Langdon, but in her death the Langdons are prompted to educate deserving Black youth because her goodness wins them over. Mr. Langdon is awed by Caroline's sacrifices and admits, "'child, you have taught me a lesson. I can no longer doubt the capabilities of your race'" (285). Goodness had its own rewards.

Conversely, in *Of One Blood* Hopkins finds a space for both critique and hope. *Of One Blood* was published in the *Colored American Magazine*, which had a mostly Black readership. In it, Hopkins made clear that being born Black is an act of chance just as it is to be born white. Therefore, chance should not be a determining factor in a system that defines human worth based on skin color. Reuel, the main character, who is passing as white, is so smart that his colleagues are awed by his intelligence. When Reuel meets his African kin, they are mesmerized by his presence. Like Tillman, Hopkins hoped to prove a character's worth and intelligence by showing that Black and African people are as smart as white people given that "Of one blood [has] [God] made all races of men" (621). All are equal; thus, racism is arbitrary and unnecessary. Life, however, is bleak in *Rachel*. As an observable phenomenon, chance aggravates the racial conditions of the characters. The young adults in the play are educated; they have acquired literacies in specific areas of study. Unfortunately, there are no happy endings, so readers are left to read about the day-to-day struggles of Black people trying to eke out a living that brings them little joy. The result has everything to do with racial hatred. There is an insistence in *Rachel* that full freedom ought not to be denied and justice should be given to good and hardworking Black families whose literacy practices, ethos, and work ethic mirror those of their middle-class white peers, even though such a thesis is problematic. This example of race literature from the first decade of the twentieth century encapsulates much of what Cooper and Matthews proposed in their essays about the value of race literature. As a form of art, it is creative; and as a form of resistance, it takes white people to task for their inhumane treatment of Black people, particularly those who are linked to white cultural norms adopted by the middle-class characters in *Rachel*.

CLASSIC BLUES

While Grimké's middle-class characters struggle against racist forces meant to keep them in second-class status, the personas the classic blues singers take on in their music react against patriarchal norms and racist forces trying to keep them not only second-class but invisible. Whereas Grimké considered the influence of racial violence on the psyches of Black mothers, the classic blues singers articulated a vision for Black womanhood that subverted the Victorian norms embraced by their late nineteenth-century predecessors and some twentieth-century contemporaries. With the aid of the recording industry, the classic blues singers brought about their own shifts and transformations in the cultural landscape of the 1920s and '30s. Rather than turn to literacy to transform people and institutions to accept palatable versions of Black people, the classic blues singers turned toward a self that embraced working-class identities in which vernacular language, cultural traditions, and values were centered instead of marginalized. This turning inward, mirroring the shared values, traditions, and beliefs of a subset of the Black working class, is a practice I call specular literacy. This literacy practice does not seek to transform Black people into temperate selves acceptable to white gatekeepers or the Black middle class. Rather, this practice is always already acting as both a metaphorical and literal mirror. The classic blues singers' lyrical content entertained, critiqued oppressive systems, and provided a healing balm for a weary people as performative and embodied acts of resistance. Hazel Carby writes, "What has been called the 'Classic Blues,' the women's blues of the twenties and early thirties, is a discourse that articulates a cultural and political struggle over sexual relations: a struggle that is directed against the objectification of female sexuality within a patriarchal order but which also tries to reclaim women's bodies as the sexual and sensuous subject of women's song" ("'It Jus Be's Dat Way'" 231).

I want to extend Carby's definition to include the thematic and intellectual rejection of motherhood and domesticity as central to liberation. This was a departure from the conventional wisdom expressed by these women's predecessors in the late nineteenth century and some contemporaries in the New Negro Era. In fact, their songs expressed disinvestment in those norms replaced by investment in situations in which love and pleasure bring about individual liberation albeit in the face of white domination of Black bodies. Although Carby later rejects the definition of classic blues by arguing the "label is inadequate" ("They Put a Spell" 52), I argue the classic blues provided its fans an escape from their troubles and, in a large sense, validated members of the Black working class at a crucial time in America. Their music thrived from the 1920s and into the early 1930s. This music and the entertainment it provided to their fans gave them access to the broader public inaccessible to other working-class Black women who surely had their own ideas about race. Yet working-class Black women's opinions were not sought after by the Black intelligentsia of the 1920s and '30s. Thus, in many ways, Mamie Smith, Alberta Hunter, Gertrude "Ma" Rainey, and other Black women entertainers who worked as vaudeville stars and women on the traveling theater circuit were bound to connect to the working class. The family origins of many of the classic blues singers also linked them to members of that class.

The classic blues singers' themes were wide-ranging, including but not limited to intense love and passion, retribution and violence, state action, natural disasters, intraracial tensions, and same-sex attractions as well as freedom and justice. These themes resonated with people who yearned to be visible and to be made whole by entertainers who knew how to connect to their fans' sorrows and joys. The lived experiences of Black people necessitated a blues feeling, but not all of the cultural products produced by the writers, artists, and singers of New Negro Era captured the interiority of those blues feelings. In a real sense, classic blues laid bare for Black and white alike the private pains of a life lived under legal constraints and social customs that kept Black people under constant surveillance but also made members of the Black working class the object of intense scrutiny from members of their own racial group. As well, classic blues captured the spirit of the folk, whose subversions against the politics of respectability brought delight and joy through the lyrical fantasies played out in classic blues music. In many ways, their impact is immeasurable. Writing about their geographical imprint and regional fame, Paige A. McGinley describes the classic blues singer this way: "these stars corporealized as well as represented the changes in the racial geographies of the nation; traveling the highways and sound waves, these women's voices conjured forgotten and imagined corners of the nation for both white and black listeners" (42). These listeners in theaters and to records became part of the specular performance embodied by the classic blues singers. When these singers interlaced their voices with pain and power, they gave the working class a window into their everyday experiences. In their lyrics, they did not ask their listeners to yield to demands to adopt modest behaviors or to change their communication styles; rather, they asked their listeners to come alongside them as they described the folkways of a life lived on the margins.

Just what is the blues, and where did it come from? Origin stories can be murky, and the beginnings of blues music are no different. According to Larry Neal, scholars believe the blues may have originated as early as the end of slavery and developed forward from there (42). Whenever and however the blues started, the music struck a chord with its fans. Gates and McKay provide this technical definition of the blues: "Blues music borrowed harmonic and structural devices and vocal techniques from work songs and spirituals. But unlike these other forms, [blues] was usually sung not by a chorus but by a single voice and accompanied by one or more instruments. Blues . . . involved a compellingly rhythmical sound that relied on patterns of call/response between singer and audience, and at times between singer and instrument too" (22). A less technical definition of blues by Angela Davis suggests "what is distinctive about the blues, however, particularly in relation to other American popular musical forms of the 1920s and 1930s, is their intellectual independence and representational freedom" (3). Some prominent writers of the Harlem Renaissance as well as other members of the Black elite and middle class found value in the folk music created by Black singers and musicians, yet failed to appreciate what Davis calls classic blues' "intellectual independence and representational freedom." The radical independence of the classic blues singers and their lyrics represents public resistance to norms they found deficient. Those norms did not value these singers and their folkways. This distinctive brand of folk music provides a window into the creative and intellectual milieu of a subset of the Black working class that reveals, revels in, and imagines lives lived without the constraints that kept many in the elite and middle class from enjoying a musical form created by members of their own racial community. Davis's critique underscores the negative views of blues music held by much of the Black intelligentsia of the 1920s and '30s:

> One might expect that because the classic blues era coincided with the Harlem Renaissance, this musical articulation of African American culture would have been treated extensively by the writers and intellectuals of the day. However, because women like Bessie Smith and Ida Cox presented and embodied sexualities associated with working-class black life—which, fatally was seen by some Renaissance strategists as antithetical to the aims of their cultural movement—their music was designated as "low" culture, in contrast, for example, to endeavors such as sculpture, painting, literature, and classical music. (xiii)

Despite the ambivalence toward blues by some of the intellectuals and writers of the New Negro Era (James Weldon Johnson, Langston Hughes, Zora Neale Hurston, and a few others were exceptions), blues music was popular with its fan base. Record sales and theater attendance attested to the popularity of blues music performed by Black women. Paige McGinley describes the source of blues women's popularity, particularly in the South: "in spite of mass migration, the rural South was home to a large and dynamic populace that, particularly before the widespread availability of the record player and movie houses, maintained its own distinct regional entertainment culture" (38). According to McGinley, Ma Rainey, Bessie Smith, and other classic blues singers toured the South, performing in tent shows and on the Theater Owners Booking Association (TOBA) vaudeville circuit and entertaining fans with their wild tales of life on the road (38). Purchasing blues records and attending theaters to watch their favorite artists allowed blues fans to enjoy an entertainment style that openly rejected the moral standards they were told they were supposed to adopt. Some enjoyed hearing about the secular world inhabited by the personas described in blues verses. Reality mixed with absurdity gave blues fans momentary pleasure away from the harsh truth of their lives.

Mamie Smith's recording of "Crazy Blues" was overwhelmingly successful. Ann Douglas reports that "The record of 'Crazy Blues' went for a stiff $1, but in four weeks an astonishing 75,000 copies had been sold; in seven months, the number was 1 million" (391). From there, the blues craze and race records were born. In addition to helping create a Black consumer culture willing to spend money on blues music, the classic blues singers' music began to reflect something equally interesting: Black communities looking to find solace in entertainment of a secular nature. The public face of Black entertainment would never be the same. Instead of writing lyrics that reflected middle-class angst, the classic blues singers sang about the personal, economic, and social problems confronting members of the Black working class and especially working-class Black women. Angela Davis writes, "it is important . . . to understand women's blues as a working-class form that anticipates the politicization of the 'personal' through the dynamic of 'consciousness-raising,' a phenomenon associated with the women's movement of the last decade" (42). Classic blues performers' lyrics linked those who had moved to the urban North and those who remained in the South to a people and land they knew intimately. The classic blues singers' lyrics embodied the homes their fans missed and the land they once traversed, reminding them of families they loved and the lovers they'd lost. McGinley highlights this value of blue singers to their fans:

> These traveling performers of tent shows and TOBA acts traversed a landscape infused by the possibility of a new life elsewhere, as well as the psychic rupture and loss engendered by the departure of loved ones. For those kin who remained in places such as Natchez, Yazoo City, and Rosedale, these traveling performers served a unique function in making migration visible and audible, providing aesthetic and affective parameters to a phenomenon impossible to conceive in its totality. (38)

This give and take between the blues performers and their audiences, with its mimetic and situational praxis of the people, land, behaviors, and traditions, defines the specular nature of their literacy practices.

The blues form allowed the classic blues singers, particularly those who wrote their own lyrics, to merge aspects of their specular literacy practices into a dynamic musical form that presented their fans with sometimes funny and sorrowful tales but also subversive critiques of life's most difficult challenges. Moreover, along with instrumental accompaniment, the classic blues singers utilized harmony, melody, and borrowed and original lyrics as well as their vocals to insert themselves into public discussions about race. Their specular literacy practices reflected the communicative styles of a subset of the Black working class; Paul Oliver describes those styles as "an expression of a working-class subculture, or rather, of several" (9).

Rhetorically, the blues form relies on verbal play, repetition, indirection, and subversion as vernacular modes of expression. Ultimately, the cultural products the classic blues singers helped create were not a propagandistic art form, but rather an art form that reflected the imagined and sometimes real experiences of a people looking for representational entertainment and secular salvation. The Black women singing blues during the second and third decades of the twentieth century were willing to tell stories in ways that made the invisible visible. Simply put, the specular literacy practices employed by the blues women were not intended to domesticate Black women but rather to liberate them from the Black and white elite and middle-class rules that they saw as rigid. Whatever the early intentions of the blues singers, their brand of art included rather than excluded dimensions of Black working-class life in ways both decadent and noteworthy. In many ways, the classic blues singers' philosophical and discursive departure from their peers in the Harlem Renaissance as well as their predecessors in the late nineteenth century was a natural extension of new technologies like the automobile and the phonograph as well as greater access to education that gave working-class Black women opportunities to join public discussions on race that their predecessors lacked. As rank-and-file members of the vast underclass, they could now create race literature different from that of Black women of an earlier generation.

MAMIE SMITH'S "CRAZY BLUES"

Blues music may not have been what Anna Julia Cooper or Victoria Earle Matthews imagined as race literature, but once it was released for public consumption, there was no stopping its societal impact. Classic blues became its own kind of uplift, a form of literacy that was specular rather than transformational. Mamie Smith is probably best known for making the first blues record performed by an African American woman: "Crazy Blues" in 1920. The song was written by Perry Bradford, who convinced "Fred Hager, a white executive at OKeh Records," to let Smith record it (Gussow 9). Although "Crazy Blues" did not follow W. C. Handy's usual blues format, a "twelve-bar form: three lines of four beats each, the first line repeated twice and followed by a third end-rhymed line" (Gates and McKay 22), it is a blues song. Moreover, even though Mamie Smith did not sing the lyrics in the slow, sad tempo made famous by Ma Rainey and Bessie Smith, the narrative that unfolds is a blues story. A female lover feels hopeless because her man has left her without notice or apparent cause. Mamie Smith sings the words in a medium tempo backed by the sounds of a trumpet, trombone, and clarinet that provide the sad backdrop to her vocals. The female persona at the center of the song has the crazy blues. She cannot get over the man who left her, and this makes her crazy. She longs for his return, singing, "since my baby went away, I ain't got no time to lose. I must find him today" (Smith). In those verses and throughout the song, the jilted female lover is not a demure woman willing to forgo the shame of abandonment in silence. Instead, she actively seeks his affections. Unable to find him and going crazy thinking about him cause her to contemplate his demise, warning that "what you gonna need is an undertaker man." The willful contemplation of his death does not erase her longing for him. She misses him but is still angry enough to want to kill him. She also decides committing suicide is not the answer, admitting, "I went to the railroad, Hang my head on the track, Thought about my daddy, I gladly snatched it back." Anger supersedes sadness here, and the fantasy is altered: his murder and her suicide are replaced by a desire to take drugs and kill a policeman: "I'm gonna do like a Chinaman, Go and get some hop, Get myself a gun and shoot myself a cop." By the end of "Crazy Blues," the desire for revenge has still not subsided. The jilted lover wants to act out her pain by hurting someone. Surprisingly, she chooses a cop.

Such emotional responses to thwarted love are not typically featured in the fiction of the Woman's Era or even some Harlem Renaissance writers' texts, but they are not repressed in this song or in the blues genre. Additionally, there is no hint of racial mobility as central to the story in "Crazy Blues." Race and justice matter, but not in a traditional way. The Black female narrator gets to enact a brand of justice not often affirmed in the fiction of Black women writers of this period. Writing about the power of "Crazy Blues," Adam Gussow remarks, "the song is, I hope to make clear, an insurrectionary social text, a document that transcends its moment by contributing to an evolving discourse of black revolutionary violence in the broadest sense—which is to say, black violence as a way of resisting white violence and unsettling a repressive social order" (10). Thus, on one level, "Crazy Blues" reflects how one woman reacts to rejection, but on another level, it reflects how reactions to rejection are tied to class. In this story, the woman uses drugs to gain courage to shoot a cop. These two indiscretions, drug use and murder, would most certainly be condemned by more conventional writers of the late nineteenth and early twentieth centuries; yet Smith's song became a smash hit.

When Rachel and Tom in Grimké's play *Rachel* become angry due to systemic racism, they react by suggesting that sex and procreation may be off limits. Thus, love and family become dangerous rather than fulfilling. They plan to deny themselves the pleasures of life that are both ordained by God and embraced by the broader society. In so doing, they do not react against the legal and political systems that have caused them so much pain. Grimké does not portray such actions in her play. In contrast, Smith, as interpreter of Perry Bradford's "Crazy Blues," articulates a fantasy whereby a Black woman strikes back against a symbolic force of power that polices the behaviors of Black people. This never happens in *Rachel* even though the characters have many reasons to fight back. When Jimmy is attacked by the white boys who had called him a racial epithet, Rachel does not turn to rage but rather to sorrow. Grimké provides no real or imagined space to avenge Jimmy's attackers. When Mrs. Loving's husband and son are lynched, Grimké does not even imagine a scenario in which retaliation takes place. Instead, the Loving family flees to the North for safety. In Smith's "Crazy Blues" record, however, sadness and rage are made audible and visible. In classic blues music, love, anger, and sadness are emotions articulated by female personas who valorize active participation in one's own lived experiences even as those experiences in real life are considered immodest or even criminal.

Although Smith did not write "Crazy Blues," the song came to embody a kind of brazen New Negro woman. The woman in the song suffers, but rather than suffer passively, she acts. The female lover in "Crazy Blues" shares little with the women described in Tillman's *Beryl Weston's Ambition* and *Clancy Street* or Hopkins's *Of One Blood*. In Tillman's novellas, at times the two main characters, Beryl and Caroline, are in distress, yet benevolent forces intervene in their lives. Internal and external forces encourage the continued acquisition of sophisticated literacy skills and education and promote good and respectable behavior. In *Of One Blood*, the female lead, Dianthe, needs to be rescued by men to be made whole. In the fictitious world of "Crazy Blues," no one intercedes on behalf of the spurned female lover. She alone imagines acting out violent responses to her lover's abandonment. Her passion for revenge seals her fate, not a desire for education, respectability, or salvation. This jilted lover who has the crazy blues marked a pivotal point in Black women's agency. Love for her is lustful, not procreative or domestic. Anger is expressed without much regret. Hence, the difference between the women portrayed in "Crazy Blues" and *Rachel* is startling since Rachel is so troubled over race hatred that she decides marriage and the possibility of having children will be too traumatic. She turns inward and suffers mental strain from her inability to intervene effectively on her own behalf as well as that of her adopted son and any future children she might have.

In contrast to Rachel, the woman at the center of "Crazy Blues" has a fleeting moment when she seeks to do harm to herself but decides against it. Also unlike Rachel, she is unwilling to be silent and invisible. There's no evidence that Perry Bradford and Smith discussed how Black women's agency would be represented in "Crazy Blues." But what I can say with a certain amount of certainty is that Bradford's lyrics and Smith's interpretation of his lyrics refused to dismiss Black grief and rage or to subsume those emotions under the cloak of moderation and piety. Smith and many other Black women singers of the New Negro Era would thus come to embody a new modern Black woman as described by Erin Chapman:

> Ultimately, the blueswoman was not only a woman who performed and recorded the popular black music of the Mississippi Delta and of the urban migrants. She was a particular manifestation of the New Negro womanhood, an iconic image of modern, performative black womanhood born in and made possible by the sex-race marketplace. Shaped in the marketplace that consumed and produced popular knowledge of black womanhood, the blueswoman was in many ways emblematic of all black women. She was the New Negro woman writ large—larger than life, larger than reality. (81)

As Chapman makes clear, the blueswoman was a new bold Black woman who was unafraid to challenge established norms. In her musical repertoire, this new Black blueswoman turned inward to express outwardly the cultural conventions of her own milieu. Often, her vernacular modes of expression born from the language and cultures of the South gave back to the South what it gave to her. This specular manifestation literally and figuratively affirmed a subset of the Black working class by figuring those individuals centrally in the women's blues narratives. In doing so, the song's thematic and character-driven plots did not demand change either within or without, but simply told the tales the musicians imagined, experienced, or bore witness to. Thus, the classic blues singers were unlike their predecessors and contemporaries who deployed literacy and advocated for literacy to transform individuals and communities into middle-class facsimiles of the white middle class suitable for admission to the public square owned and dominated by whites. Rather than seeking entry to the public square that demanded imitation of white norms, the classic blues singers' musical content operated in a public sphere not as a racial other seeking validation but as a racial self that was living, dreaming, acting, misbehaving, and providing critiques among the people. While classic blues music was affirmative for some members of the Black working class, tensions regarding it arose among other social classes.

Evelyn Brooks Higginbotham writes that "the nineteenth century had witnessed the ascendancy of the middle class as the literate public voice of the race. The twentieth century witnessed the ascendancy of the black working class as the oral narrator of modernity" ("Rethinking Vernacular Culture" 165). Although Higginbotham is writing specifically about members of the Black religious working class who were using race records to promote their public message of salvation, the race record market for classic blues was also operating within the scope of what she calls "the oral narrator of modernity" for those members of the Black working class who listened to classic blues by women who expressed themselves in a vernacular with which they were familiar. Sales of Smith's "Crazy Blues" verified the public's desire for music with secular themes. According to Gussow, it has been estimated that "within seven months, hundreds of thousands of copies of 'Crazy Blues' had been sold nationally, perhaps even a million, the great majority of them to a black public delighted at the chance to consume, in endlessly replayable form, a commodified narrative of one black woman's romantic abandonment" (9). After Smith recorded "Crazy Blues," many more Black women were recorded singing blues.

Chris Albertson, blues writer and critic, argues that "Crazy Blues" would be an insignificant blues song but for its being important historically. He writes, "if 'Crazy Blues' cut on August 10, 1920, had not been the first vocal blues record issued, it would probably be long forgotten, for it is an undistinguishable blues composition rendered by a singer whose métier was the so-called sweet song" (24). Albertson's criticism is harsh. Even though Smith's vocals are not comparable to Ma Rainey's or Bessie Smith's, it is the content of the song more than the vocals that make it a distinctive blues composition. The song cannot be forgotten because it expressed viewpoints and behaviors familiar to members of the Black working class who were often ridiculed, rendered silent, or deemed deviant. The record is also unforgettable because it provided a window into the imaginative space of a working-class artist with a working-class ethos whose artistic contributions were as much a part of the formation of the new modern age as any writer of the Harlem Renaissance. Gussow affirms its revolutionary nature, writing, "overdetermined or not, the extraordinary success of 'Crazy Blues,' was at least partly a result of the complex symbolic rebellion it enacted, the truth it spoke to white power" (12). I would say the truth it spoke was against both white power and Black middle-class constraints and repression.

As the physical embodiment of the blues women they sang about, the classic blues singers did not court favor from an invisible white or Black middle-class presence hovering between the lines of their lyrics. They did not seek forgiveness for their sexual experiences. In fact, in many blues songs, they beseeched God's guidance on how to deal with their love troubles, even those outside of marriage. Those kind of imagined scenarios where Black women's sexual agency is indicative of more modern sensibilities helped to distinguish them from their predecessors and peers. For example, Tillman's novellas had revealed some of the trappings of Black middle-class angst around transformation and acceptance. In *Beryl Weston's Ambition* and *Clancy Street*, the working-class characters need literacy instruction, religious education, and refinement to become fully embraced in their communities. In other words, they need to be reformed and transformed to join the ranks of the middle class even if they join only ideologically instead of economically. Once they do so, they can become visible in a way that is proper and appropriate; they become homogenized, integrated in what Cook-Gumperz calls "socially approvable" communities (1). To remain as they are, untutored, unrefined, and irreligious, means they will remain outsiders. For example, in Tillman's *Clancy Street*, Hettie, Caroline's good friend, is considered wayward. She accepts the attentions of a young white man, Mr. Howard, who thinks she is attractive. This is, of course, problematic because of the dangers of miscegenation. When Hettie confesses to Caroline that she enjoys this man's affections, Anne happens to be listening, and she tells Hettie she disapproves of Hettie's behavior. In this novella set in the early 1880s, Anne worries about the intentions of Mr. Howard and the harm to Hettie's reputation if she decides to become romantically involved with him. Anne admonishes Hettie, saying, "Mr. Howard means no good to you. Let him alone" (272). Anne then explains how Black girls gain respectability: "Every colored girl that wants the respect of black folks, and white folks as well, must stay in her place and keep white men folks in theirs" (273). Sexual liaisons with white men will only bring shame to Hettie, her family, and her community.

The information about race and respectability Anne tries to communicate to Hettie falls on deaf ears. Hettie does not tell Mr. Howard to leave her alone as she was encouraged to do. For a brief time, she is engaged in "unacceptable" behavior with him. But as a poor girl being raised by her grandmother, Hettie needs all the guidance and the instruction she can get. As Hettie's story unfolds, it is obvious she does not abide by the standards of behavior set forth for the newly freed people a mere nineteen years removed from slavery. Eventually, Hettie's reputation will be restored when she repents of her sins and accepts Christ. Religious instruction and Christian acceptance are what saves her. As a young working-class woman, she can become respectable and visible in her community through a saving grace. There is, however, tension among Black women within and outside the church seeking to determine what respectable behavior looks like. Higginbotham writes about this tension among Black women:

> It was in the church, more than any other institution where black women of all ages and classes found a site for "signifying practice"—for coming into their own voice. And theirs was a dissonant voice in a society in flux. Massive black migration and urbanization, employment patterns, the heightened materialism of consumer culture, the growing dominance of industrial education, the suffragist movement, and world war—all evoked responses from black women. (*Righteous Discontent* 185)

Black women blues singers add to the many voices expressing ideas on a range of topics related to the race. Theirs, however, are voices of sublimation and specularity. They offer competing ideological and cultural models though speaking to the same God in supplication and asking for grace. The immediate popularity of "Crazy Blues" shows that many Black people were looking for alternative ways to gain self-worth, self-love, and God's favor. Equally important, the Black women writing and performing blues songs were suggesting that the old ways of demureness and assimilation were not the only ways by which African Americans might find their place in America. In "Crazy Blues," the jilted female lover does not seek redemption from a god figure or an upstanding community member after admitting a desire to commit murder and suicide. Instead, she expresses rage and discontent, and the lyrics do not carry her from being a bad woman to a good one. There is a kind of expressive freedom in "Crazy Blues" that has resonance for people in the real world. Listening to these classic blues singers, members of the Black working class could cast off a respectability ethos and let loose. There, in the lyrics and literacies of blues verses, many working-class Black women could see themselves as part of Black communities looking to force their way out of repression and hopelessness.

THOSE SPECULAR "CRAZY BLUES"

The classic blues singers were not the first Black artists whose art was specular in function and form as it mirrored back to audiences their shared values, vernacular, and culture. In the late nineteenth century, Paul Lawrence Dunbar employed the vernacular of the folk in his poetry specifically in two poems, "An Ante-Bellum Sermon" and "When Malindy Sings," published in 1895 and 1903 respectively. Each beautifully and subversively captured and reflected the communicative styles of the vernacular of Black southerners. Dunbar's best vernacular poetry reflected cultural experiences and linguistic practices that were meant to value experiences and language practices rather than mock or transform the language and the people—just as the classic blues singers did years later. Although Smith's vocals in "Crazy Blues" did not necessarily reflect Black southern vernacular speech patterns, the vernacular turn of phrases did reflect the kind of expressive nuances of the Black vernacular associated with "the folk." Moreover, because values and cultural traditions are embedded within language conventions, Perry Bradford's song reflected a particular kind of working-class ethos. For example, there was the threat of violence directed at the self, a lover, and a policeman, as well as the potential use of drugs to anesthetize fear and longing. Although these are the imagined fixations of a woman scorned, the mere fact that Bradford wrote them and Smith sang them connected songwriter, singer, and audience in a triad that linked all of them to fans who loved the blues. In this song, the folk have spoken: here was no redemption or transformation of the soul at the end of "Crazy Blues." Love has driven the jilted lover crazy, and sometimes this needs to be uttered, even publicly.

Folk expressions and Black vernacular were often either exoticized or criticized, both in Mamie Smith's time and today. For instance, in her "Value of Race Literature" speech, Victoria Earle Matthews made a disparaging remark about Black vernacular, hoping that future writings by African Americans would eradicate it because its use was associated with those belonging to the lower strata. Her hope was that race literature "will undermine and utterly drive out the traditional Negro in dialect" (173). She expressed this hope even though she wrote a short story using Black vernacular. In her essay on Matthews, Shirley Wilson Logan highlights Matthews's attempt at writing Black vernacular in her short story "Aunt Lindy," noting that, "stereotypical depictions aside, *Aunt Lindy* represents one of the first attempts to feature a dialect-speaking folk character as the central figure in a narrative" (274). While the main character uses dialect, her class status is more akin to the religious middle class, whose language use is merely representational rather than a commentary on character. In the texts by Tillman and Grimké that I examined, each writer made it clear that characters speaking "improperly" needed to learn to speak "proper grammar." What these women reveal is "the ways in which American culture links literacy to social power" (Babb 366). However, one's literacy practices are more than the sum of their parts. Since literacy is not simply how one reads, writes, and speaks, but also what one reads, writes, or listens to, literacy reflects and responds to particular kinds of value systems and political structures. As vocal interpreters of original blues lyrics and writers of new blues verses, the classic blues singers demonstrated that class-identified literacies most associated with the Black working class belonged alongside all so-called socially approved literacies. As Jacqueline Jones Royster contends, definitions of literacy ought to be more inclusive and expansive rather than too narrowly conceived. Royster uses as an example Sojourner Truth's admission that "You know children, I don't read such small stuff as letters, I read men and nations" (qtd. in "Perspectives" 106). Although Truth was referring to the "literacy requirements for the right to vote," Truth acknowledged, and Royster affirms, that in its oral and written form literacy is multivalent: "becoming literate does mean gaining the skills to read and write; beyond that, it also means taking the power and the authority to know in multisensory ways and to act with authority based on that knowing" ("Perspectives" 106–7). I would add that literacy is also about embracing the literacy practices of one's social group. Smith, as the interpreter of Bradford's "Crazy Blues," represented the shared vernaculars and values of a subset of the Black working class. In specular fashion, Smith and the other classic blues singers put on public display, vocally and linguistically, how, as race women themselves who had their own ideas about the race, freedom could be expressed musically and justice enacted without calling on literacies that sought transformation of the individual and the community within the boundaries of middle-class conventions; instead, they turned inward to find ways for the full selves of African Americans to be affirmed.

Although Smith did not write "Crazy Blues," her recording of Bradford's song gave it power and meaning, particularly as it related to how expressions of a fully immersive self can be realized as a specular literacy practice. In Smith's version of "Crazy Blues," this is enacted in the ways that the central figure is unapologetic in her proposed solutions to solve her heartache. Certainly, the decision to turn to violence to mitigate suffering is fictive, but even the act of imagined revenge moves Black pain beyond the abstract and into the real. When emotions are not tempered or policed as in Tillman's novellas, the characters who express them suffer personal and communal consequences as was shown with Hettie in *Clancy Street*. Lyrically, the mercurial woman in "Crazy Blues" is not scorned by her community because she longs to be with the man who does not want her. She is not admonished because she wants to seek revenge against her man; she is also not rebuked for seeking to exorcise her anger by shooting a cop. There is no interceding voice that tells this woman with crazy blues to calm down and act like a lady.

She is allowed to express her frustration. That is the beauty of classic blues. In its vernacular tradition, outrage is a legitimate expression, in contrast to the outrage that is stifled in Grimké's *Rachel: A Play in Three Acts*. When Rachel kills the roses because she cannot handle Jimmy's race-based suffering, she is unable to even explain her own rage to John, her suitor, who asks, "Rachel,—why—why—did—you—kill the roses—then?" (88). She tells him, "it hurt—too much—to talk about it yet,—please" (89). When Rachel kills, she acts quickly, but shame and middle-class decorum do not allow her to fully comprehend or explain the pain she is experiencing. John wants her to be calm and explain herself, yet Rachel wants and needs to express her rage even more. Sadly, her timidity and inability to forthrightly discuss racial prejudice with John are manifested in a discourse of modesty, which allows her very little language with which to explain the origins of her disappointment and rage. Because transformational literacy practices in some ways buckle under dominant forces, Grimké's characters were unable to manifest powers of expression to challenge it. Rachel has the blues, but she is no blues woman.

LUCILLE HEGAMIN'S "THE JAZZ ME BLUES"

After Smith's "Crazy Blues," other blues characters were developed and stylized in songs recorded by the classic blues singers. Lucille Hegamin was the second Black woman recorded singing blues music. Her "The Jazz Me Blues" and "Everybody's Blues" were recorded in 1920, though the recordings were released in February 1921. Tom Delany wrote "The Jazz Me Blues," but Hegamin's recording gave it life. "The Jazz Me Blues" was not like Smith's "Crazy Blues." There is no jilted lover who looks for her man, threatens to kill her man, contemplates suicide, or imagines killing a cop. In fact, the themes of rejection and revenge do not appear in "The Jazz Me Blues." In it, the tempo is fast, the vocals are light, and the instrumental accompaniment provides a fun and lighthearted backdrop to Hegamin's high-pitched voice. This song steps over the boundary line of decorum respected by the Black elite and middle class since fun and indulgence are centered, rather than social uplift. The following lines are instructive. Hegamin sings, "come on professor and jazz me, jazz me, you know I like my jazzin' both day and night, and if I don't get my jazzin' I don't feel right." Excitement and fantasy are delights for the singer; without them, life is drab. As an artistic expression, blues music in content and form provided Black people on the margins, especially many in the Black working class, an opportunity for public expression. Much of the literature written by Black women intellectuals and creative writers of the late nineteenth and early twentieth centuries was by women whose ideas about art and the race were reactions against allegations of Black inferiority. This makes sense, of course, given the historical and political realities they and other members of their race faced; however, in the 1920s Black women were recorded singing blues, writing blues verses, and even composing and arranging blues songs that imagined, embellished, and revealed truths about desires and behaviors usually kept hidden by their middle-class predecessors and contemporaries. The classic blues singers were a group who unabashedly found delight and agency in playing out the worldly pleasures of a blues life in their songs. In so doing, their employment of specular literacy informed the narratives at the heart of their music and simultaneously shaped their ethos.

James Cone provides an apt definition of the ways blues songs function by positing "they are not propositional truths *about* the black experience. Rather they are essential ingredients that define the *essence* of the black experience. And to understand them, it is necessary to view the blues as a *state of mind in relation to the Truth of the black experience*" (114; emphasis in original). The state of mind Cone refers to marks the blues narrative as both inventive and experiential—and, I would add, culturally disruptive. It is an art form that sought to prove the worth of neither its creators and performers nor the race to which they belonged. In many ways, the creators and performers could just be. Nevertheless, market forces changed early blues music. Ann duCille describes how popularizing the form altered some folk aspects of the music:

> The fact what was once local lore could be packaged and distributed, I would argue, altered and institutionalized the form irrevocably.... the classic blues, the variety of blues sung and recorded by professional performers such as Bessie Smith and Ma Rainey, are so called both because they standardized and universalized particular, recurrent lyrics, themes, techniques, and because they re-formed the ritualistic elements of a once private or communal African American folk modality into public entertainment available for mass consumption. (72–73)

Yet the blues form did offer the lyricists and singers artistic malleability even as it succumbed to the demands of consumer culture. That does not make the lyrics they wrote any less impactful. Nonetheless, Hegamin, not as a songwriter but as a performer of "The Jazz Me Blues," articulated a version of life that was not a direct reaction against racial injustice but one that was more tacit and specular. Her performance of the song created race literature that acknowledged the need for fun and excitement in the face of racial oppression. When she sang, "don't want it fast, don't want it slow, take your time professor, play it sweet and slow," she indicated she wanted to have a good time despite the circumstances of life. In 1920, however, good times were circumscribed. How might Black people enjoy themselves in an era when much of their life was regulated by Jim Crow and the gaze of the emerging Black elite and middle class? Listening to blues on records and going to venues where the classic blues singers were performing were ways to ease their burdens. Yet this music gave some Black intellectuals pause because of its vast reach. As the director of the Atlanta School of Social Work, Forrester B. Washington worried about the leisure activities of Black people, advising that some activities such as church, tennis clubs, and golf clubs were acceptable but listening to race records was not. In fact, race records, he thought, were destructive rather than constructive. Arguing that white-owned record companies were using race records to encourage immorality among African American consumers, Washington protested:

> The general practice of the larger talking machine companies of America, of almost forcing on the Negro race records that are distinctly immoral in their title and context. Some of these records are so obscene that the companies have not the courage to advertise them in their regular catalogs, but issue special booklets for Negroes. Not content with issuing these booklets to Negroes, these companies also flaunt the suggestive titles of these records, accompanied with obscene pictures, in Negro newspapers. (279)

Washington's critique is illustrative of the degree to which middle-class angst was pervasive among Black leaders who feared their attempts to establish respect for their race would be undermined by what they saw as obscenity and immorality portrayed in blues music.

For example, Washington would have likely been bothered by a 1927 advertisement for Ma Rainey's blues song "Soon This Morning Blues" in the *Chicago Defender*. In the ad, there is a drawing of a man with his left arm holding onto a window ledge and his right arm and the rest of his body outside the window. In his right hand is his satchel. The man just needs to drop his left arm, and his whole body would be on the ground, and he could freely walk away from the house. Next to the sketch of the man is a drawing of a small community. One of the more prominent buildings in this drawing looks like a church with a steeple, with the sun rising over the community. The quiet community scene is disrupted by the man leaving through the window while his female lover watches in distress. Beneath the drawing of the community is a sketch of Ma Rainey, who smiles contentedly. Beneath Rainey are a couple of lines from her song "Soon This Morning Blues": "Seen this morning, just about the break of day, I caught my good man making his getaway." In addition to the quoted lyrics, there is a description of the song that reads "there's hard luck, remorse, unsatisfied love, and worlds of yearning." As incendiary as was the image of the man sneaking away from his lover, it is not a leap to suggest that the words accompanying the image were similarly offensive to Washington. One can assume that, for Washington, sexual liaisons were immoral and therefore not respectable, especially for Black women and men in the early twentieth century. To twenty-first century eyes, the drawing and the words are not obscene, yet it is understandable why Washington would be aghast at such a depiction of Black male-female relationships in 1927. The ad does not denounce sex outside of marriage; rather, it is a representation of a sexual liaison between two adults. Washington knew all too well how many white people perceived the so-called hypersexualized behaviors of Black men and women. Nevertheless, the recurrent themes in classic blues regarding sexual relationships between adult women and men, as this advertisement illustrates, were not concerned with the social mores of white people or of the Black elite and middle class. There was no consideration for their feelings. In this way, specular literacy operated in both an imaginative space but also a material one where the private moments of casual sex were not obscured by moderation and obfuscation.

The tone and content of Washington's indictment of race records were indicative of a race man who recognized how ideology worked within a consumer culture that profited from Black artists but devalued their humanity. Aside from the sexually explicit content that worried Washington, he failed to recognize how race records likely forged bonds among their fans and how valuable it was for individuals often ostracized within Black communities to see themselves reflected in the music they loved. He did not consider how the vernacular expressions in blues songs such as "Crazy Blues" or "The Jazz Me Blues" acknowledged publicly the vibrancy of folk language. Slang, indirection, and verbal play, which are common in the vernacular, are pervasive in blues music, helping to give it vivacity. When Hegamin sings, in "The Jazz Me Blues," "I got those doggone, low-down, jazz me, jazz me blues," "jazz me" takes on varied meanings, making the verbal play multilayered. "Jazz me" can be interpreted as having a case of the bad blues because the music feels so good that it makes the vocalist feel bad. Other words in the song like "doggone" and "jazz me" are slang terms that convey a funky, bluesy feeling and, because they are familiar, help to forge connections with their listeners. People who were usually told they needed to change how they communicated and what they believed must have felt affirmed by blues songs like "The Jazz Me Blues" and probably felt as if they were resisting the status quo.

Like Washington, critics of classic blues music paid attention to the explicit and implied sexual content in blues lyrics. "The Jazz Me Blues" serves as one example among many that likely gave critics pause. The most provocative lyrics in the song are playful, but they do not obscure the sexual innuendo when Hegamin sings, "don't want it fast, don't want it slow, 'take your time, Professor, play it sweet and low'" or "you know I like my jazzin' both day and night, and if I don't get my jazzin', I don't feel right." When Hegamin sings these lines, she teases playfully, not explicitly sexually, but one can hear the sexual tension. The double entendre present in those lyrics can be read either to mean the musicians need to play the music just right to halt a blues feeling or to mean the intimate encounter needs to be right. Critics of blues understood the representational power of implicit and explicit content like those found in "The Jazz Me Blues." Yet, for all the worry of some Black critics of classic blues, there is no denying its sonic and cultural power. Hegamin's and Mamie Smith's recordings of the blues introduced a different dynamic into the consumer culture expanding rapidly in the early decades of the twentieth century. Black people of various social classes could seek diverse forms of entertainment that affirmed parts of themselves in the creative expressions of Black artists. Erin Chapman writes about how Black performers of the time took advantage of modern principles connected to capitalism and agency, suggesting, "on the whole, New Negroes, acutely aware of the sex-race marketplace and its machinations, sought by various means to use their commodification to their own advantage" (82). In the early twentieth century, Black women had very little agency over their lives, yet the race record industry provided some with new opportunities for economic advancement and personal agency. The race record industry allowed Black women entertainers such as the classic blues singers to participate musically in public discussions on race and to do so in a language familiar to them. In so doing, their specular literacy practices sometimes affirmed but more often challenged the ideals of race literature voiced by most Woman's Era and New Negro Era writers.

Hegamin's "The Jazz Me Blues," for instance, can be contrasted to Grimké's play *Rachel*. There are no moral choices to make in Hegamin's song, whereas moral choices are central in Grimké's play. In Hegamin's verses, the secular world of jazz and blues momentarily forgets the daily humiliations tied to Jim Crow laws portrayed in Grimké's play. Black middle-class dissatisfaction, an important part of Rachel's world, is of no concern in "The Jazz Me Blues"; having a good time is. Writing about Black consumer culture and identity formation, Chapman suggests, "It was the music, and through the purchase of clothes, cosmetics, race records, and other luxuries and entertainments, as much as through travel, work, and politics, that African American migrants became urban, sophisticated, undaunted New Negroes. As much as any other factor, the clothes and the cosmetics, the music, and the nightlife helped them forge new identities, develop new attitudes, and shape their destinies in this period" (81). These New Negro identities forged in the music of the blues in songs such as "The Jazz Me Blues" provided alternate ways to explore how discussions about race might be addressed differently in the new, modern age. Staid discussions of proper dress and speech or quiet and reflective religious experiences were not the only way to mitigate their second-class status; adventure and fun, sex and passion, music and dance were also. African Americans' race need not be an impediment to having a good time as "The Jazz Me Blues" showed. Perhaps reflecting good times back to the people where they were as a specular part of their and the audience's literacy practices could also serve as a kind of uplift, rather than making them feel excluded even from their own race if they failed to satisfy the moral dictates of many in the elite and middle class.

In 1922, the year after the release of Hegamin's two blues songs, came Alberta Hunter's "Down Hearted Blues," notable for being the first song written by Hunter and composed by Lovie Austin, a Black woman pianist and composer. "Down Hearted Blues" was one of her signature songs recorded by many others including Bessie Smith. This blues song continues in the spirit of the two discussed above. The three songs share an up-tempo beat despite their lyrical content. In "Down Hearted Blues," a woman laments that she loves a man who does not love her, saying, "gee . . . it's hard to love someone, when that someone don't love you, I'm so disgusted, heartbroken too" (all lyrics qtd. in A. Davis 273). In the middle verses, the woman hopes for better results but recognizes too that trouble, including man trouble, might "follow me to my grave." By the end of the song, the man she loves still does not love her. His rejection of her fuels vengeful impulses. Karma, she hopes, will avenge his mistreatment of her; should that compel him to come back to her, she requires that he "come under my command." This bold declaration provides the dejected lover with some agency, at least an imaginative agency, in which her man suffers for breaking her heart. The song suggests that Black women deserve spaces to express their forbidden desires and hidden pains and to do so in a manner not associated with middle-class respectability.

In addition to the working-class ethos articulated in the lyrics of "Down Hearted Blues," Hunter's phrasing reflects the linguistic flourishes of a subset of the Black working class. Throughout the song, she shifts between standard and vernacular idioms. In one place, the written lyrics are, for example, "Thought you mistreated me, and drove me from your door. You mistreated me, and drove me from your door." However, Hunter sings the word "door" as "doe." Geneva Smitherman identifies these kinds of differences as "tonal semantics, which refers to the use of voice rhythm and vocal inflection to convey meaning in black communication" (134). When Hunter changes the pronunciation of words like "your" and "door," she also changes their meaning and intent. The transcribed lyric is "you mistreated me and drove me from your door." If she were to sing those two words without changing the standard pronunciation, the degree to which she feels mistreated by her man loses its emphasis. For her man to throw her out of *his* "doe" [door], a door she has presumably walked in on numerous occasions, is doubly insulting and upsetting. Smitherman explains that "Intonational contouring is the specific use of stress and pitch in pronouncing words in the black style" (145). The ability to shift from standard speech to a Black style gives Hunter linguistic options that reveal the different language practices and experiences of the Black working class. Kari J. Winters writes that Hunter's unconventional responses to commonplace problems allow her to "participate in the blues philosophy that, resisting Master Narratives, inspires energies that undermine, bypass, subvert, and exceed patriarchal logic" (205). In so doing, Hunter enacts and embodies specular literacy by emphasizing both the linguistic and cultural forms of the racial community she knew intimately. She signifies as she sings the blues to the blues community.

At first glance, it may not be obvious how Hunter's "Down Hearted Blues" extends Cooper's and Matthews's calls to create race literature that will uplift the race. The leap, though, is not a far one. Hunter participated in the continued formulation of music that allowed Black women to speak to everyday issues that affected women from similar social classes who longed for love, protection, and visibility. Hunter and the other classic blues singers showed that middle-class status should not be the only outcome of the racial struggle and that art can be powerful even as it reflects the folk at their best and worst selves. Specular literacy, the practice of reflecting back what one sees, has a function, and the blues singers utilized it to masterful effect. Langston Hughes's essay "The Negro Artist and the Racial Mountain" underscored much of what is inherent in the practice of specular literacy. Hughes argued that Black artists should be inspired by their own cultural traditions and, in so doing, might find the best of themselves reflected in their ways of being. Hughes wrote, "But then there are the low-down folks, the so-called common element [who] furnish a wealth of colorful, distinctive, material for any artist because they still hold their own individuality in the face of American standardizations. And perhaps the common people will give the world its truly great Negro artist, the one who is not afraid to be himself" (1312). Hughes also suggested that art does not have to function as race propaganda. Great art can feed the soul even as it affirms elements of Black lives and experiences that may be considered unseemly by the more conservative members of the race.

Many of the working-class classic blues singers featured in this book embodied Hughes's artistic manifesto as well as those not examined like Bessie Smith, who provides another example of specular literacy in action. Smith lived a kind of blues life and, as a performer, imagined its possibilities for communal healing and uplift. In a 1926 article, Mable Chew wrote in the Baltimore *Afro-American* that Smith hoped her traveling show would inspire young people: "Bessie Smith . . . nationally known Blues singer . . . is not 'upstage' in manner, nor has she forgotten her struggles before she became famous. Miss Smith says her greatest ambition now is to carry her marvelous voice into the small towns and villages so that young people of our race may be inspired to use their talent and develop themselves" (4). Smith was one of the most highly paid and notable blues singers of her time. In some ways, she was more myth than singer; but this does not belie the fact that Smith recognized her status as an influencer of young Black people. She hoped her presence and her talent would convince them they could rise above negative perceptions about the race and that remaining true to one's cultural roots had value. She was a living embodiment of this reality. Rather than adapt her musical style to fit the cultural tastes of the Black middle class, she remained wedded to a vernacular tradition rooted in her southern community. Smith and other classic blues singers reflected a dynamic, diverse, and fluid language that reflected the place and time of a people whose folk traditions were existing alongside their New Negro Era counterparts looking to find solace and status in the new modern age. What these blues women illustrated is that discussions about race could be expansive, varied, and evolving rather than static and regressive. Moreover, they refused to abide by fixed uses of literacy as a transformational practice enacted for acceptance into white spaces controlled by white gatekeepers. The classic blues singers found fun and adventure as well as provided critique and condemnation by turning inward and leaning on specular forms of literacy that met them and their fans where they were artistically and racially.

Chapter Four

LITERACY, LITERATURE, AND CLASSIC BLUES

Jessie Redmon Fauset and Gertrude "Ma" Rainey

Jessie Redmon Fauset and Gertrude "Ma" Rainey are creative heirs of Anna Julia Cooper's and Victoria Earle Matthews's race literature aims. They were Black women of the New Negro Era who turned to their art to speak to and for the needs of the race. Fauset sought to resolve how race impacted the lives of the Black middle class, while Ma Rainey helped many members of the Black working class appreciate approaches to the race problem that were sometimes eccentric and outlandish but no less important. Although Fauset and Ma Rainey approached the race question differently and utilized different forms of literacy to do so, what makes their contributions important sites of inquiry is that both illustrate the philosophical investments in Black people by Black women from different social classes at critical moments during the New Negro Era. Many studies cite Fauset's contributions even when her work was considered too bourgeois. Few studies acknowledge the contributions of Ma Rainey as a race woman invested in her community or place her work alongside her New Negro women peers. However, in many ways I see Fauset and Ma Rainey contributing to the same racial meal. One cooks protein, and the other one prepares vegetables. A human body needs both. Each in her own way used her creative skills to help the race during the New Negro Era and to address W. E. B. Du Bois's famous summation of the "Negro problem":

> Between me and the other world there is ever an unasked question: unasked by some through feelings of delicacy; by others through the difficulty of rightly framing it. All, nevertheless, flutter round it. . . . They say, I know an excellent colored man in my town; or, I fought at Mechanicsville; or, Do not these Southern outrages make your blood boil? At these I smile, or am interested, or reduce the boiling to a

simmer, as the occasion may require. To the real question, How does it feel to be a problem? I answer seldom a word. (9)

Du Bois, of course, was not actually silent on the question, and neither were Fauset and Rainey, who found creative ways to try to improve the poor state of Black life.

In her novel *Comedy: American Style*, Fauset critiqued a form of literacy utilized by characters who viewed racial advancement as a zero-sum game. This form of literacy, transactional literacy, is a commodified form of literacy meant to enhance the social position of certain members of the Black race and their families without consideration for the social advancement of their racial communities. Forms of transactional literacy have a long history. Henry Louis Gates Jr. describes one form of it as existing for certain enslaved persons like the poets Phillis Wheatley and George Moses Horton: "writing, for these slaves," Gates notes, "was not an activity of mind; rather, it was a commodity which they were forced to trade for their humanity" ("Writing 'Race'" 9). Both Wheatley and Horton had masters who freed them, and they were freed, Gates argues, because as highly skilled writers they were Black oddities. Thus, they won their freedom because their masters could profit from their literacy skill. That their literacy skills were objects of trade for their freedom constitutes the exchange as a transaction. This promise to exchange an enslaved body for a freed body due to literacy is peculiar, but as Gates notes, for Europeans and white Americans, writing meant that one could reason and, if one could reason, one might be human. Thus, it was inhumane to keep a literate person enslaved. Gates emphasizes that "writing, especially after the printing press became so widespread, was taken to be a *visible* sign of reason. Blacks were 'reasonable,' and hence 'men,' if—and only if—they demonstrated mastery of 'the arts and sciences,' the eighteenth century's formula for writing" (8). Wheatley and Horton had little in the way of power in that literacy transaction between master and enslaved person. In the early twentieth century, commodified aspects of literacy remained a complicated part of Black life as Fauset made clear in *Comedy: American Style*. The comedy of race was enveloped in a form of transactional literacy that commodified the very soul of the central family in the novel.

Fauset's contemporary, Ma Rainey, was already a star when she recorded her first record in 1923. She had long been on the theater circuit performing with Pa Rainey and the Rabbit Foot Minstrels. Hailing from Georgia and spending much of her career traveling in the South and Midwest, Ma Rainey remained artistically connected to her southern roots. In doing so, her blues was an outward expression of her keen observations of a blues life lived on the racial margins. The blues life she captured reflected the language, geophysical places, behaviors, and attitudes of the folk whom she knew well. This way of seeing the racialized manifestations of a people in song was part of her unflinching blues aesthetics and her specular literacy practices. Ma Rainey's corpus of classic blues music was recorded over five years from 1923 to 1928. Her music encapsulated the milieu of a folk people looking for fun and salvation by worldly means. Although Ma Rainey's specular literacy practices differed from Fauset's, each represented the hidden voices in plain sight occupying the liminal spaces where alternate ideas and oppositions were emerging but were obscured by the more dominant ideas and men of the New Negro Era.

FAUSET'S *COMEDY: AMERICAN STYLE*

Comedy: American Style is an intriguing novel. The title suggests comedy will be a central element in the story or that, in some way, readers will find a comedic release from their troubles. The title, however, is misleading. The novel is more tragedy than comedy, with hardly any funny moments. Fundamentally, the novel is about the absurdities of race, which on one level can be maddingly funny but on another level is so absurd as to be ridiculous. What qualifies something as funny is an idea Fauset considered in a 1925 essay titled "The Gift of Laughter." In the essay, Fauset complicated notions of race and comedy, primarily through the lens of the Black stage actor. Fauset recognized that the history of minstrelsy meant that Black people were often the butt of the joke even as they were, in fact, making the joke about themselves on the stage. But she caustically mused in the essay that "no genuinely thinking person, no really astute observer, looking at the Negro in modern American life, could find his condition even now a first aid to laughter" (162). And while African Americans understood that truth, Fauset reminded us that some Black stage actors brought the gift of laughter to genius level on the American stage. Thus, Fauset recognized the value of comedy to render painful truth visible and to do so with humanity, humility, and grace. With *Comedy: American Style*, the comedy of race was rendered tragic as she acknowledged explicitly in her essay: "not without reason has tradition made comedy and tragedy sisters and twins, [so] the capacity for one argues the capacity for the other" (167). These twins, comedy and tragedy, make the novel an important one, even as elements in it have been criticized. Alain Locke, Fauset's contemporary, wrote: "This situation Miss Fauset has admirably documented, so that an important segment of Negro life is opened up; but the characterization is too close to type for the deepest conviction, the style too mid-Victorian for moving power today, and the point of view falls into the sentimental hazard, missing the deep potential tragedy of the situation on the one hand, and its biting satire on the other" ("Saving Grace" 222). Locke's critique, though debatable, had an effect on the way early critics analyzed Fauset's work.

In the novel, Fauset exposes the racial absurdities occurring in America and abroad. On a systemic level, the racial absurdities were caused by generations of racial propaganda and laws that defined one drop of Black blood as inimical to intelligence. Today, we understand race as a social construct; but for those racial essentialists, certain kinds of biological pairings defined whether one was part of an inferior (Black) or superior (white) race. Writing about race as relative, Bridgett Fielder identifies how biological determinists have used biology to define race: "Scientists and others in the US have debated the nature of race as well as its location—in quanta of imagined 'blood' according to the 1705 Virginia Colony or the Indian Reorganization Act of 1934 in the 'scarf-skin,' or even the 'bile' as Thomas Jefferson posits . . . or in the shape and size of the skull as Samuel Morton argues" (11). The less one had of African blood, the theory went, the better one was and the more intelligence one had. The more Nordic blood one had, the more social capital one could accrue, and the more economic opportunities were extended. However, the results of biology were not fixed in that the so-called visible signs of biology produce phenotypes that are not always determinative of one's race. Fielder underscores the relativeness of race, writing that "while race may be visible, visual, material, geographical, and cultural, its biology is actually miniscule and suspect" (12). Thus, the following questions were raised for Fauset and others: How do we make sense of the ways race operates societally if a person chooses a kind of racial exile? What "racial" obligations do Black people have if their phenotype allows them to pass for white? What should we do about the attitudes and institutions that uphold racial categories to the detriment of building and maintaining stable Black communities? Is race performative? These are just some of the questions Fauset poses in *Comedy: American Style*.

Some of the racial absurdities in this novel are systemic, while others are a by-product of other causes. Some of the psychological harm that affects the characters is a direct result of generations of racism against Black people, but other harm results from acceptance of that racism by the Black characters. This direct and causal relationship impacts nearly every facet of their lives even though nearly all have acquired the literacy or vocational skills to live middle-class lives. Many of the characters could theoretically escape some of the harsher conditions that racism foists on members of the large Black working class. Yet racism extends its tentacles because the matriarch in the Cary household is so susceptible to racist ideologies and practices that she becomes the literal and metaphorical killer that causes the death of one family member, socially annihilates another, and nearly destroys the rest. As an enforcer and proponent of literacy as transactional, the matriarch epitomizes all the problems associated with the more commodified understanding of education and literacy. There is nothing funny about that.

The novel is divided into six chapters. Three of the six titles are the names of three very different but interconnected characters: Teresa and Oliver Cary and Phebe Grant. Teresa is Oliver's older sister, and Phebe is one of Teresa's childhood friends. These chapter titles do not hint at the trouble that underlies much of the novel. For the most part, the novel follows the lives of the Cary family and the childhood friends of the Cary children. Olivia Cary, the wife of Dr. Christopher Cary Sr., is a destabilizing force. Her husband is a passive figure. Their children—Teresa, Christopher Jr., and Oliver—are victims of their mother's machinations and their father's docility. Olivia, their mother, is obsessed with light skin color, and it rules every part of her life. It is this obsession, of which Fauset is critical, that drives the action in the novel. Oliva is so obsessed with white skin and is so class-conscious that she refuses to acknowledge the harm she is causing her family. She believes to be of brown or dark skin is to be discounted by the larger white world. To be able to pass as white is the highest value for her. Since Olivia valorizes light or near-white skin color, all other familial duties are aligned with that, even if and when it means that her husband and their children suffer.

In many novels written by Black writers of the nineteenth and early twentieth centuries, the Black characters suffer because they are discriminated against due to their race. Hence, in some instances, race precludes success. Poverty is a way of life to which families acclimate and try to live the best possible lives they can despite the dire circumstances. Because they are Black, they are forced to exist on low wages, deal with inadequate or no education, live in dilapidated housing, and have limited or no reading and writing skills. This causes some characters to suffer immensely. In *Comedy: American Style*, by contrast, many of the characters are highly literate. They have high levels of education or vocational training. They speak "standard" English and are well regarded in their communities. For the most part, very few characters in this novel suffer because they are poor, and when they lack money, it is usually because they are in an apprenticeship phase that will end soon. Ironically, in *Comedy: American Style*, some of the main characters suffer because they have accepted the premise that Black skin is inferior to white skin. Love of self, knowledge of the self, and knowledge of Black history are for the most part absent in the lives of the characters who suffer the most: Teresa and Oliver. Their suffering is caused not by a failure to acquire literacy per se but because the literacies that hold the most social capital are the ones that cause them the most damage. This is, of course, a result of their mother's blind acceptance of one type of literacy practice. Olivia rejects literacy practices that teach love of the self and one's racial community. She sees literacy as strictly a transaction that takes place for the self and not as a communal action that benefits the race. Thadious Davis identifies Olivia's marriage to Christopher Cary Sr. as a business transaction (xxvi). In fact, Olivia views all her life as a business transaction. She is motivated to act only to conduct exchanges. Although race is relative, it has material outcomes.

OLIVIA'S RACIAL ORIGINS

Olivia is the only child of Janet and Lee Blanchard, who love their daughter but find her to be distant and unaffectionate. Aside from her lack of warmth toward her parents, Olivia has another attribute that interferes with parent and child bonding. She loves status and power. As a young child, she already knows the value of white skin, having been called a "nasty little n----r" by a white child she mistakenly hit with a snowball (Fauset, *Comedy* 4). The other children had not realized Olivia is Black because she is so white in appearance. Now that they know, they stop playing with her except for one other child, "as nut-brown and as curly-haired as Olivia herself," who tells her that color "'doesn't make a difference'" (4). Olivia is not appeased by these words. She is disgusted not so much by the white children's racism, but that they force her to acknowledge her racial difference. She becomes angry with her parents for making her Black. The narrator describes her feelings towards them: "Olivia almost hated them both with a flaring intensity no less violent for the immaturity of heart which engendered it. How could they—how *could* they have made her colored? How could they lead the merry, careless life that was theirs with this hateful disgrace always upon them?" (4). Olivia cannot reconcile how her parents can be both Black and happy.

Other incidents in the novel reinforce Olivia's desire to shed her Black identity in exchange for a white one. When her father dies, her mother moves to a new town seeking work. In her new school, Olivia's teacher thinks she is Italian, not Black. Olivia does not correct her teacher and, in fact, tells her she is "proud to be an Italian" (6). On another occasion, Olivia asks her mother if she has told the townspeople they are Black. Janet replies no. Her mother has her reasons for passing: she needs work, fair wages, and decent housing. It is not because she is ashamed of her race. Olivia, however, wants to keep the townspeople from knowing the truth because she has internalized the idea that being white is better than being Black. White skin offers material goods and social status that Black skin does not, but Olivia understands that even if Black people prosper despite their skin color, they are still marginalized. Janet tries to dissuade her child from thinking so negatively of her Black identity, even though in her response to Olivia, she too justifies caste systems. She tells her daughter:

> "There are many white people in the world who are no better off than we today. You're too young to understand all of this just now, Olivia, but you'll find out that you'll have a much better time as a colored girl who eventually will come to know some of the best people of her group than as an ordinary white girl who will always know and go with ordinary white people." (10)

Olivia is not convinced by her mother's declaration. She will spend the rest of her life running away from her Black identity—to devastating ends.

In some ways, Janet is a foil to Olivia (Phebe, Olivia's childhood friend, is also her foil). Janet embraces her Black identity, even though it is an elitist one. She is a social striver who hopes to leave the mill and make a better life for herself and her daughter. Janet seeks to gain knowledge to better herself, but she also wants to attract highly educated men for the purpose of social interaction and perhaps remarriage. Reading is one way she tries to enhance her life and to still the loneliness she feels without her husband: "at night now, not so weary as she had once been, she read, she made notes, she remembered.... she enjoyed the English reading, especially the poetry and the essays" (12–13). Janet even decides to take "extension courses at Harvard" (13), which means she actively participates in literacy activities to enhance her life and give her access to a better class of Black people. After Janet takes courses for two years, her next goal is to move away from the mill town to Boston or Cambridge, Massachusetts. Janet wants to go back to life as a Black woman and be in the company of Black people and Black culture. Olivia is loath to return to a Black life where she will forever be marginalized. In a powerful moment between mother and daughter, Olivia expresses her true feelings about Black men and her father specifically: "Olivia, it appeared, had thought of the young men whom she might meet in Boston. 'All of them black or brown,' she raged, 'and all of them looked down on! If you think I want my children to feel toward their father as I felt toward—'" (15). *Mine* is the word she dare not utter. It is a devasting admission, but one in which Olivia speaks her true feelings.

Fauset is in a peculiar position as a Black woman writer—a novelty in some regards. In the early twentieth century, the mere term "Black woman writer" shatters stereotypes. Carolyn Wedin Sylvander wrote that "being Black in America, being Black woman in America, and being Black writer in America are all experiences historically fraught with pressures, conflicts, frustration, irony, and exploratory creativity" (4). Fauset was also a highly educated Black woman in the early twentieth century, yet another novelty: she earned a Cornell BA, Phi Beta Kappa, and a University of Pennsylvania MA in French Literature. Her insistence that Americans' obsession with racial caste was destructive beyond its individual impact was not quite novel, but the way she allowed its destruction to take hold of the Cary family illustrated a kind of fresh brazenness. She satirized her own people's colorism obsession to devastating ends. Vashti Crutcher Lewis writes, "*Comedy, American Style* is the first sustained and effective satirical novel authored by an African American woman" (378). Ultimately, the novel acts as a truth serum, designed to dismantle notions about racial caste that might help to rid Black communities of the odiousness of colorism, but not before Fauset lays out the ugly truth for her readers. Olivia is only nine years old when she becomes reconciled to the idea that whiteness yields power. To tell these stories of racial caste and familial destruction, Fauset used her own sophisticated literacy skills to write about the devastating impact of obsession with whiteness. If literacy can act as a panacea to help snuff out racial discrimination on an individual level with hopes at the macro level, then Fauset skillfully was weaving a tale of woe using all the conventions of writerly prose one can use. But on an even starker level with regards to the function of literacy in the lives of the characters in *Comedy: American Style*, the characters' sense of isolation—and here I am referring to others besides Olivia—make visible how their transactional-only literacies fail to help them make sense of a world that envelops them in notions about white superiority they are not even able to contemplate, much less contest. Too many of the characters see literacy as a transaction that helps to advance their personal ambition. Cherene Sherrad-Johnson argues that Olivia is an "anti-race woman" (xxiii). Concomitantly, Dr. Cary Sr. is an *anti-race man* and his daughter Teresa is an *anti-race woman* like her mother. They are not in the tradition of characters like Beryl in *Beryl Weston's Ambition* or Caroline in *Clancy Street* who actively seek to use their literacies to transform the lives of the race.

LITERACY, MARRIAGE, AND RACIAL CASTE

Olivia has the intelligence to mature into a proactive race woman, helping lift others up. Instead, she chooses to exchange her literacy practices—her ability to read and write effectively—to selfish ends. What is more, she chooses to trade her white skin to gain social advantages. In this sense, then, her literacy practices and white skin color in the marketplace of consumer goods are commodified and exchanged for self-marketability and sustainability rather than a social good that might provide economic advantages for her racial community. Even her mother, Janet, sees early on Olivia's commodified understanding of literacy and education. In a conversation with her fiancé, Ralph Blake, Janet tells him that Olivia has no desire to marry a Black or brown man: "'My dear, she wouldn't marry you or Christopher Cary or any other colored man, no matter how little he showed his Negro blood. My daughter, your future stepchild, is a confirmed Negro-hater. She thinks there is no health in us'" (Fauset, *Comedy* 23). These are harsh words from Olivia's mother, but she is right in many ways. Strangely, though, Olivia has a change of heart with regard to marriage. She decides to marry Christopher Cary Sr., a man who has even lighter skin than Olivia, because of his social status as a medical doctor. Also, the possibility that they might have nearly white children changes her mind about marrying a Black man. She conceives of the idea to marry him because her mother had recently given birth to twins with her new husband and the twins "were so completely white" (28). Olivia rationalizes that perhaps she and Christopher will have nearly white children too. Love, lust, and longing do not figure into her desire to marry and to have children; only the prospect that she and her husband might be able to enter into the white world thrills Olivia.

Indeed, the marriage between Christopher Cary Sr. and Olivia is a strange one. The narrator describes Dr. Cary as not focused on race or ambition. In other words, he is not a race man or social striver. He wants to be moderately successful and will go to no great lengths to distinguish himself from his peers. For the most part, racial issues are not in his purview. Race is what happens when he is directly affected by a racial slight, which is not often since his skin is so white as to make him almost indistinguishable from white men. This is how he lives most of his life as it relates to race. Racial acts against him or a family member force him to confront the issue; otherwise, he stays silent and in the background, although he cares for Black patients against his wife's wishes. Dr. Cary is unlike his step-father-in-law, Ralph Blake, who at one time delayed medical school to go to Alabama to educate poor Black people there. As an educated Black man, Ralph is inspired by a professor to go south to help educate the poor. He explains to Janet: "The colored people there, poor things, wanted the school because they thought there was necromancy in higher education. That it would bring palpable and material results. Of course a few of them saw beyond that. The white people didn't want the school because they were afraid it might make their 'n----s uppity' and they didn't mean to stand for that. Yet they realized the benefit to the town" (20). While Ralph and some of the community members understood the reward for gaining literacy was ambiguous at best, Ralph nevertheless recognized that a life without reading and writing skills would most certainly guarantee ongoing poverty. Harvey J. Graff's concept of the literacy myth echoes Ralph's own analysis: "Major elements of the literacy myth exert powerful influence, for example . . . the myth of literacy's link to economic development, and social advancement; and the myth of literacy and democracy. In contemporary popular discourse, literacy is represented as an unqualified good, a marker of progress, and a metaphorical light making clear the pathway to progress and happiness" ("Literacy Myth" 640). Hence, Ralph's cynicism is warranted because he knows that the structural blocks that impede Black progress remain in place. In other words, if literacy accrues as its own product that can be exchanged for a material good or social capital, then one might assume that exchanges between sellers (white people in power) and consumers (Black buyers) are fair. Unfortunately, the sellers and/or owners of the goods do not always uphold their end of the bargain even when Black consumers have acquired the right amount of knowledge, money, and prestige. Despite what he knows to be true about the literacy myth, Ralph is at least willing to teach those who need it the most. Dr. Cary, on the other hand, is in many ways handicapped in marriage and is unable to pass on his academic and cultural knowledge to those who need it the most. He does, presumably, communicate his medical literacy to his patients, so that they will heal. But he does not, it seems, transfer a type of social literacy that might help to uplift the race; consequently, Dr. Cary's view of the world is symptomatic of a literacy practice that is more transactional than transformational.

LITERACY AND RACIAL SELF-HATRED

The best kind of literacy practice is one that provides an individual with the means to ask critical questions of the self and society. The worst kind of literacy is one that inoculates the self against the self and the world and asks no critical questions. Olivia's behavior epitomizes the worst kind of transactional literacy practices. Literacy is simply a means to an end. It provides no safeguards and no critiques in its commodified form. Throughout the novel, Olivia never asks why racism exists. She simply takes it as a natural fact of life and decides the best way to defeat racism is to become white. I suppose on one level that all signs to the contrary have proven true for her. It is better to be white than to be Black if one wants to live without racial persecution, acquire the best possible material goods, and gain social capital. Yet her mother tries again and again to teach her that there is nothing wrong with being Black especially if she is among the better class of Black people. This is, in and of itself, contradictory, but nevertheless it is obvious that her mother wants Olivia to rid herself of the shame of being Black.

The narrator of Fauset's *Comedy: American Style* describes a time when Janet could have denied her race but chose instead to tell the truth. Janet wants to improve her material and social conditions as well as improve her knowledge, so she decides to take classes at Harvard Extension. Her time at Harvard Extension is good for her on two levels: it expands her knowledge and emboldens her entrepreneurial plans. She wants to open a "rooming house for colored students" (16). Janet explains her plans to Professor Inness, a white professor with whom she has built a relationship. Professor Inness likes her plans and allows her to "use his name both in order to obtain a house and a security for credit" (16). Professor Inness tells Janet he trusts her because "'I know you've told me you are a colored woman when you might just as well have let me think you white. That assures me that you may be foolish but you certainly are honest,' he told her dryly" (16). This message to Janet is a mixed one. Professor Inness gives her credit for being truthful but acknowledges the difficulty faced by Black people. It signifies to readers that Janet wants her racial heritage to be acknowledged and accepted. This message, though paradoxical, is among many others that Olivia likely encounters at school and in her local communities. It is to Janet's credit, however, that she does not deny her race, at least when she is in Massachusetts. This act of racial acknowledgment should remind Olivia that acceptance of one's racial heritage can yield positive results, but Olivia does not receive this message.

It is obvious why Olivia hates being Black or rather hates that being Black disallows certain kinds of access. She has already accepted that being racially identifiable as Black comes with a set of outcomes she is unwilling to take on. Her social interactions at home, at school, and in town have reinforced the difficulties Black people experience due to the color of their skin. Those who cannot pass have a hard time traversing white-dominant spaces. Thus, her concerns are practical and ideological and have been passed on through instruction in various educational, physical, and psychic spaces. One way is through literacy instruction as described by J. Elspeth Stuckey:

> Literacy is an economic and social regulation, it is . . . taught. The functional issue of how literacy comes to distribute class relations *and*

race involves ways of teaching.... Acquisition becomes the mediator of social relations; teaching, the arbiter. This is to say that literacy is a function of culture, social experience, and sanction. Literacy education begins in the ideas of the socially and economically dominant class and it takes the forms of socially acceptable subjects, stylistically permissible forms, ranges of difference and deviance, baselines of gratification. (19; emphasis added)

As Stuckey makes clear, what people come to know as good and acceptable behavioral and linguistic norms are passed on through social interactions, and those social interactions are communicated with the literacy practices of those in power. These social interactions are exchanged in everyday social communications as well as in schools and in the workplace. Hence, it would make it almost impossible for any of the characters in *Comedy: American Style* not to be influenced by racist ideologies embedded in literacies most valued in educational settings and existing in elite and middle-class discourse practices. Olivia does attend school, and she has built relationships with the youth in the mill town, all of whom are white. She watches as her mother passes in order to earn a decent living as a widow. All around her, in school and at home, she is taught that being Black is a handicap. Hence, she becomes victim to a set of ideologies that negate her very being, which Cooper and Matthews believed that race literature could overturn. Yet Olivia is making choices because she values money and status over integrity. She has a one-dimensional understanding of literacy as a transaction that earns her rewards above others rather than one drawn from its transformational value that could enhance her life and members of her racial community.

Transformational and specular literacy practices are modes of communication that offer challenges to oppressive conditions, but transactional literacy as practiced by the characters in *Comedy: American Style* provides limited opportunities for intellectual and personal struggle. Transactional literacy is merely a by-product of reaching a selfish end. Hence, Olivia recognizes that passing offers her freedoms she cannot have if she identifies as Black. Thus, she does not question social and political systems that reward lighter skin. Conversely, contesting the systems that reward white skin can happen if the literacies she is taught or embraces acknowledge the beauty of Black life, yet so much of what she encounters is a kind of miseducation and a misapplication of different types of literacies. Carter G. Woodson's *The Mis-Education of the Negro*, published in 1933, is apropos here. In the preface, and developed throughout the book, Woodson explains the ways Black people have been miseducated:

> No systematic effort toward change has been possible, for, taught the same economics, history, philosophy, literature and religion which have established the present code of morals, the Negro's mind has been brought under control of his oppressor. The problem of holding the Negro down, therefore, is easily solved. When you control a man's thinking you do not have to worry about his actions. You do not have to tell him not to stand here or go yonder. He will find his "proper place" and will stay in it. You do not need to send him to the back door. He will go without being told. In fact, if there is no back door, he will cut one for his special benefit. His education makes it necessary. (xiii)

Woodson's explanation of the miseducation of Black people is a damning indictment of educational systems that rendered Black achievement invisible and Black self-worth negligible. Woodson knows that education is not value-neutral. How one is instructed, what books are used for that instruction, and what language and literacies are privileged over others matter in the construction of a positive self-identity. This is precisely why Cooper and Matthews argued so vehemently for race literature created by Black writers. Black writers would know what to say and how to say it textually, unlike white authors, even those with good intentions. Cooper and Matthews hoped the values embedded in the literacies they employed and advocated would help establish a dynamic and strong people who could be embraced and imitated by the large poor Black underclass. Reading texts written by Black writers, they argued, could be a transformational experience. They understood if Black people lacked basic knowledge about their racial past, they would continue to be subject to the whims and imaginations of white people. Olivia embodies this miseducation process. Her education and transactional approach contributed to her self-loathing. She therefore accepts literacy for personal gain with economic outcomes for her benefit alone. Sadly, Olivia has acquired and uses literacy practices that offer her little help in combatting the racism she refuses to confront. She has rejected the kind of social and transformational literacies that could have provided her with the means to contest the racial oppression she experiences.

As a child and even as an adult, Olivia never alters her thinking. Her education both formally and informally makes this inevitable. Olivia is so race- and status-conscious that she does not want Teresa, her daughter, to play with racially identifiable Black children and does not want those children in her home. After school one day, Olivia denies Marise, a dark brown child, entry into her home but extends an invitation to Phebe, whose skin color is white. The exchange between Olivia and the two children highlights her racial self-hatred: "'Good-afternoon children. I'm afraid it's not best for Teresa to have so much company today. . . . I don't mind if one of you stays. Phebe, suppose you come in and play with her a while, and Marise, you can come back another time'" (Fauset, *Comedy* 33). This is, of course, a ruse. Marise will never be invited to enter her home. Meanwhile, Phebe refuses to go inside the Cary home to play with Teresa. She chooses, instead, to go home with Marise as she has been instructed by her own mother and because she intuitively knows the race game Olivia is playing. After Marise and Phebe leave, with an exasperated tone Olivia explains, "'now, Teresa, it isn't worth going all over this matter again. I don't mind your having Phebe here; in fact, I rather like Phebe. But I don't like to have colored people in the house if we can possibly avoid it'" (34). Incidents like these are ever-present in the novel. They illustrate Olivia's profound sense of self-hatred and self-alienation as well as the cruelty she is willing to exact against others, even children who have shades of brown skin that mark them as Black. It is as well a reflection of a kind of literacy practice that values white cultural and social norms over ones that affirm Black people and their cultural traditions. It is, in fact, an exclusive focus on transactional literacy that will nearly destroy the Cary family.

Considerations for her daughter's feelings or the racist ideologies and the values she passes on never figure into self-reflective moments. Olivia acts on her own self-hatred and imposes those feelings on her children. She warns Teresa that Black life is so abject as to be objectionable, telling her, "'I just don't want you to have Marise and people like that around because I don't want you to grow up among folks who live the life that most colored people have to live . . . narrow and stultified and stupid. Always pushed in the background . . . out of everything. Looked down upon and despised'" (36). This novel is set in the 1920s in urban areas such as Boston, Philadelphia, and New York City. In one sense, Olivia is right that life is difficult for millions of Black people living in the United States. Despite the difficulties, however, many of them were living fulfilling and stable lives in spaces where love and progress flourished. Olivia's own Black family is the epitome of social advancement. Her husband is a doctor, her now-deceased father was a doctor, her stepfather is a doctor, and her father-in-law has a successful upholstery business. Her daughter's childhood friends' parents are successful. One has a successful catering business and the other a funeral business. Their lives are certainly circumscribed by their race, but none are so terrible as to make them unlivable. In another way, Olivia is blind to other realities, and her life is defined by her obsession with whiteness and her utter failure to turn her literacy knowledge into positive good. Passing, Gayle Wald surmises, can be considered a "transgressive act" out of the bounds of white supremacy and into a life of freedom (8). Yet such transgressions may come with consequences, including exile from race and family. Olivia does not consider how the acceptance of color consciousness and eventual exile might impact her family.

Her specific interpretation and employment of transactional literacy for selfish ends make this so, despite her coming from a racial group that has historically employed forms of transformational and specular literacy to challenge racial oppression. Writing about the power of African American language practices, Carmen Kynard maintains that "language is more than a mere reflection of an existing reality; it creates the reality" (368). As the author of *Comedy: American Style*, Fauset was engaging in intellectual exercises that call on the communicative powers of her language and literacy practices by responding to and creating realities centered on the lives of the characters inhabiting her novel. In *Comedy: American Style*, Fauset created characters who reflected both the fragility and the strength of Black life. That fragility is where the combination of tragedy and comedy is revealed— demonstrating the psychic harm of racism but also the fortitude with which Black people overcome racism. Katherine Tillman, one of Fauset's predecessors, created the characters Beryl in *Beryl Weston's Ambition* and Caroline in *Clancy Street* as exemplars of Black womanhood who are well on their way to becoming race women. Tillman's heroines combat the idea that Black women are incapable of being intelligent and honorable. Conversely, Fauset employed her literacy skills and creativity in *Comedy: American Style* in the service of intraracial critique, a good that might shift the consciousness of the race. Olivia's behavior is so detestable that perhaps no readers will want to model their behavior after hers. She is an antiheroine. Fauset refracted back to American society a monster of its own making, showing what happens when literacy that does not affirm the self is enacted one-dimensionally. Olivia's detestableness is best reflected in her treatment of Oliver, her namesake and youngest child. While pregnant, Olivia hopes Oliver will be "'the handsomest and most attractive of [them] all'" (Fauset, *Comedy* 40). When Olivia sees Oliver for the first time, to her horror he "had the exact bronze gold complexion of Lee Blanchard! She had reckoned without her own father" (41). She wants nothing to do with him because he is racially identifiable even though he is, in fact, "more attractive than her other children" (41). Unfortunately, Olivia had decided long ago that any hint of Black blood is objectionable; thus, she subjects Oliver to cruelty no decent mother would ever impose on her child. He suffers greatly from her cruelty. The problem is that Oliver reminds Olivia that she is Black, which makes it difficult for her and other family members to pass as white. Rather than try to love Oliver despite his color, she chooses not to love him at all.

LITERACY, RACE, AND EDUCATION

Fauset's *Comedy: American Style* is a difficult read not because it is so esoteric as to be hard to understand. It is difficult because the behavior of the lead character is grotesque and the decent characters are too passive. The decent characters try to be life-affirming, yet even they fall victim to colorism and classism. The most flawed character, Olivia, has a reach so far and wide she harms not just her family but her children's friends. Nevertheless, by all measure, many of the characters are social strivers who succeed at a time in American history when few Black people did. They attend Ivy League colleges and one, Marise, becomes a famous entertainer. Others attend medical school, while others succeed in their vocations. In many ways, even though they are living under a racist system, their lives are enviable. Yet beneath the surface of their successes lies a fundamental flaw. Very few of them reflect on what it means to be Black in America. Certainly, there are some characters who contemplate the challenges brought on by racial discrimination, but their musings rarely cause them to be civic-minded or socially engaged. They are not race women and men. In other words, their literacies, gained in various academic and vocational spaces, do not serve as transmitters of knowledge from themselves to their racial communities.

At one point early in the novel, it is revealed that Dr. Christopher Cary Sr. wants Teresa and Christopher Jr. to learn about Black heroes, so he teaches them about great Black men and women. The children are excited and willing to learn, but soon their enthusiasm wanes—mainly, it seems, because their father does not continue teaching them about their racial history. When Teresa is a teen, passing as white while attending an elite all-white girls' school in New England, and is confronted with an existential question regarding race, she at first remains quiet while the other students rattle on about who should and should not be allowed to attend their school. They wonder what they would do if a Black student were admitted. Some of them accept the idea, while others reject it. Those who accept the idea argue that Black people are just like white people. Some girls point out that some Black people strive, and others do not; some are successful, and some are not. The most vociferous supporters of Black humanity are Ellen and Jennie, two white girls who recognize that there are all kinds of Black people in the world. Some of the other white students, however, turn to stereotypes and innuendoes about Black people to argue against admitting them to the school. When Teresa finally responds, she at first acknowledges that Black people are as diverse as any other group and should be judged accordingly. Yet she cannot help but make the case that Black humanity is connected to skin color. She explains to the students that the most popular girl in her former school was Marise, whom she describes as "'a dark brown girl; not black, you know, but brown like—like a young chestnut. Her skin was just as thin. You could see the red under it'" (77). Teresa, Olivia's daughter, has internalized that goodness is related to skin color. Thus, as Woodson explained, her education and, I argue, her mother's narrow vision of what literacy can do for her and members of her racial group have produced a Black person who does not know or understand herself. Teresa values what the dominant group values. The lighter the skin, the more honorable and intelligent the individual is.

This is precisely the problem of the social practice of a kind of racialized literacy that denies the humanity of some and valorizes the humanity of others. A social practice of literacy is not necessarily a critical practice. As literacy relates to human experience, J. Elspeth Stuckey writes:

> We must remember who we really are. We are not just private individuals in whose private minds the printed word works powerful deeds. We are, to be sure, natural individuals, but we are social before we are born, and the commerce we do with literacy is always, fundamentally, social. We are arranged by our relations to literacy, to how and why literacy is produced, and to the effects of what literacy is about. The extensions of these relations describe how close to the edge of survival we live. (95)

As much as Teresa recognizes many Black people are like many white people in their abilities and desires, she cannot help but note the difference between skin color and likability, and ultimately respectability. As Stuckey notes, literacy has a social component, and humans are fundamentally social beings. Social beings can be taught to be critical if they engage with the right kind of literacy practices. With that, literacy has the power to influence interactions between the self and the community. Teresa, however, is a product of her home and school environment and, as such, consumes literacy as a one-dimensional transaction to be used for class acceptance rather than communal uplift. She makes comments about Black and white lives based on the prevailing racist ideologies that define white as normal and Black as aberrant. The closer people are to having white skin, the better they are and the more socially advanced they can become. It is a kind of literacy that turns the self against the self. Thus, Teresa's home life as well as school literacy has failed her. She asks no critical questions.

Truthfully, Teresa is a victim of her mother, the dominant white society, and literacies that uphold values anathema to pride of the self and the community. This is made evident with the arrival of Alicia Barrett. The hypothetical question regarding a Black girl's attending Teresa's elite all-white school becomes real when Alicia arrives. There is no question about her race and her racial pride as Alicia is Black and proud. She clearly has had a different familial and educational background as well as a foundation in literacies that are life-sustaining. The narrator describes Alicia's disposition this way: "Alicia's whole attitude said serenely: 'Here am I, the best of my kind and I am perfectly satisfied with my kind'" (Fauset, *Comedy* 83). Alicia and Teresa become friends; Teresa admires Alicia. Soon they become so close that Alicia invites Teresa to go home to Chicago with her while they are on vacation from school. Alicia likes Teresa so much that she wants Teresa to date her brother, Alex. Pressed by Alicia's longing to pair Teresa with her brother but for the fact that Teresa is white, Teresa decides to reveal her true identity. She tells Alicia she has been passing as white, saying "'I'm not white really.... I'm colored. I love being colored ... but Mother has always been so set on passing'" (88). Teresa's confession does not derail their time together, but it does highlight Teresa's passivity and alienation from herself and her culture. This is made all the more so when Teresa observes Alicia's family and friends who are Black and proud, which also reveals to Teresa that she is disconnected from her own racial group. The narrator describes Teresa's dissociation in this way: "emotionally, as far as race was concerned, she was a girl without a country.... Later on in life it occurred to her that she had been deprived of her racial birthright and that that was a great cause for tears as any indignity that might befall man" (89). Because Olivia demanded Teresa deny she is Black, Teresa suffers other indignities, none of which her transactional literacy practices can remedy.

While Teresa is vacationing in Chicago, she meets Henry Bates, Alicia's former beau. Henry and Teresa fall in love and become engaged while she is in Chicago. He is an engineering student at Massachusetts Institute of Technology (MIT), and Teresa will soon be a student at Smith College. For two years, they continue in a long-distance relationship without the knowledge of her mother. They plan to marry after Henry's graduation. Teresa knows her mother will never approve of their marriage, but she invests her time and energy into loving Henry and planning their lives together. Although Teresa loves Henry, there are secrets she cannot utter to him, one of which is that her mother detests Black people. Teresa hopes that marriage to Henry will provide both emotional and physical distance between her and her mother. She wants to live out her life in Chicago with Henry as a happily married Black woman, and she also hopes to rescue her younger brother, Oliver, from her mother's tyranny. As a narrative strategy, Henry enters the plot where race, education, love, and comedy intersect. Henry and Teresa love each other dearly, but love will not be enough to overcome racial caste and intraracial conflict.

Fortuitously perhaps, while Teresa and Henry are walking down the street after his graduation ceremony, Olivia sees the couple as they set off to seal their union. She confronts them. When Henry tells Olivia they plan to marry, Olivia is outraged and forces Teresa to make a choice: go with her mother and leave her fiancé or deal with her mother's rage and the consequences of living as a Black couple. Teresa decides to leave Henry because she can't escape the racialized view of herself she learned from her overbearing mother that sees value in passing. Moreover, Teresa's education has not provided her with the kinds of literacy tools to engage her mother in a debate about race and passing. Perhaps, this is Fauset's point. The interplay that follows among Olivia, Teresa, and Henry is so absurd as to be unreal. The comedy is in word and deed. In their ensuing conversations, Henry asks Olivia why she refuses to allow Teresa to marry him. After all, he has a degree from MIT. Unfortunately, Henry's degree from a prestigious school is not good enough for Olivia because it does not erase his color. He is, in the end, identifiably Black. She tells Henry, "'I'd rather see her married to one of these Portuguese down on the Cape in the cranberry bogs. I'd rather see her dead!'" (143). How can such an outrageous statement be made in a novel Fauset calls a "comedy"? Albert Sergio Laguna explains that "the comedy of race [is] to explain how comedy is *of* race, how the very architecture of comedy and what makes us laugh can help us better understand how race itself works with and independent of comedy. Comedy stages the mechanics of racialization" (105). The very idea of race is a comedy as Fauset hopes to emphasize in her novel. The scenes with Henry, Teresa, and Olivia are so absurd as to be funny, but no one is laughing. These actions by Olivia will cause Teresa's familial and racial exile. Viewing Teresa's relationships as a transaction that moves her closer to whiteness will bring on her social death. In the moment, even though Teresa is heartbroken, she is unable to stand up to her mother's interference. She lacks a strong literacy foundation to respond to her mother's foolish statements. She ultimately loses Henry and falls into despair. Olivia's behavior is unconscionable, but she does not care how much she has hurt Teresa or even Henry. She only knows that, for Teresa to advance socially, she believes her daughter cannot marry a racially identifiable Black man.

Henry is deeply troubled by Olivia's and Teresa's actions. He is a proud Black man who is aghast at their willingness to deny their race. When Teresa suggests to Henry that he could pass as a Mexican and they could marry and live without the burdens of race, he responds by saying: "'Are you crazy, both of you? I'm perfectly satisfied to be an American Negro, tough as it is. I can help other men to work their way to better conditions. What am I going to do, throw aside all my traditions, all my old friends and be a damned gringo just to satisfy the vanity of two make believe white women!'" (143). It is a poignant tragicomic moment with the last line as a zinger. It releases pent-up tensions for Henry but also for readers. He boldly confronts the problem of racial passing and racial self-hatred. He scolds the two women while making the case that race pride means more to him than the benefits of passing. What readers witness is the profound weight that colorism and class have on the Black psyche. Part of the literacy experience is that it can provide individuals like Olivia and Teresa with the language to process the profound alienation from the race caused by white gatekeepers who insist on whiteness as the norm. J. Elspeth Stuckey suggests "that literacy provides a view from which to survey the history and future of social formations . . . thus, the questions of literacy are . . . matters of enforcement, maintenance, acquiescence, internalization, revolution" (64). Olivia and Teresa are experiencing all but the revolution part of literacy.

Teresa could be a version of the new modern Black woman setting out with the aid of her husband to help build up the self-confidence and self-worth of members of their racial community. She could be like the nineteenth-century female protagonists in Tillman's *Beryl Weston's Ambition* or *Clancy Street* who considered the acquisition of literacy to be what Logan calls "the essential tool for change" ("Literacy as a Tool" 194). Instead, Teresa's mother, her education, and her literacy practices make this all but impossible. Teresa cannot comprehend that "African American language and literacy practices are dynamic and fluid cultural matrixes from which revolutionary life and culture-sustaining ideas and practices can be fashioned" (Richardson 678–79). All that Teresa can see is the effect of the color line and her mother's disappointment and rage. Unfortunately, she has acquired no literacy tools from which to fashion an alternative narrative that would allow her to confront her mother's and the broader society's warped view of Black life. Her view of life and literacy functions simply in a consumerist model of take rather than give, while learning passively instead of asking critical questions.

DESTRUCTIVE LITERACY FORCES

There will be no revolutionary acts for Teresa or Olivia through the employment of their literacy practices. There will be, however, several destructive acts they commit by way of their transactional literacy practices. After Olivia causes the dissolution of Teresa and Henry's relationship, she destroys her youngest son, Oliver. Of the three children, Oliver is described as the most sensitive and artistic of the Cary children. He is also the most alienated member of their household. Because he can be identified as Black, at times throughout his young life he is sent away to spend time with his paternal grandparents, Aaron and Rebecca Cary, and with his maternal grandparents, Janet and Ralph Blake. These two sets of grandparents love him dearly, but their love is not enough to shield him from psychic harm. When Oliver is home with his mother, she ignores or uses him. In the chapter dedicated to Oliver, the narrator describes a time when Oliver sees his mother walking down the street with a group of women. Oliver tries to get his mother's attention, shouting, "'Mother'... 'Mother'" (Fauset, *Comedy* 200). Olivia ignores her son in the ensuing shocking scene: "with the other ladies (he did not know whether they were white or colored since there were none fairer than she), she turned and faced him, let her eyes, like theirs, rest on his face with a strange and awful lack of recognition. Then she turned away again. He stood still" (200). Oliver is devastated. At home, he confronts his mother; she admonishes him for yelling in public. At no point does she apologize to Oliver for ignoring him when she was with her white friends. In a separate incident, Olivia hosts a committee meeting in her home. Embarrassed that she does not have a butler to impress her white friends, Olivia explains her predicament to Oliver. She knows Oliver will do anything to please her, and when he offers to act as the family butler, she obliges. When her older son comes home to find his brother pretending to be the butler and not Olivia's son, he becomes enraged. He tells his mother, "'You've made me despise you! I never expect to know a sadder day than this'" (213), though a sadder day will come.

At the end of the chapter focused on Oliver, readers learn that he killed himself with a pistol because he finally learned why he has been rejected by his mother. He reads a letter written by his mother to his father while she is away in France with Teresa. In the letter, Olivia describes places she has visited in France. She is enamored with those French cities and suggests to her husband that they and their oldest son, Christopher Jr., should move there. In France, she surmises they can pass, and no one will know. The only problem, she admits, is that Oliver is too dark and will thwart her plans to pass as a white family. She acknowledges to her husband how difficult it has been living with Oliver's skin color: "*I know you don't like me to talk about this . . . but really, Chris, Oliver and his unfortunate color has certainly been a mill-stone around our necks all our lives*" (221; emphasis in original). Oliver also learns that his sister, whom he had hoped would rescue him from his mother, has explained in a letter that her new French husband will not want him around because of his "*tell-tale color*" (225; emphasis in original). Even Teresa has forsaken Oliver, and their letters devastate him. Each points out something about him that he cannot control. He will always have his bronze skin, which means he will always be identifiably Black. His spirit is shaken. Only death can bring him comfort. Sherrad-Johnson says Oliver's suicide "stands as a stern chastisement for everyone in the book, even the unfeeling Olivia" (xxvi).

For all the trouble Black people faced during the second and third decades of the twentieth century, when the novel takes place, much of their trouble was caused by external forces. In other words, it was white people who directly impacted their lives. White people's laws, social policies, and political and economic structures dictated where Black people lived, worked, and were educated. Their racist beliefs caused much consternation and pain among Black people. In many ways, Olivia is the arbiter of the suffering that takes place in the novel. It is her refusal to see love, education, and literacy as a political act that causes so much heartache. Mary Jane Lupton writes that *Comedy: American Style* "can be read as indictments of discrimination within the Black community itself, and only secondarily from white society" (40). Certainly, Olivia is a victim of a society that has demonized Black people, but she has some agency. Unfortunately, she chooses to use her agency to meet her needs first. She chooses to commodify the institutional literacies she has acquired along the way and to use her racial ambiguity for her own ends. Everyone else is secondary, so much so that at no point after her son's death does the narrator share any moments when Olivia reflects on the cause of Oliver's death. She just goes on living her life and meddling in her other children's lives, particularly Teresa. Her husband, however, is nearly destroyed by his younger son's suicide. The narrator reports that "the older man had lost his grip. After Oliver's death his interest in his work died away; he spent long days in his office, refusing to see patients; the seriousness of his financial plight seemed to impress him not a whit" (Fauset, *Comedy* 279). Dr. Cary Sr. may be devastated, but he is not innocent either. He has no racial pride, and he did not intervene against his wife, whose obsession with colorism has literally destroyed the family.

The Cary family is at a critical juncture after Oliver's death. All are educated people who have the cognitive skills to process the cause of his death.

Yet no one in the family gathers its remaining members together to discuss why Oliver committed suicide. This is a familial failure as well as an educational one. There are varying degrees of literacy operating within the Cary family. Unfortunately, the one they rely on the most, transactional literacy, gets them nowhere as a family. In the early twenty-first century, writing about his father's education, James Ray Watkins Jr. asks "what it meant and might mean to be a literate member of the middle-class" (19). Watkins asks this question decades after publication of Fauset's *Comedy: American Style* in a much different context and for a different racial group; but his question is instructive. What did it mean for the Cary family, a middle-class Black family with all the education they had, to exist in a space where the mother and father allowed self-hatred and passivity to almost destroy nearly all the members of their family? To what extent did the kinds of literacy practices advanced and supported by the dominant class participate in their downfall? Watkins provides some hints, writing that "literacy and, by extension, education" are "not a singular skill or knowledge, acquired once and for all, but a series of interrelated, more or less successful learning experiences occurring over stretches of time and space and rooted in the specifics of both individual biography and social history" (19). What had the Cary family learned over time that allowed them to acquiesce, for the most part, to their mother's racial caste obsession? Why had they not utilized their sophisticated literacy skills to combat Olivia's destructive behavior? Fauset's objective, it seems, was to give readers an up-close view of the destructive nature of racism by showing the ways self-hatred is disseminated in and through institutions like home, school, and work. Its harms are tangible and long-lasting. The socialization process that humans experience while acquiring various forms of literacy is fraught with values and traditions that interfere with their self-perceptions. Thus, when confronted with racial constructs that are damaging, members of the Cary family passively watch and hope for good outcomes. By the end of the novel, readers know how dangerous that passivity is. Highly functioning and intelligent individuals like Olivia and her husband are not absolved from their direct participation in the near destruction of all their children.

Fauset illustrated the unique function of literacy and education in this novel. Learning to read and write also means learning about the self. While engaged in a process of acquiring knowledge, learners (receptors of the educational transactions) like Olivia, Dr. Cary Sr., and Teresa should seek to engage their instructors (providers of information) and the broader world (interceptors and distributors of that knowledge) in communicative practices that actively seek to dismantle notions about Black people that damage their self-image and the image of their racial communities. Yet Fauset laid bare sophisticated literacies that obscure or ignore the problems of race and can have profound consequences, one of which for the Cary family is an actual death and the other is a social death. The attainment of high status at the expense of the self and in conflict with one's family and community is no success at all. Neither is a narrow vision of literacy that teaches people, Black people specifically, to negate themselves. Thus, the matriarch of the Cary family stands not as a role model of a new modern Black woman but the antihero despite what she claims are good intentions. Carolyn Wedin Sylvander writes that "all of Olivia's motivations are from her desire to be white, her hatred of Black. Superficially, she justifies her actions in relation to her marriage, her social life, and her children by saying that it is for their own good" (212). Readers know her self-justification is a patent lie.

In one sense, it seems, the purpose of *Comedy: American Style* is to trace the destructive nature of human absurdities. Among the many absurdities humans have created are the distinctions among the races. In America, the debates that have raged since the first Africans landed on American shores include questions like this one asked by white people: Are Black people like us, meaning, are they like people whose skin is classified as white? This is, of course, a simplified version of the early encounters in the Americas between Black and white people. The point here is that, even though prejudice and discrimination against dark-skinned people existed long before the United States was established, early in the formation of America as a country and America as an ideal the white majority decided that Africans and their descendants were not, in fact, like them and constructed laws, social practices, and language to ensure continuing white dominance. Writing about the legacy of enslavement, Patricia J. Williams says, "we are all inheritors of that legacy . . . for it survives as powerful and invisibly reinforcing structures of thought, language, and law" (61). Olivia's insistence on passing is a result of a nation unwilling to let go of its racist ideals. Although physically free but psychologically in bondage, Olivia inherited a debased notion about Black inferiority and white superiority.

At school, at home, and in the communities where Olivia lives, life has reinforced those racist notions, which she then passes to Teresa, her impressionable daughter. Despite that, there are moments in the novel when alternate notions could surface and take hold, especially after Oliver committed suicide. Speaking about his death, processing her failures as a parent, and facing the state of affairs she experiences as a Black woman living in Jim Crow America could have helped to provide a different lens through which Olivia understood her role as a relatively privileged Black woman. Unfortunately, she does not ever consider that her behavior should be adjusted. She is the commodified product made real by a social and consumer culture that privileges white people over Black people. She has not the literacies—or, more precisely, she rejects those literacies—that might have helped her challenge systems of racial oppression in which she is an active participant. The novel ends with Olivia living alone in France because her husband is unable to pay her fare to return home to America. The truth is he does not really want her to come back, with Oliver dead and Teresa in a loveless marriage to a Frenchman living in a small French city. Only her older son, Christopher Jr., and their father narrowly escape Olivia's tyranny. On a happier note, Christopher Jr. marries Phebe Grant; his father goes to live with them and slowly comes back to life.

During her lifetime, Fauset was often criticized for writing about bourgeois issues confronting the Black middle class (Goldsmith 258). Certainly, *Comedy: American Style* is about the Black middle class, but it is not merely a chronicle of their bourgeois lifestyles or a simple story about their lives as middle-class Black people held back from success from white gatekeepers. In the novel, Fauset asks readers to consider what the stakes are for African Americans to gain access to the white world and its material goods if it is at the expense of family and community. Readers are asked to consider the nature of race. What does it mean to be Black? Does having white skin color make one white or Black? What are the specific causes of racial self-hatred? Is it self-induced or imposed from outside? Less explicitly but equally importantly, Fauset also asks readers to consider the nature of literacy and education. In *Comedy: American Style*, functional literacy is not a vehicle that carries one out of poverty and into middle-class life. Sophisticated literacy skills do not open the door to selfhood. A one-sided view of the transactional nature of literacy is dangerous. The death of Oliver, the social death of Teresa, and the exile of Olivia from her husband and older son illustrate the existential crisis that follows when literacy objectifies the self. Fauset's discussions of race are a far cry from Woman's Era notions of equality based on literacy, education, and respectability. Literacy acquisition and its use in daily life cannot function as a one-to-one exchange between those with power and those without power. For literacy to have value, particularly for Black families and their communities, transformational and/or specular literacy must be actualized.

Comedy: American Style is valuable in presenting a nuanced understanding of the shifting dynamics of race relations in the early decades of the twentieth century. It enumerated both the possibilities and limits of literacy where literacy instruction, specifically in its sophisticated dimensions, loses its appeal as the crushing defeat of racial caste takes hold in the lives of the emerging Black middle class. The ideals of race literature that held so much promise and power in the late nineteenth century for Black women writers shifted as the world changed and Jim Crow became ever more entrenched. These changes marked in the pages of Fauset's *Comedy: American Style* reflected a shifting dynamic that would combine with new technologies in the second and third decades of the twentieth century when race records came to be a major source of entertainment and public discourse. At that time, informed by their social and economic conditions, geography, and the vernacular of the folk, Black women blues singers like Ma Rainey engaged the specular dimensions of their literacy practices on matters of race.

GERTRUDE "MA" RAINEY: MOTHER OF THE BLUES

Gertrude "Ma" Rainey and Fauset could not be any more different as public figures responding to challenges affecting the Black race. Their differences, though stark, demonstrate that Black women from various social classes had distinctive ways of engaging in questions related to race. Rainey's creative and discursive energies were focused on the lives of a subset of the Black working class. Her blues lyrics and vocal performances reflect both the real and imagined stories of a people longing to exist freely in a world that deemed them unworthy of full citizenship. Rather than seek acceptance of their art by the white majority and the small but influential Black elite and middle class, blues singers like Ma Rainey found beauty and joy in the expressive dimensions of the folk. Including aspects of folk culture in their vernacular provided representation often lacking in the fiction of these women's predecessors and contemporaries. Ma Rainey's blues embodied and forecast a divergence among Black women of the 1920s and '30s. The classic blues women turned inward and looked outward toward their physical and linguistic environments to reflect the sensory, visual, and auditory worlds they and their fans inhabited. Rather than portray those environments as deficient and needing change, they deployed their creative spirits to reflect the joys, disappointments, and sensualities of their surroundings. This is how specular literacy works. In practice, specular literacy reflects instead of demands change. It expands notions about race, freedom, and justice rather than mimicking the status quo. Hence, Ma Rainey became part of a contingent of Black women looking to stake their claim as free thinkers unafraid to deviate from more modest and conservative Black public voices of the early twentieth century.

Ma Rainey's five-year recording career extended from 1923 to 1928. Space will not permit me to provide an exhaustive study of her blues songs. Rather, I have chosen a few representative songs from her 1925–1928 recordings to illustrate how the classic blues singers included dimensions of Black women's sexual and sensual experiences that were unexplored in Cooper's and Matthews's concepts of race literature or in most Black women's fiction of the late nineteenth and early twentieth centuries. Music written and performed by Ma Rainey explored working-class Black women's losses and loves, rejection and revenge, crimes and injustice, pains and triumphs, desire and violence, same-sex attraction, and many expressions of Black female agency. Ma Rainey and the other classic blues singers thus imagined and reflected in their music alternate ways to deal with racial issues. As Angela Davis points out, "these songs provide a rich and complex backdrop for working-class women's lives" (45).

For the most part, the women including Ma Rainey who wrote and performed classic blues music did not overtly consider literacy and education in their lyrics, though Rainey mentioned writing a few times in her songs. Essentially, the women cast as central figures in classic blues were not doting mothers sitting by the hearth reading to their young children or extolling the virtues of writing. These songs did not portray literacy instruction as an activity shared by mothers and children or transferred from the literate to the semi-literate or illiterate as a democratic good needed for liberation purposes. Yet Ma Rainey's values and literacy practices were present. She wrote many of her blues songs, and she wrote verses in the vernacular of her southern roots. Some of the women in her songs compose letters. For Ma Rainey's blues women, however, writing has a sometimes ominous purpose: it warns rather than legitimizes writing as a democratizing force for good. In those cases, writing serves to warn women to stop behaviors that anger their estranged lovers.

In Ma Rainey's blues, the folk could see themselves come to life, which was in many ways a democratic experience. Ma Rainey once described the blues by saying, "the blues aint nothing but the easy going heart disease" (qtd. in "'Blues' Mama 'Ma' Rainey" 4). Ma Rainey's blues were more expansive than she revealed in her statement. She recognized both the lyrical power of the blues and its performative import. Sandra Lieb, author of a biography of Ma Rainey, describes the connection between the singer and her audiences this way:

> For the rural audience, listening to Ma Rainey's blues was an act of identification and communion, but for its displaced urban counterpart

in the North and Midwest, the same music symbolized a quickly vanishing world, which lived faintly through letters and an occasional visit. Even for those with no wish to return South, attending a concert or listening to Ma Rainey's records was a way of witnessing, testifying to the strength of black cultural roots and shared communal experiences, recapturing the past and the values of a lost culture, while in a strange land. (169)

In those strange and familiar places, Ma Rainey reminded her audiences that their cultural expressions and lives deserved to be elevated artistically. This is how specular literacy functions. The artist both reflects back to the audience their ways of being and helps them imagine ways of being that comfort them and thus serve as both entertainment and salve.

MA RAINEY'S CLASSIC BLUES

It is perhaps easy to reduce Ma Rainey's classic blues music to the trivialities of life. What do estrangement, travel, hoodoo, violence, sensuality, and personal agency have to do with racial issues? And how can considerations concerning specular literacy help make sense of Ma Rainey's classic blues in the context of the New Negro Era? For all the hoopla surrounding the transgressions of the classic blues singers of the 1920s and '30s, I argue that their entry into the public imagination simply extended race literature to new dimensions, though admittedly not as it was envisioned by Cooper and Matthews. Whether writing new lyrics or adapting lyrics circulating among blues singers, Ma Rainey's classic blues shows that working-class Black women like her had something to say about life. Instead of waiting to be rescued by elite and middle-class Black women who may have wanted to police their behaviors both in real life and in their creative works, Rainey took it upon herself to envision a world where women took care of their own troubles without consideration for respectability politics. Women in her songs act without restraint. Sometimes they fight back violently, other times metaphorically. One of her most popular blues songs, "Broken Hearted Blues," recorded in 1926, is about Black female agency of a different sort. Ma Rainey sings part of the song in the first person singular "I" and at other times refers to herself in third person singular (as "she" and "her"). The female persona has many worries, one of which is concern about her lovers. In the opening lines Ma Rainey sings, "Lord, I wonder, what is it worryin' me" (all lyrics qtd. in A. Davis 209). She seeks the Lord's help to understand her worries. It is the men in her life who give her so much trouble, both in the present and from the past: "if it ain't my regular, must be my used to be." Her invocation to the Lord is both a sacred and secular plea for help. The Lord helps those who are weary, which she is; she hopes too that the Lord will help even those who cross the boundaries of the marital bed. It is obvious the embattled "I" is not married to the man she worries about, yet she loves him enough to worry about him. To ease her worries, the woman decides to go in search of her man with the help of some dogs. She sings, "I'm going to buy me a pair of meat hounds to lead this lonesome trail, if I don't find my good man, I'll spend the rest of my life in jail." Rather than wait on the Lord to answer her pleas, the woman decides to act and remedy the situation on her own even if it means she acts criminally. In her warning, she declares she is willing to suffer the consequences, even if she has to go to jail. She confesses, "Good morning, judge, Mama Rainey's done raised sand, she killed everybody, judge, she's even killed her man." Speaking of herself in the third person, Ma Rainey confesses to the judge she has transgressed biblical and legal boundaries.

One interpretation of "Broken Hearted Blues" is that it is about a mad woman who kills in a fit of rage. This is true in one sense. Rejection has driven her mad. But, in another way, this song can be understood as a cathartic expression of rage, in which a Black woman is permitted to act out vengeful desires in a world that tells women like her to suppress their emotions, particularly emotions that lead to physical actions. In the literature of the Woman's Era and much Harlem Renaissance fiction, such outbursts, even imagined ones, had no place in art to be consumed by both Black and white readers. For some of the elite public intellectuals of the era, such expressions of rage only reinforced what white people already believed about Black people. To counter white people's negative perceptions, Black women in both fiction and the real world should act modestly. This was not the position of Ma Rainey. In the fictive world of her blues, women like the one in "Broken Hearted Blues" can act and react without consideration for middle-class respectability politics, responding instead with all the emotional, vernacular, and cultural tools at their disposal. In this way, Ma Rainey granted the license for Black women to be more emotive, something they had been counseled not to do.

Writing about working-class Black Baptist women, Evelyn Brooks Higginbotham describes the fervor with which they sought to gain respectability in the eyes of both Black and white society: "By claiming respectability through their manners and morals, poor black women boldly asserted the will and agency to define themselves outside the parameters of prevailing racist discourses. Notwithstanding the sincerity of the Baptist women's appeals to respectable behavior, such appeals were also explicitly rejections of Social Darwinist explanations of blacks' biological inferiority to whites. Respectability was perceived as a weapon against such assumptions" (*Righteous Discontent* 192). Neither the fictitious Mama Rainey nor the real Ma Rainey worried about respectability politics. The policing of behavior was anathema to the creative spirit of the blues. A desire to express hurt and rage is part of the human condition. Steve Goodson writes about Ma Rainey's broad appeal, saying, "as much as these songs are about black migrants from the South, the travails of working-class black women, and the 1920s, they are also—in a broader sense—about what it is to be a human being" (161). Whether in a typical twelve-bar blues or an atypical blues form, the songs provided these Black women songwriters and performers, who were largely from poor and working-class families, a way to narrate stories and truths that were meaningful to them and their fans. Certainly, blues lyrics were viewed as obscene by some; for others, they opened a voyeuristic window into the lives of some members of the Black working class. Nonetheless, classic blues singers created paradigmatic schemes for personal and civic justice. As the broken-hearted woman in her own song, Mama Rainey seeks justice for mistreatment experienced at the hands of a former lover. In the song, she acts outside the boundaries of a legal system designed to punish wrongdoers. In this case, the justice system was moving too slowly, and Mama Rainey, in this revenge story, remedies the situation in her time and with her own methods.

Upon first hearing "Broken Hearted Blues" or reading the lyrics, one may think the scenario imagined by Ma Rainey leaves no room to consider race questions. The song tells a story about the stresses of life, with rejection at its center. It is a fact of life that Black men and women struggled over love and lost love in the 1920s. It is a fact that some Black men and women resolved their relationship struggles in counterproductive ways. Resolution sometimes meant that police intervention was necessary, or violence might be an outcome. These realities take shape in the music written and performed by Ma Rainey. She took anguish and made it beautiful. The beauty lies in the complicated nature of the story she narrates as well as in the vocal delivery of her lyrics. Love is part of the discourse of race, particularly how one loves. Love is revolutionary. It can be a political act especially for Black people, whose enslaved ancestors were not always allowed to choose their partners and lovers. In Ma Rainey's blues, Black people can choose their lovers, how they love, and how their relationships with their lovers evolve. The outcome may be as horrific as it is in "Broken Hearted Blues," but the fact that it happens is significant.

In a slow tempo, Ma Rainey sings "Broken Hearted Blues" in a southern regional vernacular that captures the essence of pain experienced by the broken-hearted female lover. Over the course of the song, there is much consternation for the female lover who worries about the men in her life. Ma Rainey's southern-inflected vocals emphasize the degree to which the lover worries. This is obvious because an elongated emphasis is placed on the word "worrying," which is sung as "wor-re-in." Her pronunciation emphasizes that the worrying is deeply bothersome and endless. In the latter part of "Broken Hearted Blues" Ma Rainey's southern regional vernacular continues to capture the essence of African American Vernacular English (AAVE). When Ma Rainey sings, "Good morning, judge, Mama Rainey's done raised sand," instead of the grammatical structure favored in standard American English (Mama Rainey has raised sand), singing "done raised" announces her allegiance to a grammatical structure in AAVE, which signals her commitment to a language practice that both is authentic to her and notes the emphatic nature of her action. Furthermore, it indicates that her misbehaving action has already taken place, and there is no way to remedy the situation. The deed is done; everyone is dead. Writing about the "perfect *done*," William Labov notes: "AAVE has always possessed the perfect particle, *done*, which is found both in white Southern states English and in Caribbean creoles. In AAVE, *done* precedes a verb that makes reference to an action completed in the recent past. If that is a telic verb, which implies a change of state, *done* will indicate that the action is completed" (124). The colloquial expression "raised sand" also reflects a connection with the folk. Thus, the specular literacy practices rooted in Ma Rainey's "Broken Hearted Blues" are reflective of a singer who finds purpose and beauty in the vernacular expressions, speech, and vocal inflections of the folk.

Ma Rainey's 1925 "Rough and Tumble Blues" is another song that focuses on interpersonal violence and heterosexual relationships. The song opens in the future present tense by a jilted lover who declares her intention to send a telegram to expose her cheating lover to everybody who will listen and says she is willing to die as she seeks revenge against the women cheating with her man. This public shaming she hopes will stop his cheating ways and embarrass the cheating women. The story in these blues verses is really a private story about heartache, but the function of the blues is that it allows the private to become a communal experience. Other people hurting at the hands of cheating lovers can commiserate while listening to the record or console each other as they watch Ma Rainey perform it. In other words, fans get to work through their pain privately or in community with others. Although public expressions of pain are often frowned upon, this song gives private pain a public place. This move is where specular literacy deviates from transformational or even transactional literacy. Where transformational literacy suggests uplift as a central function of its ethos, and transactional literacy embraces the singularity of success over communal good, specular literacy allows emotive and physical reactions to be part of a communal cathartic experience. Hence, Ma Rainey's specular literacy operates on two levels. First, as a creative artist she holds up one side of a metaphorical and literal mirror to divulge the inner workings of a blues tradition that exposes to the world one of life's most difficult emotions: human heartache. Second, the other side of the mirror discloses private thoughts usually kept from public knowledge and scrutiny as they relate to heartache. How does one deal with rejection and deception in a secular world focused so much on restricted covenants designed to modernize and "civilize" the poor Black underclass? Ma Rainey describes in her music how to negotiate such complex terrain. This too is part of race work. The love and sensual lives of Black people also needed to be attended to. That interiority is as much a part of race work as trying to work out how Black people seek better employment opportunities, decent housing, and critiques the status quo.

Private pain cannot be contained, and thus the story in this song begins with an announcement that all must hear this first-person revenge story. Fury animates the beginning of "Rough and Tumble Blues." The abandoned lover is so angry that she wants everyone to know why death is an option. Death is a viable option for her given the love and money she has invested in her lover. Regrettably and even dangerously so, the male lover does not appreciate the time, money, and care she has given him; thus, the women who have charmed her good-looking man away from her must pay the price. The angry lover mocks them at first: "then every little devil got on my man's road, . . . Mama Tree Top Tall and Miss Shorty Toad" (all lyrics qtd. in A. Davis 239). In these humorous descriptions of the women who have taken her lover's attentions away, the jilted lover raises the stakes even more by belittling the physical attributes of her man's new lovers. The derisive comments, an aspect of "signifying," are a part of a vernacular tradition in Black culture. Geneva Smitherman explains that it "refers to the verbal art of insult in which a speaker humorously puts down, talks about, needles—that is, signifies on—the listener. Sometimes signifyin (also siggin) is done to make a point, sometimes it's just for fun" (118–19).

This signifying has two purposes. First, the signifying works to elicit laughter, which helps ease the tension listeners might be experiencing in their own relationships with a philandering partner. Second, within the narrative framework of the song, the signifying is designed to humiliate the women who have themselves humiliated the cheated-on female lover. This, in turn, works to alleviate the felt pain of women or men whose cheating mates have chosen lovers who may not be their physical equivalents. Later in the song, the sassy and funny descriptions continue when the rejected lover finds her man with his new lovers: "Tree Top Tall give a stomp as I stepped in the door . . . Miss Shorty Toad and my man was shimming down to the floor" (all lyrics qtd. in A. Davis 239). Being caught in the act of a sensuous dance with Miss Shorty Toad sends the disrespected lover into a violent rage, and listeners learn she "got rough and killed three women 'fore the police got the news, 'Cause mama's on the warpath with those rough and tumble blues." All rationality has ended in the last verse. To rid herself of the pain of betrayal, the bewitched lover chose to murder instead of walking away from her troubled relationship. In addition to appreciating Ma Rainey's vocal abilities, such over-the-top behavior described in these classic blues is what likely captivated her fans. They could live vicariously through her lyrics since so much of Black life was policed by white people and advocates of Black respectability politics. James Cone writes eloquently about this appeal of the blues: "The blues were living reality. . . . They are bitter but also sweet. They are funny and not so funny. . . . They are part of that structure of reality in which human beings are condemned to live. And because the black person had to live in the midst of a broken existence, the reality of the blues was stark and real" (122).

The "living reality" of the blues bore witness to love triangles in "Rough and Tumble Blues," but also to the humanity and frailty of love often denied to Black people in a world that viewed and treated them as second-class citizens. The matter-of-fact tone in which Ma Rainey sings "Rough and Tumble Blues" belies its provocativeness and its profound departure from the modesty politics embraced by her New Negro Era peers. First, the jilted lover writes a telegram that describes her rage. Next, she makes disparaging remarks against the physical characteristics of the two women cheating with her man. As well, she admits that murder is not in opposition to her morality. Finally, she admits she killed three women in a rage after she found her man dancing sensually with Miss Shorty Toad. The song is both humorous and incendiary. It is also a song that reveals the precariousness of human life. Simply put, the blues were not written or sung to be a wholesome representation of sorrow; rather the blues, as Ma Rainey shows in "Rough and Tumble Blues," were meant to express and reflect the gut-wrenching emotions humans experience in daily life. Ma Rainey's specular literacy practices in "Rough and Tumble Blues" as well as her other blues songs allow the hyperbolic and the real to occupy an in-betweenness that affirms and cajoles working-class sensibilities while critiquing systems of oppression.

In "Broken Hearted Blues," Ma Rainey morphs into the jilted lover seeking revenge. In "Rough and Tumble Blues," she embodies a witty lover seeking love justice. In "Black Dust Blues," recorded in 1928, Ma Rainey sings as the frail and vengeful lover. The mistress is haunted by her man's main lover. The haunted mistress feigns ignorance, while the vengeful lover turns to writing and voodoo to seek retribution. Ma Rainey sings, "she sent me a letter, says she's gonna turn me down. . . . She's gonna fix me up so I won't chase her man around" (all lyrics qtd. in A. Davis 203). Writing serves as both a warning and a poetic catharsis. In this revenge blues, the stakes are high, and the consequences immediate. The haunted woman reveals she "begins to feel bad, worse than ever before . . . started out one morning, found black dust all 'round my door." The black dust signals to the haunted woman that trouble is on the way. First the letter and now the black dust, which is causing her to feel ill. The warning has come to life. The black dust performs its desired duty; the mistress suffers for her transgressive actions. The mistress says she "began to get thin, had trouble with my feet. . . . Throwing stuff out my mouth whenever I tried to eat." Whatever power is in the black dust is making the mistress so sick that she is losing weight and regurgitating her food. Moreover, the black dust is working so well that "black dust got me walking on all fours like a cat." The deed is done; the dust has made a fool of the cheating female lover. She should no longer be desirous to the man they share. Even more, she should no longer want to cheat with the other woman's man, given how much the voodoo practiced against her has changed her life.

Ma Rainey sings "Black Dust Blues" in a slow melancholy tempo that mirrors the progression of the cheating woman's sickness. From feigned ignorance and good health to an open warning and failing health, the cheating woman turns into a fool who is exposed for crossing her man's love-sick lover. As Ma Rainey sings the verses while embodying the cheating lover, listeners can get a sense of the realization that her cheating ways will bring about consequences that she is unprepared to stop, much less deal with. Listeners know this by the lyrics, but they also are made aware of the seriousness of her actions by Ma Rainey's haunted vocals, which give credence to the black magic practiced against the cheating woman.

On the one hand, "Black Dust Blues" embodies the old adage "you reap what you sow." On the other hand, it represents a religious and cultural practice that was sanctioned by certain groups of Black people wrestling with existential and spiritual questions relating to the body and interpersonal relationships. Timothy J. McMillian writes about the history of black magic and its connection to Black people's spiritual practices: "Blacks throughout the New World modified their African beliefs to deal with the novel and . . . oppressive situations which presented themselves. The syncretism of Catholicism and West African belief which resulted in voodoo is perhaps the best known of these transformations of African religion in the face of New World pressure" (101). As a result, some African-descended Americans turned to voodoo spiritual practices to punish their enemies for personal and civic transgressions. These practices made some more modest Black middle-class Americans uncomfortable, as Katherine D. C. Tillman alludes to in her late nineteenth-century novella *Clancy Street* in which the narrator disparages these beliefs and practices by referring to them as "a diabolical form of worship brought from Africa by Negro slaves. . . . Voodoo or Vaudoux when properly carried out means a well-organized band of men and women who worship the devil under the form of serpents and who lend themselves to all sorts of evil schemes in order to be revenged upon their enemies" (261). Only the uneducated, the narrator asserts, continue such practices (262). Whether or not readers subscribed to the moral principles of the narrator regarding Voodoo, the fact is there were many who believed and valued the spiritual practices of their African ancestors and imbued them with meaning that allowed African Americans to function within an oppressive system that confined them in small physical and psychic spaces. Ma Rainey's "Black Dust Blues" and her other blues songs opened up those physical and psychic spaces for her listeners by appealing to and singing in a vernacular language they understood while imagining scenarios they wished for or related to. Writing about Ma Rainey's gifts to her fans, Steve Goodson asserts that "through her music—and in particular through a new musical style to which she helped to give birth—Gertrude would assert her dignity, her autonomy, and her humanity, all the while tacitly encouraging her listeners to do the same" (149). The strength of Ma Rainey's stories and her down-home southern blues warmed many a soul at her public performances and those listening to her records at home with friends. Her lyrics also affirmed for some of her fans that their spiritual beliefs and practices—those mocked within and outside their racial communities—had a place in her blues.

    Many of Ma Rainey's blues songs explore rejection and retaliation in heterosexual relationships. There are, however, songs that focus on same-sex love and desire such as "Prove It on Me Blues" and "Sissy Blues." "Prove It on Me Blues," recorded in 1928, is an upbeat and mischievous blues song that speaks openly about same-sex relationships. Ma Rainey opens the first verse by describing a woman in search of her female lover with whom she had had a "big fight" (all lyrics qtd. in A. Davis 238). The lover leaves after their fight, which compels the girlfriend to search for her woman: "where she went, I don't know, I mean to follow everywhere she goes." Early in the first two verses, there is no shame admitting same-sex attraction, although there is recognition of societal disapproval by acknowledging that "folks say I'm crooked, I didn't know where she took it, I want the whole world to know." Instead of hiding her true self, she openly admits she is searching for her female lover, expressing her willingness to circumvent social convention. At the same time, she may be ambivalent regarding her same-sex attractions as the lyrics continue, "they say I do it, ain't nobody caught me, sure got to prove it on me," while also disclosing she prefers women over men: "It's true I wear a collar and a tie. . . . Talk to the girls like any old man." It does not matter if her same-sex attractions can be proven. Acknowledgment of a lesbian relationship has already been stated as fact in this song. "Prove It on Me Blues," according to Hazel Carby, thus "engages directly in defining issues of sexual preference as a contradictory struggle of social relations" ("'It Jes Be's Dat'" 237). Even as the song reveals how Ma Rainey deals with the ambivalence of same-sex desire as the site of physical desire over civic responsibility (since heterosexual relationships were then generally defined as the foundation of nation-building and respectability), her bold declarations stand in stark contrast to traditional values and behaviors embraced by Black and white alike. It was a political decision to reject such patriarchal and gender norms.

Although classic blues music written and performed by Ma Rainey and other singers was shunned by some in the Black elite and middle class, the *Chicago Defender*, an important Black newspaper of the early twentieth century, advertised the release of blues music alongside spirituals as well as important news stories of the day. The September 22, 1928, issue featured an advertisement for "Prove It on Me Blues." With a broad smile, Ma Rainey stands next to two attractive feminine-presenting women. She is wearing a masculine suit coat, vest, and tie, with a man's fedora on her head. The women next to her wear modern dresses and fashionable hats. All of the women seem comfortable with each other. In the background stands a vigilant cop watching the women interact. Is there something askew going on at the corner where they stand, his presence asks? The description of the song plays along with its suggestive title: "What's all this? Scandal? Maybe so, but you wouldn't have thought it of 'Ma' Rainey. But look at that cop watching her! What does it all mean? But 'Ma' just sings 'Prove It on Me' in this great new Paramount Blues" (7). The advertisement's description is deceptively playful. And as Ma Rainey stands next to the women, the sexual tension is muted, but it goes without saying what the true nature of their relationship is as they linger on the corner next to each other. The lyrics are direct: she "talked to the gals just like any old man" (qtd. in A. Davis 238). Her attraction is to women not men.

MA RAINEY'S SPECULAR LITERACY PRACTICES

Ma Rainey could write and sing "Prove It on Me Blues" and other blues songs in a modern world because modernity had brought with it new views of the world and bold new ways of being. Rather than maintain a staid persona intent on earning the respect of the wider white world and the emerging Black elite and middle class, Ma Rainey turned to the specular and reinvention as modes of entertainment and survival. Carby explains the potency of Black women's blues: "what a consideration of women's blues allows us to see is an alternative form of representation, an oral and musical women's culture that explicitly addresses the contradictions of feminism, sexuality, and power" ("'It Jus Be's Dat'" 231). The contradictions that Carby describes and that Ma Rainey embraced illustrate a profound understanding of an evolving people who wished to capitalize on their talent and culture. Ma Rainey was an extension of this desire. To that end, Ma Rainey's specular literacy practices, rooted in both the personal and the communal, reflected a woman masterfully writing and singing songs for and about the folk. As Daphne Duval Harrison writes, "the blues artist speaks directly of and to the folk who have suffered pain and assures them that they are not alone; someone understands" (6). Ma Rainey had to be aware not just of pain but also female desire.

Ann duCille problematizes classic blues singers as both giving agency and exoticizing black female sexuality and "subjectivity":

> Identifying women blues artists as the site of a struggle for black female subjectivity necessarily raises complex questions about agency and interpellation, self and subject, person and persona. . . . Perhaps the answer to the question of agency and interpellation lies somewhere between the two possibilities—in exploring the reflexive nature of ideology and invention, in examining critically the ideological aspects of the epoch that made possible the invention of both the explicitly sexual black female subjects sung in the songs of blues women like Bessie Smith and Ma Rainey. (74)

Although duCille is right to express the contradictory nature of women's blues as a "the site of a struggle for black female subjectivity," I offer an addition to rather than a counter to duCille's concerns. The music did give a public face to ideas, behaviors, and emotions that needed exorcising. Too often, the concerns, desires, ideas, attitudes, and language practices of the folk were absent from the creative texts of both the Woman's and New Negro Era writers. Blues singers like Ma Rainey illustrated the diversity of thought existing among Black women creatives. Her music gave space to working-class Black life. Rather than allow Black working-class people to remain hidden, Ma Rainey's blues reimagined and reflected the lives of women whose stories would have remained on the back porch and whose language and literacy practices would not have been elevated to masterful effect on blues records. Black people had been policed since their forced arrival on American shores. Finally, they could, even in commodified form, remove the shackles momentarily.

The classic blues music that Ma Rainey wrote and performed helped to dispel the myth that Black art and Black culture are monolithic. I doubt that Ma Rainey's approach to uplift was what Cooper and Matthews imagined for race literature when they encouraged Black writers to create works with positive and realistic portrayals of Black people. Fighting injustice, creating strong and proud race men and women, and being creative, however, changed as modernity, travel, and a consumer culture allowed Black working-class women to engage in their own debates about how best to represent and uplift their people. No longer forced to accept and practice transactional or transformational literacies to rise in social status, Ma Rainey and her classic blues contemporaries found ways to employ forms of specular literacy to produce works that reflected working-class linguistic and cultural practices, thus affirming the value of the lives they imagined and lived in the new modern era. In the hands of classic blues singers like Ma Rainey, ideas about how Black people respond to racial oppression looked as different as a poem is to a novel.

Chapter Five

LITERACY, THE FOLK, AND CLASSIC BLUES

Zora Neale Hurston and Victoria Spivey

Jessie Fauset's anti-heroine Olivia Cary in *Comedy: American Style* is exiled from her Black American family when she is forced to settle in France, and she is also exiled from the French middle class she had hoped to join because of her daughter's marriage to a Frenchman who lives in a small, pedestrian French town. Olivia's dream of living in Paris and enjoying life passing as white with her family in tow is dashed. Her husband and remaining son have no desire to join her in France. Alone and poor in a dingy room at the end of the novel, Olivia will most likely fade into invisibility, but not the kind of invisibility she wanted. Thus, her sojourn into whiteness is an utter failure. The social currency she had hoped to capitalize on in France only serves to reinforce the dangers of employing literacy as a transaction. In contrast, the characters who populate Ma Rainey's blues proudly embody aspects of their Black vernacular culture while confronting interpersonal issues. As a result, on record and in her live performances, Ma Rainey succeeded in utilizing and demonstrating forms of specular literacy to entertain and affirm the folk dimensions of a subset of the Black working class.

If classic blues music captured the spirit of working-class souls, then Zora Neale Hurston's fiction gave those souls form as fully realized characters. As a masterful storyteller, she described Black southern rural life like few others in her time. Using the vernacular of the folk, Hurston took what was considered by many inside and outside her own racial community to be a linguistic embarrassment and elevated it to lyrical beauty. In so doing, Hurston's fiction represents and reflects Black people at ease with themselves even as some of the behaviors and attitudes described are deeply troublesome. The ability to represent in fictional form the lives of the people she knew so well and to bring their strengths and foibles to the fore is what makes her literary and literacy efforts daring and revelatory. Her short stories and novels revel in the culture and traditions of a people whose lives she helped give meaning to as the world was moving into modernity. In capturing the rhythms of Black speech patterns, particularly in the novel analyzed in this chapter, Hurston did not imitate to shame but rather to present Black speech in its natural forms. Ultimately, *Jonah's Gourd Vine* acts as a place where Black life exists as it is rather than what some thought it ought to be. This makes both the linguistic and cultural aspects of her novel forms of specular literacy.

While Hurston is best known for her 1937 novel, *Their Eyes Were Watching God*, I have chosen to focus on her first novel, *Jonah's Gourd Vine*. Published in 1934, it tells the story of John Pearson, a preacher who loves women as much as he loves the word. When readers are introduced to John, his verbal skills are already highly developed; he will utilize them as a preacher and in his other work environments. As a teen, John seeks to acquire written literacy skills, which will serve him in his capacity as a lover, brother, and community member. As a handsome and dynamic preacher, John lives his life by satisfying his carnal needs even when doing so destroys him and those he loves. While John is the main protagonist of the novel, the sub-protagonists are Lucy Potts and literacy. Learning to write and signifying are the ingredients that keep life moving in this novel. John talks himself into and out of trouble because of his facility with words. He captures Lucy's imagination with his love letters and poems and later with his earnest and rhythmic sermons. Lucy impresses John and others with her spelling and oratory skills. After he meets his new love, Sally Lovelace, John writes her love letters every day. Oral and written forms of literacy are central in this novel; literacy is also both mocked and admired. In every way, Hurston compels readers to see the folly and the possibilities of literacy.

During the same period in which Hurston was writing these novels, the classic blues singers continued to write, record, and perform their music. This chapter features the work of the classic blues singer Victoria Spivey alongside Hurston. Spivey was a contemporary of Ma Rainey and Bessie Smith. Lesser known than Rainey and Smith, Spivey was no less important in classic blues. She too wrote lyrics about broken hearts, but her lyrics also reflected the everyday challenges of people dealing with racial injustice. In her songs, densely populated neighborhoods give way to disease and death, drug use empowers, and love follies continue. Spivey's musical heyday was in the mid-1920s, though she resurfaced in the 1960s as an entertainer and writer before dying in 1976. Like the lyrics and vocals of the other classic blues singers of the 1920s and '30s, Spivey's were a reflection of the folk. Her music and her literacy converged to tell their stories.

JONAH'S GOURD VINE'S JOHN PEARSON

In Hurston's *Jonah's Gourd Vine*, John Pearson, also known as John Buddy Pearson, is the biracial son of Amy Crittenden and stepson of her husband, Ned Crittenden. The Crittendens are poor sharecroppers in Alabama struggling to survive. Their children, including John, also work the land and help around the house. Even with the children's help, the family remains very poor. Amy loves her children, but she often finds herself at odds with Ned, who hates John. The sight of Amy's only biracial child irritates Ned. At sixteen, John is tall, strong, handsome, and sharp-tongued. What Ned at first loves about the younger John—his complexion—he grows to despise. He often threatens to harm John for what he perceives is his stepson's youthful impertinence; however, John is simply responding to Ned's tyranny. In an early scene, Ned screams at John to close the front door. John retorts, "'I wazn't de last one inside'" (2). John's backtalk infuriates Ned, who yells back at him, "'don't you gimme no word for word.... You jes' do lak Ah I say do and keep yo' mouf shet or Ah'll take uh trace chain tuh yuh. Yo' mammy mought think youse uh lump of gold' cause you got uh li'l white folks color in yo' face, but Ah'll stomp yo' guts out and dat quick! Shet dat door!'" (2). Ned's threat is heard by Amy, and it forces her to challenge Ned because he has threatened to beat John. Regretfully, life with Ned becomes unbearable for John.

In another early scene in the novel, John is forced to intervene in a domestic dispute between Ned and Amy. Ned, reeling from Amy's backtalk and her love for John, attacks her violently under the pretense that she fed seconds to the younger children when he had not yet had his first plate of food. John reacts to Ned's violence against his mother by hitting him so hard Amy believes he may have mistakenly killed him (8). A humiliated Ned tells Amy that John must go. In fact, Ned had already decided he did not want John in the house and, without Amy's knowledge or consent, had "bound" him over to work on a plantation operated by a brutal and unscrupulous poor white man (7, 10). John decides it is better for him to leave, even though his mother wants him to stay. John leaves with peace, work, and other "people['s] ... daughters" on his mind (12).

"OVER THE CREEK" JOHN

To John's surprise, he will find he also wants literacy and education after he moves to an area on the other side of the local creek. The narrator describes John's amazement when he sees a school for the first time: "So! This must be the school house that he had heard about. Negro children going to learn how to read and write like white folks" (13). Since John's parents needed him to work alongside them as sharecroppers, he was not allowed to attend school. Thus, to see a school on his way to find work on his first day in the new town is magical. At the school, Lucy, a smallish girl, attracts his attention. He decides he wants to get to know Lucy, and he wants to learn how to read and write. Once in school, John learns quickly; he is intent on learning and does so even when school is out for "cotton-picking time" (27). Life "over the creek" is going well for John, so well in fact that he is encouraged by his employer, Alf Pearson, to visit his mother and ask others to come to work there. When John visits his mother, Amy is happy to see John and to learn he is getting an education. She exclaims with joy, "'Jes' tuh think, mah boy gittin' book-learnt! Ned, de rest uh dese chillum got tuh go to school nex' yeah. Sho is'" (28). Amy understands why learning to read and write is so important for her children and for Black people more broadly.

Amy was once an enslaved person on Alf's plantation, and she gave birth to John while there. John's paternity is never clarified, but Alf seems to recognize something about the young man at their first meeting, telling John, "'your face looks sort of familiar but I can't place you'" (17). Amy never talks about John's biological father, although she sent John to Alf's plantation and told him to tell Alf that Amy sent him there to look for work. John never seems to make the connection about his possible parentage, but the narrator points the way. In their early interactions, Alf shows affection toward John. He even encourages him to go to school when work is slow, saying, 'Well, John, there's nothing much to do on the place now, so you might as well go on down to the school and learn how to read and write. I don't reckon it will hurt you. Don't waste your time, now. Learn'" (21). Alf's encouragement to learn may be because John is his son, and he wants the young man to at least have a functional level of literacy and to be a good person. Whatever was motivating Alf's encouragement, the reality is that children like John desperately needed an education. Born during a time when employment prospects for newly freed African Americans were limited, they understand the benefit of formal education. John's mother and stepfather's struggles show how difficult life was without adequate reading and writing skills. Thus, the joy Amy expresses when she learns John is in school reflects a dream of literacy held by many Black people of her time. With the right literacy skills, Amy hopes John will have a better life. Harryette Mullen writes about "the African American tradition of literacy as a secular technology and a tool for political empowerment" (673). Mullen notes that the secular dimensions of literacy give users an opportunity for advancement but also for personal growth.

Outside the schoolhouse on his first day, John unexpectedly meets Lucy, who is the smartest student at the school. Her ability to spell impresses John, who tells his friend Charlie about it. A humorous conversation ensues between Charlie and John that captures the way literacy and education could give a person what seemed to be miraculous skills. When Charlie praises John for his friend's spelling abilities because John can spell the word "baker," John replies that another student can spell more complex words. He tells Charlie that he "'aint ez smart ez some. Take Lucy Potts for instink. She's almost uh 'fessor now. Nobody can't spell her down. Dey say she kin spell eve'y word in Lippincott's Blue-back Speller'" (Hurston, *Jonah's Gourd Vine* 27). John's amazement is palpable. He admires Lucy's intelligence so much that he wants his friend to know she is smarter than he is. Yet, in the exchange between John and Charlie, the narrator seems to imply something else is going on regarding Charlie's admiration for John's spelling skills and John's admiration for Lucy's spelling skills. John's spelling abilities are below Lucy's but more advanced than Charlie's; Lucy can spell small and big words better than both. At this point in Lucy's young life, however, it is not apparent if or how her advanced spelling skills impact her day-to-day life. Thus, when Charlie declares that Lucy's ability to spell long words such as "compresstibilty" (27) means she has learned all she can, his declaration comes too soon. His pronouncement is so ridiculous as to be comical. There is so much more that Lucy and others like Charlie and John need to learn in school. The acquisition of a thing, in this case learning to spell, is merely that. It is a thing unto itself. For spelling to have real value, the speller needs to learn what to do with the words to give them meaning. This is what John and Charlie need to understand but cannot because they are so enthralled by the thing itself. This is the lure of literacy as merely transactional. Transactional literacy is an accrual of language for the purposes of status and material gain. Charlie is impressed with John's and Lucy's spelling skills, but their skills for that time are mere ornaments.

WHAT IS THE POINT OF "BOOK LEARNING"?

Lucy is awarded the honor of giving a long speech during a program to celebrate the school year. One might assume that community members attending the program would be proud to listen to Lucy's oration. After all, such public recognition of Black students would have been unheard of in the not too distant past. But the banter between two unnamed characters provides evidence of Carter G. Woodson's prophetic warning about "the mis-education of the Negro." The two characters are polar opposites regarding literacy and education. One sees no value in literacy and education that does not result in immediate returns. The other values the acquisition of literacy even if the results are esoteric. Their exchange is revelatory. One character admiringly says, "'Dere's Lucy Potts over dere in uh fluted dress. Dey allus gives her de longest piece tuh speak'" (36). The other character retorts, "'Naw, 'tain't, dey muches her up. Mah Semmie could learn jes' ez long a piece ez anybody if de give it tuh her—in time'" (36). One praises Lucy's intelligence; the other criticizes it. On one hand, their discussion about Lucy might seem superficial. It can be read as gossip between two friends. On the other hand, their conversation matters greatly. There is a bit of jealousy revealed in their exchange. One character believes her daughter could give speeches like Lucy if she had time to learn the speech. The other one recognizes Lucy's talent for giving speeches.

The more illuminating revelation in the conversation between the two women occurs when Semmie's mother boldly admits she would rather her children work than attend school. She declares "'Ahm gwine take mah chillum outa school after dis and put'em tuh work. Dey ain't learnin' 'em nothin' nowhow. Dey makes cake outa some uh de chillum and cawn bread outa de rest'" (36). Semmie's mother's pointed declaration highlights the conundrum brought on by systemic issues that hinder outcomes for literacy and education for Black people, particularly those in the late nineteenth and early twentieth centuries. Speaking of them insightfully, Semmie's mother rationalizes that literacy and education ought to have immediate returns. In thinking about Lucy's oration, Semmie's mother thinks beyond the esoteric and into the real. Who does it serve, she might ask, if Lucy's literacy skills showcase her individual talent but do not provide meaningful change in her life or her family's life? This attitude reduces literacy and education to a mere commodity, a one-to-one transaction. It fails to recognize that, beyond a technology, literacy serves a humanistic end because, in the right circumstances, literacy can teach the self about the self. Readers can assume, however, that sociopolitical and economic concerns compel Semmie's mother to think of literacy as a consumer product. This was not what Cooper and Matthews envisioned or enacted as Black women who used their literacy skills in service to their communities.

The negative reaction to Lucy's recitation has roots in the famous disagreement between Booker T. Washington and W. E. B. Du Bois. Washington argued in his 1895 Atlanta Exposition Address that:

> Our greatest danger is that in the great leap from slavery to freedom we may overlook the fact that the masses of us are to live by the

productions of our hands. . . . no race can prosper till it learns that there is as much dignity in tilling a field as in writing a poem. It is at the bottom of life we must begin, and not at the top. Nor should we permit our grievances to overshadow our opportunities. (128–29)

By what means can Black people newly freed from bondage find their place in society? Washington believed that physical labor served as a noteworthy way to earn a decent living as well to bolster the social capital of the race. Why waste time writing poetry that does not actually change Black people's condition but merely reports on their condition? The real value of a vocational education such as the one Washington advanced would serve dual aims. It would provide Black people with certifiable skills and make them assets to their local Black communities and to the broader white community their skills could serve. This perspective seems to align with Semmie's mother's attitude toward literacy. Both Washington's and Semmie's mother's perspectives signal the transactional value of literacy, not its humanistic and transformational functions supported by Cooper and Matthews and by the other unnamed character as well as some of the named characters in Hurston's novel.

Du Bois, Washington's rival, disagreed that vocational education and common toil were the only means to elevate the race and to fight against white tyranny. In his rebuttal of Washington published in his 1903 *The Souls of Black Folk*, Du Bois urged resistance: "By every civilized and peaceful method we must strive for the rights which the world accords men, clinging unwaveringly to those great words which the sons of the Fathers would fain forget; 'We hold these truths to be self-evident: That all men are created equal; that they are endowed by their Creator with certain unalienable rights; that among these are life, liberty, and the pursuit of happiness'" (45). Du Bois's words reminded Black people that the rights accorded to their white countrymen and -women are the same rights accorded to Black women and men. They too should therefore pursue paths forward that allow them to exercise their intellectual powers to participate as full citizens. If that includes writing poetry to challenge their conditions, then they should pursue those ends. Narrow conceptions of citizenship and activism, according to Du Bois, should not exclude intellectual pursuits. In fact, as Derrick R. Spires has noted, enslaved and free Black people were already participating in citizenship activities of the intellectual sort: they understood how the activity of writing and publishing, for example, was as much a part of citizenship and liberation as any physical work used for the same ends. According to Spires, "citizenship and struggles for citizenship happened outside of official state institutions, in those very spaces black writers consistently cite as life sustaining. And it is through these sites that restrictive notions of belonging can be contested and in which alternate models can be theorized and practiced" (4). Citizenship activities are inclusive rather than narrowly conceived and include intellectual pursuits that contest racial oppression. Thus, as Du Bois emphasized, Washington's theory of labor and citizenship was mediated by a vision that undervalued the contributions of written communication. Hence, Du Bois's position aligned more with Cooper's and Matthews's visions of the transformational power of literacy.

The disagreement between Washington and Du Bois is analogous to the discussion of Lucy's oration by two unnamed women characters in Hurston's *Jonah's Gourd Vine*. Semmie's mother's contempt for what she views as decorative learning is indicative of Washington's critique of the arts. The other character's acknowledgment that Lucy always gets the longest speech suggests admiration for the girl's intelligence. Semmie's mother seems to think, at least momentarily, that labor is more important than "book learning." She equates labor with money; she equates orations with aesthetics. Ironically and rather comically, Hurston also includes in the novel a conversation between Hambo and John that directly parallels the positions of Washington and Du Bois. In their conversation, Washington is lauded for his intelligence, invitations to speak on behalf of Black people at the White House, and founding of Tuskegee Institute; Du Bois, however, is mocked for writing books. The presumptive theory is that writing produces nothing tangible. Thus, one of the friends asks: "What did Du Bois ever do? He writes up books and papers, hunh? Shucks! Dat ain't nothin', anybody kin put down words on uh piece of paper. Gimme da paper sack and lemme see dat pencil uh minute. Shucks! Writing! Man Ah thought you wuz talkin' 'bout uh man what had done sumpin. Ah thought maybe he wuz de man dat could make sidemeat taste lak ham" (148). In this hilarious harangue, Du Bois's accomplishments are deemed worthless because the speaker alleges his writings have not changed the social condition of Black people, whereas a man who can alter the taste of food has more value. For all the comic relief in the passage, questions concerning the value of literacy and education are real. The conversation about Washington and Du Bois as well as the discussion about Lucy's oration captures people at the crossroads of new lives. What kind of learning would best prepare Black people for success? What kind of literacy practices might enhance their economic and emotional lives? The characters and the narrator in *Jonah's Gourd Vine* provide sometimes contradictory, condemnatory, and complex answers to these questions.

On the question of the value of literacy and education, the narrator in *Jonah's Gourd Vine* takes time to condemn the behavior of a schoolteacher who is accused of "prid[ing] himself on his frowns . . . He yearned to hold his switches in his hand. He had little ambition to impart knowledge. He reigned" (25). Such descriptions of a stern disciplinarian might not be that unusual for the late nineteenth century. However, a Black teacher who is described as lacking a desire to "impart knowledge" to his pupils is clearly not a good teacher. Thus, there is no equivocation here as the narrator offers an opinion about the teacher, who is Lucy's uncle. The narrator does not condone this kind of instruction, especially from someone who would have first-hand knowledge of why education is so important to the overall success and well-being of Black learners. The schoolteacher and Semmie's mother are not the only characters who undervalue learning. Ned too is suspicious of education and declares its uselessness after John's mother, Amy, celebrates him for going to school by exclaiming "'Jes' tuh think, mah boy gittin' book-learnt'" (28). Ned declares:

> "What fur? So dey kin lay in the peni'ten'ry? Dat's all dese book-learnt n----rs do—fill up de jails and chain-gangs. Dese boys is comin' 'long all right. All dey need tuh learn is how tuh swing uh hoe and turn a ferrer. Ah ain't rubbed de hair off mah haid 'gin no college walls and Ah got good sense. Day ain't goin' tuh no school effen Ah got anythin' tuh say 'bout it. Jes' be turnin' 'em fools." (28)

Ned scoffs at Amy's joy and declares that learning corrupts. Part of his reaction is linked to jealousy. He wants to be the central figure in the household; he wants to be in power. However, Ned might be right that learning can corrupt, though not in any pathological way. The novel takes place in the early twentieth century. Although Black people were then legally free, their lives remained circumscribed by social custom and laws that made advancement nearly impossible for the large Black underclass. Thus, education was not the great equalizer. Those Black people who gained an education might become embittered because white gatekeepers refused to employ them in professional and skilled jobs. This problem is one that Grimké explored in *Rachel*. Three of the characters in her play, Rachel, Tom, and John, have earned college degrees. Rachel has a degree in domestic sciences, and Tom and John earned engineering degrees. However, none of them are hired for jobs in their fields of expertise due to racism. They are all psychologically impacted by the refusal of white employers to hire them. The characters experience anger, hurt, and resignation brought on by a corrupt system. Rachel, Tom, and John do not seek revenge, so they are not corrupted in the way that Ned describes.

Deferred dreams are not easy to manage, and learning the truth about one's condition is also troubling. One value that literacy imparts is that it allows learners to decode social and political systems. This was revealed to Frederick Douglass when he overheard a conversation between his master, Mr. Auld, and Mr. Auld's wife. Mr. Auld tells his wife that she should not teach Douglass how to read. Doing so, he explains, "would make him discontented and unhappy'" (47). Douglass admits Mr. Auld is right, explaining, "As I read and contemplated the subject, behold! that very discontentment which Master Hugh had predicted would follow my learning to read had already come, to torment and sting my soul to unutterable anguish. As I writhed under it, I would at times feel that learning to read had been a curse rather than a blessing. It had given me a view of my wretched condition, without the remedy" (53). At that time, Douglass was powerless to change the political and legal systems that upheld slavery. Thus, his despondency had much to do with the recognition that simply learning to read was not going to change his slave status. Although Douglass's revelations are insightful, they are also hyperbolic. Had Douglass not learned to read and write, he may not have been able to critique enslavement and racism so forcefully. This was true for Hurston's characters as well. On several occasions in *Jonah's Gourd Vine*, some characters reduce literacy and education to a mere transaction; but the main character, John, is so enamored with the word that the subtext of the novel suggests Hurston supported the kinds of literacies that affirm folkways and traditions and those that critique racism. Her deft handling of the rhythms and pacing of southern Black speech is masterful, and the value she places on the humanity of the Black characters suggests the people and the culture they represent need no linguistic or social reformation, but merely to work on themselves as humans belonging to the human family. In this way, specular literacy as deployed by Hurston functions to reflect the folk at their best and their worst. Specular literacy in this instance operates at a psychosocial level, gesturing that racial, cultural, and linguistic difference is not an indication of Black inferiority to white cultural norms and linguistic practices, but merely different. John's literacy practices embody the practice of specular literacy and provide an insightful illustration of literacy's pitfalls and possibilities.

JOHN'S LITERACIES

John's formal education does not last very long, but what he learns as a sixteen-year-old student serves him well for his practical and sensual needs. His love for words lasts beyond his teen years and well into his adult life.

John's literacies are functional, personal, and spiritual. His verbal skills are superb. Eventually, John's reading and writing skills impress Alf enough that he hires John as his bookkeeper and supplier. About John's literacy acquisition, Sharon L. Jones notes, "learning to read and write permanently changes his life. John gains in self-confidence" (78). He writes love letters and poetry to Lucy during his courtship of her; he writes letters to his brother Zeke; he writes letters to his children; he writes letters to his new wife, Sally; and he writes letters to collect old debts. As a preacher, John's orations are rhythmic recitations so mesmerizing that the congregation is willing to look past his infidelities with other women. John speaks and writes to live. In his speaking as a preacher, John gives life to God's word as well.

Although Semmie's mother and Ned see the benefits of education as a one-dimensional transaction for the purposes of acquisition, production, or compensation, John soon recognizes that learning to write helps him express his love for Lucy and ultimately sustain the life he wants to live. Gary Ciuba writes, "As John progresses from discovering his voice through speaking to reading and writing, and finally to preaching, he engages in the kind of hermeneutical enterprise that has been described by Paul Ricoeur, who examines how speaking brings the meaning of experience to language, how writing surpasses the limits of spoken discourse, and how reading may disclose new possibilities of being in the world" (120). John's oral and written communication skills provide him the visibility, status, and admiration he craves. His communicative style and ethos as well as those of the other characters in the novel support a vision of literacy that Hurston values. John and Lucy write and speak in a southern rural vernacular. The secondary characters also speak in a southern rural vernacular. The story centers on the lives of rural Black people who communicate in the vernacular of the folk, and the folk are never held up to scorn because they do not speak in standard English. John's faults are many, but his greatest gift is his mastery of words. He is always writing, talking, or preaching. When readers are introduced to John early in Hurston's *Jonah's Gourd Vine*, they learn he uses writing to impress and court Lucy. He gives Lucy his first love letter while they are sitting in the choir stand together. This letter reads: "Dere Lucy: Whin you pass a mule tied to a tree, Ring his tail and think of me. Your sugger-lump, John" (52). Although his sweet letter contains misspelled words, it conveys his heartfelt sentiments, as well as showing his creativity. Unfortunately, his written confessions of love for Lucy do not stop him from satisfying his carnal needs elsewhere.

John is sought after by other women, whom he finds hard to resist. Nevertheless, he never stops wanting to make Lucy his main sweetheart. Soon after he begins to court Lucy, John finds his sexual exploits have angered a lover's boyfriend, who threatens to harm him. John recognizes the threat is real and leaves town before something terrible happens to him or the boyfriend. While he is away, John tells his brother Zeke to let him know if other men try to date Lucy: "'Git word tuh me iffen any ole mullet-head tries tuh cut me out. Ahm gointer write tuh you and you way-lay her an get her tuh read it fuh yuh'" (57). Even as he escapes from harm, John knows he has to rely on his literacy skills to stay connected to Lucy. Hence, writing will keep him bound to his true love. Quickly, however, John recognizes that an impediment to maintaining a relationship with Lucy and his brother via writing might be Zeke's low level of literacy. Although Zeke is a teenager, he reads at the level of a much younger child. Thus, John instructs Zeke to have Lucy read the letters he has written to his brother. Zeke rebuffs this suggestion, telling John, "'Aw, Ah kin read too. Ah kin read some'"; when John replies, "'What kin you read?,'" Zeke responds, "'In de fust reader it say, This is Ned. He has a dog. Ah kin read dat lak anything. . . . Dat's uh heap, ain't it?'" (57). Zeke is proud of his reading ability, but his basic reading skills prove John's point: his literacy skills are not developed enough for him to read John's letters or to write to John about Lucy's potential love interests. John tells Zeke, "'dat'll do, but Ah ain't goin tuh write 'bout no Ned in de fust reader, and neither no dawg'" (57). Zeke has to accept John's demand. Once settled in the new town, John writes a letter to Zeke. Weeks later, Zeke takes a letter from Lucy to John, and it makes John smile (62). John and Lucy's love thus continues through their writerly activities.

When John returns to his hometown of Notasulga, he hopes to remain in contact with Lucy. He writes her notes even though her mother, Emmeline, who is from the good side of town, does not approve of John, thinking since he comes from a landless poor family, he is not good enough for her daughter. Emmeline has already chosen a propertied man for Lucy. Nevertheless, John is persistent and is begrudgingly given permission to see Lucy but only in the presence of her mother or father. When allowed to meet, John and Lucy devise ways to communicate without her mother listening and replying to their conversations. On one occasion, as Lucy and John "keep company" (72), John slyly writes a note to Lucy on a slate board in the hopes of preventing her mother from interfering in their conversation. However, when John tries to hand the slate board to Lucy, the narrator describes her mother's reaction: "When John leaned forward and tried to hand the slate past Emmeline to Lucy, Emmeline's hand flew out like a cat's paw and grabbed the slate" (72). John's note to Lucy reads, "I got something to tell you. Let's go for a walk" (72). Although readers might initially assume Emmeline grabs the slate to read the note, the narrator explains that Lucy's mother is illiterate: "Emmeline couldn't read a word and she was afraid that no one would read it correctly to her, but one thing she was sure of, she could erase as well as the world's greatest professor" (72). Emmeline's intervention may have temporarily stopped their exchange of words, but it did not stop the degree to which John and Lucy experience what might be called the psycho-secular experience of written language. As Gary Ciuba summarizes their relationship, "John's love affair with Lucy Ann Potts . . . is a courtship in and of language" (122). In its written and physical dimensions, their love cannot be stopped.

With Lucy's father's resigned approval and to her mother's disgust, John and Lucy marry. The early part of their marriage is one of financial hardship along with John's infidelities. His penchant for cheating causes John to leave Lucy at home with the children while he spends time with his lovers. His time away proves problematic for many reasons; yet, oddly enough, it affords him opportunities to put his literacy skills to use. For example, John leaves Lucy to spend time with one of his lovers when she is soon to give birth to one of their children. While John is away, Lucy's brother, Bud, comes to collect money owed to him. Unfortunately, Lucy does not have the money, so for payment, Bud requests Lucy and John's "weddin' bed" (Hurston, *Jonah's Gourd Vine* 91), which she loves. When John returns home and sees Lucy sleeping on the floor, he asks about their bed. When Lucy explains why the bed is no longer in their home, John is so angry that he leaves in search of Bud. John finds Bud, beats him, and steals a pig to feed John's family. For his violence against Bud and for stealing the pig, John soon learns he will have to leave town to avoid being sentenced to work on a chain gang. John tells Lucy, "'Ah ain't goin' tuh no chain-gang. If dey ever git in behind me, Ah'll tip on' cross de good Lawd's green. Al'll give mah case tuh Miss Bush and let Mother Green stand mah bond'" (95). True to his word, he leaves Alabama with Alf's help. John travels on a train to Sanford, Florida. Eventually, he puts his literacy skills to use, writes a letter to his wife, and "sent her all of his ready money" (105). When Lucy and their children finally arrive in Florida, John's writing continues. He writes her poetry, which she loves (114). Although the narrator describes his poetry as "primitive" (114) as in lacking sophistication, this does not negate the fact that John uses language to express his love for Lucy and function in the world.

John's writing extends into other aspects of his life. When Lucy dies and he quickly marries Hattie Tyson, the woman with whom he cheated as Lucy lay dying, John is eventually compelled to write letters to his children to presumably inform them of his and Hattie's impending divorce. His marriage to Hattie was a disaster. She had been a terrible wife and horrible mother to his children. She had used conjuring to lure him away from Lucy, cause Lucy's untimely death, and separate him from his children. Out of necessity and to expunge his guilt, John writes "a shy letter" to each child to make amends (162). Here, literacy functions as a salve and as an olive branch.

JOHN'S ORAL-LITERATE LIFE

John's adult life was always a contradiction. He loved Lucy but enjoyed the sensual pleasures of life with other women. His infidelities, always at odds with his vocation as a preacher, never stop his behavior. He makes excuses for cheating. His failed marriage to Hattie and some church members' disapproval of his wild ways eventually cost John his church. He preaches his last sermon and decides that expectations for him as a pastor to abstain from sex outside of marriage are too much to bear. Poignantly, he tells Hambo, his trusted friend, "'ah won't say never 'cause—Never is uh long time. Ah don't b'lieve Ahm fitted tuh preach de gospel—unless de world is wrong. You see dey's ready fuh ah preacher tuh be uh man uhmongst men, but dey ain't ready yet fur 'im tuh be uh man uhmongst women'" (182). John is not ready to stop cheating; thus, he believes it is better for him to stop preaching than to stop his philandering ways. Regarding John's dilemma of wanting to be both a man of the world and a man of the word, Anthony Wilson writes: "In his efforts to master the cognitive understanding necessary to assert himself in a world he is initially ill-equipped to understand, John Pearson sacrifices a kind of prelapsarian intuitive wholeness, an idealized and ultimately unsustainable marriage of nature and self-generated language, of instinct and intellect" (66). As Wilson notes, John has trouble reconciling his sexual exploits outside of marriage with his call to preach the gospel. It is a human frailty and a linguistic failure. John wants to experience pleasure without public condemnation. This is where the collision occurs among the three forms of literacy: literacy as functional and transactional, literacy as transformational, and literacy as specular. John learns to read and write to impress Lucy and court her. His oral communication skills are so advanced that his preacherly style is unmatched. He is the embodiment of African and African American oral traditions merged to spread the word. Harryette Mullen, writing about the relationship between orality and the "African American tradition of literacy" (673), notes, "For African-American visionary writers and artists, the Bible as sacred text and sublime speech, as the written record of a divine voice inspiring its authors to write and its readers to speak holy words, mediates the historical and mythic dislocation from primarily oral cultures to one in which literacy has the power of a fetish" (674). In many ways, John fetishizes the word by acting on its primal aspects rather than its introspective potential.

Indeed, this practice of his calls on literacy to act as a bridge between his immediate desire for public recognition as a preacher and his private carnal needs. In doing so, John opts out of literacy as a transformational exercise in which language provides the means to act introspectively. Had John recognized that literacy could allow him to question his behavior as a man of faith, perhaps he would have made more informed choices. But, alas, John is not ready to embrace this aspect of literacy as he steps away from the pulpit. John refuses to abstain from sex outside of marriage because he enjoys sex with different women. This means, however, that he cannot be a man who leads his flock. With his admission to Hambo, John ultimately decides that he needs to leave Sanford, Florida, to improve his life. His beautiful, rhythmic, cultural, and linguistically sophisticated sermons are left behind to dwell in the memories of his congregants. John's leaving does not mean that he has put away his speakerly or writerly voice. John returns to writing once he lands in Plant City, Florida. His spirits have improved. Eager to express himself, John writes letters to his good friend Hambo, to Mamie Lester, a woman who once chased him, and to George Gibbons, whom he asked to return his tools. John had once borrowed money from George but never paid him back. John also writes letters to his new love, Sally Lovelace, who enters John's life just when he is ready to live again. The love they share is beautiful. He expresses his appreciation and love for her by writing her "some kind of letter every day" (Hurston, *Jonah's Gourd Vine* 195).

JOHN'S NON-REVELATORY LITERACY

John is a complex figure in Hurston's novel. He cheats on his first love, Lucy. He hits her once in anger. He tells her he will never allow her to leave him, but when life becomes too difficult for him, he leaves her, even if it is only momentarily. He beats his second wife, Hattie, with impunity. He cheats on his third wife, Sally, whom he loves dearly. She had loved him when he was at his lowest point. He cannot maintain monogamy in his marriages. Yet, for all his earthly foibles, John is a man who loves language and "loved to tell stories" (61). When he is not writing, John is talking his way into or out of trouble. Even as a young man, people around him recognized his gift with words. In an early scene in the novel, when John joins a crew cutting trees, the other men come to realize that John can tell the best lies and urge him to tell them some stories: "One night Do-dirty began, 'Y'all wanta heah some lies?' 'Yeah,' said Too-Sweet, 'Ah evermore loves lies but you can't tell none. Leave John tell 'em 'cause he kin act'em out. He take de part uh Brer Rabbit and Brer B'ar and Brer Fox jes' ez natche'l'" (61). John's facility with language is an embodied experience. His natural ability to not only tell the story but embody the characters so they come to life makes him a valuable member of the crew.

When he becomes a pastor, John enthralls his congregants with his oratorical prowess. He even amazes himself with his dynamic verbal skills. He confesses to Lucy, "'De words dat sets de church on fire comes tuh me jus' so. Ah reckon de angels must tell 'em tuh me'" (112). John's gift for the spoken word brings both his longing to be a better husband and his repentance for his sins to beautiful heights. For example, when Lucy rebukes John for cheating on her with Big 'Oman, John seeks forgiveness from Lucy and from God. He offers his prayer at church. His prayer is a rhythmic revelation:

> You are de same God, Ah
> Dat heard de sinner man cry.
> Same God dat sent de zigzag lightning tuh
> Join de mutterin' thunder.
> Same God dat holds de elements
> In uh unbroken chain of controllment. (88)

The repetition of the phrase "same God" emphasizes God's omnipotence and omnipresence, which John recognizes and highlights. His three-time recitation of the natural forces of God's creations reveals his verbal mastery. After John delivers this prayer at church and makes other great invocations, his fervent supplications to God convince Deacon Moss that John should become a preacher. John eventually answers the call to preach, never recognizing that his cheating ways are contradictory to the behavior expected of a man of God.

John's greatest assets are his literacy skills. Written and spoken language gives him access to people, which gives him access to the pleasures of life, both secular and sacred. Unfortunately, his literacies do not provide him time for contemplation, reformation, and transformation. When his wife is dying, John escapes to the arms of another woman. After her death, the narrator reveals that John "was sad but underneath his sorrow was an exultation like a live coal under the grey ashes. There was no longer guilt" (136). One day after her funeral, John and his friend Sam Mosely argue over Lucy: "'Funny thing, ain't it John—Lucy come tuh town twelve years uhgo in mah wagon and mah wagon took her uhway.' 'Yeah, but she b'longed to me, though, all de time,' John said and exulted over his friend" (136). John's quick retort to Sam reclaims Lucy as his, but his words do not honor her or express the love he once had for her. Neither do his words give him the space to contemplate the physical or psychic damage he caused Lucy in life and death. In other words, literacy does not help to make John a contemplative man. It only provides him tools of existence and sustenance. Literacy is a means to an end for him, much as it is for Olivia in *Comedy: American Style*. Olivia's literacies never compel her to think about others. Literacy for her is merely a transactional exercise meant to serve her needs and desires.

Yet, in John's life, there are so many moments when the effects of a literate mind and self-examination could have come together for good. When John is essentially forced out of the church for his sexual misdeeds and his abuse of Hattie, he never really returns to his literacies to help him consider how he might have been a better man and a more upstanding preacher. He places the onus of his downfall on others. In a conversation with his best friend, Hambo, about whether he plans to ever preach again, John reveals his less introspective side when he says, "'Reckon Ah better stay out de pulpit and carpenter fuh mah livin'. Reckon Ah kin do dat 'thout a whole heap uh rigmarole'" (182). Rather than admit that extramarital sex is his failure and that other aspects of his life are incongruent with being a man of the word, John suggests that if his congregants had understood his sexual needs apart from his role as a preacher, then all could have been reconciled. Language gives him the means to express his feelings to Hambo, but not really to atone for his behavior. Thus, in his final sermon John compares his downfall, which he says was caused by his friends and enemies alike, to what causes Jesus' crucifixion. He says, "'our theme this morning is the wounds of Jesus. When the father shall ast 'What are these wounds in thine hand?' He shall answer, 'Those are they with which I was wounded in the house of my friends'" (174). Jesus had been betrayed by Judas, and John had been betrayed by Deacon Harris and Hattie. John sees a parallel between the two, but the narrator's comments, John's behavior, and his admission of infidelity demonstrate the two men are quite dissimilar. One chooses his downfall, and the other one accepts his crucifixion to save others. John is no sacrificial lamb.

The one time that John attempts introspection is when Hattie files for divorce. In the court proceedings, John realizes his misdeeds will be on trial along with the entire race. Disgusted that his divorce is on display for the white gaze, John chooses silence rather than defending himself against Hattie's allegations. However, his private words to Hambo are powerful. He says to his friend that white people believe Black people are "ignorant" and all alike and that white people think they know Black people (169). Following this, John tells Hambo that a true assessment of Hattie and Lucy would not have changed white people's opinions of his wives and Black women more broadly. Resignedly but with his dignity, John confesses to Hambo, "'Dass how come Ah got up and said, Yeah, Ah done it, 'cause dey b'lieved it anyhow, but dey b'lieved de same thing 'bout all de rest'" (169). His analysis of race is much keener and more introspective than his ruminations on his physical abuse of his wives and his infidelities. If one thinks of literacy as a cognitive act combining acceptance and responsiveness, then John's literacy process here works beautifully. The white gaze and the power it enacts are not lost on him. In his explanation to Hambo, John reveals that he is capable of recognizing and understanding how words can harm. Unfortunately, the literacy process he uses to engage in self-reflection is lost on him when he considers other more personal actions. Hence, the one-time deep introspective confession with Hambo does not ultimately change how he uses and perceives literacy for his own ends.

HURSTON'S SPECULAR LITERACY PRACTICES

John's poor choices are as old as human existence, and Hurston wrote about them with clarity, wit, and aplomb. She wrote poignantly about how a man with so much potential squandered it because he could not control his lustful desires and refused to be introspective when he needed it the most. As well, Hurston wrote movingly about a man in love with language itself. In so doing, she foregrounded both the man and his community, whose visions of themselves were expressed in a vernacular that reflects the best and the worst of them without pathologizing Black people. The characters in *Jonah's Gourd Vine* behave in ways counter to many of the other characters described and analyzed in this book. Men and women have sex before marriage and engage in extramarital affairs. Violence against women is encouraged and tolerated. Disparaging remarks among the characters are commonplace. Church people act in ways counter to the teachings of Christ. In portraying all of these not so flattering behaviors, Hurston never suggested that how these people speak and write or the fact that they have variations of black and brown skin was biologically linked to their poor choices. In other words, she did not pathologize their behaviors as Black deviance. Rather, the characters who populate the novel speak honestly, beautifully, and rhythmically in a language they understand and value, as it is clear Hurston did too. As Deborah G. Plant asserts, "Hurston . . . worked to rescue black folk from an oblivion imposed by racist social scientists and lay scientists who believed that the oral traditions of 'pre-literate' societies were but relics, survival from the primitive stages of humanity, with no greater utility than to be mined for the benefit of the self-proclaimed more evolved group" (62). Hurston gave southern folk culture and vernacular visibility without shame. Along with her Black women contemporaries in the Harlem Renaissance, Hurston used her writing including *Jonah's Vine Gourd* to remind readers that Black lives do not have to be subsumed under the auspices of white normative values. Finding inspiration for this novel from her parents' lives, the southern towns of her youth, and her anthropological work, Hurston challenged literary frameworks that positioned the authentic voices of the rural southern Black working class as anathema to racial advancement. Instead, Hurston showed how members of this group lived as best they could, with dignity, sadness, and joy.

The characters in Hurston's *Jonah's Gourd Vine* behave, for the most part, without a preoccupation with "white" values and without considering that their actions might bring shame to members of the Black middle class. No one is chastised, and none are asked to change how they talk or to alter their beliefs or cultural practices for the sake of white acceptance or Black middle-class approval. When John remembers the past, he muses to Zeke, "'things dat happened long time uhgo used to seem way off, but now it all seems lak it waz yistiddy. You think it's dead but de past ain't stopped breathin' yet'" (142). John's utterances here are not spoken in standard English, but neither Zeke nor the narrator scorns him for doing so. The truth is John's description of how the past unaccountably enters into his consciousness is apt. That he is able to articulate it so clearly is what makes what he says so beautiful. In a 1934 review of the novel, Andrew Burris wrote that Hurston "has captured the lusciousness and beauty of the Negro dialect as have few others" (167).

The novel benefits from Hurston's ear for the Black southern working-class vernacular and her skill in reproducing folk sayings and culture. When John beats Hattie for conjuring him, he does so not out of complete disdain for this folk belief and practice, but because she uses hoodoo against him. He seeks revenge because the conjuring also causes him to mistreat Lucy while they are married. He blames conjuring for compelling him to marry a woman who is already "experienced" (Hurston, *Jonah's Gourd Vine* 143). To reverse the conjuring, Hambo suggests they go to a "hoodoo doctor and turn it back on her" (162). Neither Hambo nor John dismisses the potential value of such actions, only turning against it when it is used against them. John's final sermon, a beautiful recitation on Genesis, Jesus' crucifixion, and resurrection, is chock-full of language that captures the rhythmic patterns of southern Black preachers. His sermon is so good, in fact, that a 1934 *New*

York Times review by John Chamberlain argued, "it is too good, too brilliantly splashed with poetic imagery, to be the product of any one Negro preacher" (17). According to Carla Kaplan, John's sermon was influenced by one Hurston heard delivered by Reverend C. C. Lovelace (302).

In reaction to Chamberlain's critique, Hurston told James Weldon Johnson in a letter that Chamberlain knew nothing about Black preachers: "You and I who seem to be the only ones even among Negroes who recognize the barbaric poetry in their sermons know that there are hundreds of preachers who are equaling that sermon weekly" (302). Hurston lamented Chamberlain's lack of knowledge about Black preachers and even Black people's frequent dismissal of the beauty inherent in Black preaching styles. In Hurston's *Jonah's Gourd Vine*, John fervently and beautifully tells biblical stories with human elements as a warning or a model for his congregants. When John explains Adam and Eve's transgressions in the Garden of Eden, he depicts a man who hears and understands disobedience but also God's divine grace:

> I heard de whistle of de damnation train
> Dat pulled out from Garden of Eden loaded wid cargo goin' to hell
> ...And on her way to Calvary, when she blew for de switch
> Jesus stood out on her track like a rough-backed mountain
> And she threw her cow-catcher in His side and His blood
>   ditched the train
> He died for our sins. (181)

Lies, deceit, and bad behaviors are personified in the image of a train going awry. This train of iniquity will be stopped because Jesus died to save humanity from itself. Hurston explained in her letter to James Weldon Johnson the role of the Black preacher and the artistry with which he preached: "I wish that you would write an article about Negro preachers that would explain their hold upon their people truthfully. That is, because they are the first artists, the ones intelligible to the masses. Like Adam Bead [sic], a voice has told them to sing of the beginnings of things" (303). As a Black woman who knew southern rural dialect and culture and as an anthropologist, Hurston allowed her characters to inhabit spaces physically and linguistically that embodied lives lived as she knew and witnessed. In so doing, *Jonah's Gourd Vine* reflects and represents Black people living lives as they are, rather than what others want them to be.

Hurston's predecessors Anna Julia Cooper and Victoria Earle Matthews imagined a time when Black authors would be in control of the stories they told—and when lives lived by Black people would not be judged by white people who viewed the races in a Black-white binary in which white was superior and Black inferior. Cooper and Matthews also utilized and envisioned a world where their literacy skills would be in service to their communities. Both women practiced and advocated for literacy that was transformational for their communities and for white society. In their writings on race and the literary imagination, Black people were in control of their destinies. In many ways, Hurston's *Jonah's Gourd Vine* is a manifestation of their race literature theories. Although Hurston struggled against the expectations of her patron, Margaret Osgood, who wanted her to write about the underbelly of Black life, Hurston's narrative style exemplifies Cooper's penultimate goal, which was for Black writers to write authentic stories about Black people that demonstrated their range and complexities. John, Lucy, Ned, Hambo, and the other characters who populate *Jonah's Gourd Vine* are flawed, brilliant, lovable, and detestable. They are fully human.

Matthews's writings about race literature argued that Black women writers should be at the vanguard of the literary movement. Hurston was a Black woman whose literary works, including *Jonah's Gourd Vine*, birthed into public existence facets of Black life that added dimension to a people who were often invisible and, when not invisible, were relegated to the margins. Hurston expanded prior calls for race literature by focusing particularly on the linguistic and folk elements of southern rural Black life. Boldly, creatively, and exceptionally, Hurston allowed the Black characters in *Jonah's Gourd Vine* to write and speak in their own vernacular and to represent themselves as they are. The characters are not sideshow oddities, but humans communicating with one another as other humans do. In Hurston's deft hands, specular literacy honors their ways of being. As Matthew Heard maintains, "the black social sphere in Hurston's fiction is portrayed as linguistically sophisticated not *in spite of* its dialect and storytelling, but *because of* these traits. . . . Hurston repositioned such portrayals at the very grounds on which black authors should make a rhetorical stand" (138). Hurston rejected writing to suit the tastes of the small but influential Black elite and middle class or white society; rather, she used her powers of imagination to rescue the folk from the literary outhouse and place them firmly in the main house.

VICTORIA SPIVEY

Victoria Spivey was Hurston's contemporary. Like Hurston, Spivey turned to folk culture for inspiration, and, in doing so, her music reveals an artist whose blues lyrics reflect a dynamic and evolving people engaged in sometimes naughty behavior even as her more moderate contemporaries turned toward Black elite and middle-class concerns in their writings. Spivey's blues music also engaged in race matters. Unfortunately, Spivey's musical career is often overlooked. Her records had to compete with those by classic blues singers such as Ma Rainey and Bessie Smith, whose vocals and public personas were unrivalled. Nevertheless, Spivey's music has something to add to the crowded field of classic blue singers. Spivey's blues lyrics and vocal styles employed elements of specular literacy to capture the highs and lows of Black folk life, which included poor health conditions and relationship troubles. In the first phase of her career, she recorded classic blues from 1926 to 1937. She then had a second career as a blues entertainer in the 1960s, as well as a career writing articles for *Record Research: The Magazine of Record Statistics and Information* from 1962 to 1970. Her column "Blues Is My Business" provided historical context for some of her most popular classic blues recordings from the 1920s and '30s. Like her peers, Spivey had a number of records on which she received cowriting or single author credit. Since space does not allow for an exhaustive analysis of her collection, I have chosen four representative songs to illustrate Spivey's focus on issues of race.

"TB Blues," which Spivey wrote, became one of her signature blues songs. According to Spivey, it was recorded in 1927 at a studio at the University of St. Louis, and she wrote the song to honor one of her friends, Maggie Williams, who had died from tuberculosis when they were teenagers ("Blues Is My Business" 12). The song, performed at a resignedly slow pace, follows the slow demise of a tuberculosis patient. In the persona of the ill person, Spivey moans it is too late to heal from tuberculosis. In the first two verses, she sings, "too late, too late, too late, too late, too late, it's too late, too late, too late, too late, too late" ("TB Blues"). Spivey's ten "too lates" indicate the seriousness of tuberculosis along with its debilitating impact on the body. The next verses highlight the stigma of contracting tuberculosis. She sings, "TB's alright to have if your friends didn't treat you so low, Don't you ask'em for no favors, They even stop comin' round." Not only is tuberculosis a slow killer, but it causes the sufferer to experience isolation. There are no friends who come to the rescue in "TB Blues"; Death is a lonesome killer. In one of her columns, Spivey wrote, "in those days when you had that [tuberculosis] or people even thought you had it you were shunned and denied all the rights of society" ("Blues is My Business" 12). This explains why the verse says it is all right to have TB if your friends do not abandon you. Spivey admitted in the same column that many mothers refused to allow their children to play with Maggie. Despite the fears of others, Spivey said she continued to play with her friend: "I used to play with [Maggie] through the fence. My mother was different as she was not afraid of nothing and as a full fledged nurse she tried to help little Maggie." In the early twentieth century, tuberculosis afflicted the poor more than the well-to-do. This means many in Black communities contracted it and died from it. It often spread in densely populated communities with poor sanitation. Although Spivey's song does not mention poor living conditions as a cause of the disease, it stands to reason that she was aware of the conditions that caused tuberculosis to spread in Black communities. I suspect as well that Spivey's "TB Blues," which she wrote in the same column was "my big hit," resonated with audiences who related to the veracity of the song.

A blues song without vanity is no blues at all. In "TB Blues," speaking in the first person, Spivey reflects on the havoc tuberculosis is causing to the body of the once attractive woman. The woebegone woman is losing her good looks, admitting "when I was up on my feet, I could not walk down the street, For the men's lookin' at me from my head to my feet, But oh now, the TB's killin' me" (Spivey). Not only is TB literally killing her; it is also killing her good looks. Despite this seemingly frivolous comparison, the ultimate message that Spivey conveys is the seriousness of the stigma that accompanies tuberculosis. It causes social isolation, which in turn impacts the emotions of those afflicted with the disease. Spivey was so moved by the poor treatment and untimely death of her friend that she memorialized her in "TB Blues." In her column she wrote, "the episode stayed in my mind for years and years and when I got the opportunity with the Okey record company I wrote the lyrics and added the music of Black Snake Blues . . . to it and from there came the original TB Blues" ("Blues Is My Business" 12). Although Spivey and the other classic blues singers are often relegated to the margins in discussions on racial matters, Black women like Spivey cared deeply for the people in their communities. The tribute to Maggie in "TB Blues" demonstrates that Spivey recognized tuberculosis caused suffering not only from the disease but from the isolation it caused.

Tuberculosis was still on Spivey's mind in 1929 when she recorded "Dirty TB Blues." This recording shows Spivey at her vocal best. Its slow pace and haunting trumpet solos mirror the sorrow the afflicted feels as she knows death is imminent. In this blues death narrative, the figure at its center longs for the nurse to relieve her suffering, but the nurse does not come to her rescue. Not only is the nurse not around to help, but the tuberculosis sufferer does not even have family to ease her sorrow. Spivey sings, "I feel down, not a friend in this town, I feel all alone." She pleads for the Lord to intervene but even God cannot keep her alive. She has been "railroaded . . . to the sanitarium" and now knows recovery is improbable. According to Marion M. Torchia, some Black people who had contracted tuberculosis did not want to go to sanitariums far from home or were not wholly aware of the benefits such care could offer (157). Although the patient in Spivey's song is in a sanitarium, its care will not heal her. She also expresses sorrow that her own behavior may have caused her to contract the disease: "Yes, I run around for months and months, from gin mill to gin mill to the honky tonks.... Yes, look what I done done, I got the dirty TB." The twice-sung "done done" emphasizes both the irresponsibility and the absurdity of contracting tuberculosis. In AAVE, the word "done," according to Labov, "resonates with the sense of ... indignation" (126). Had the speaker in Spivey's song not gone to those social places, she may not now be knocking on death's door.

Spivey wrote many of her own songs, but she shared the writing credit on others. One song she coauthored with Lonnie Johnson was "Dope Head Blues," which was recorded in 1927. The pace of this song is measured. Spivey's voice plays coy alongside a slow-moving guitar accompaniment. "Dope Head Blues" highlights the strength that dope supposedly gives its users. In the song, the female drug user outlines all the physical feats dope allows. Spivey sings, "just give me one more sniff, another sniff of that dope, [and] I'll catch a cow like a cowboy and throw a bull without a rope." In another instance, the dope makes her feel so good that she "feel[s] like a fighting rooster, feel better than I have ever felt.... Got double pneumonia and still I think I got the best health." This is a song about drugs, but it is also about one woman's power to tackle even the most vicious animals and to outfox the smartest of men. At one point she boasts, "the president sent for me, the Prince of Wales is on my tail, they worry me so much, I'll take another sniff and put them both in jail." The power she wields over powerful white men in the song is certainly not indicative of the power Black women had in their daily lives. In 1927 America, Black women were subject to Jim Crow laws; their employment prospects were few; their children's access to education was limited; and their husbands, brothers, sons, and nephews may become victims of mob violence. Yet, in the verses of blues lyrics, Black women, particularly Black working-class women, were empowered to believe and to act in ways counter to traditional societal dictates. In this song about dope but about belief more broadly, Spivey envisioned a Black woman whose strength and cunning were unmatched by man and beast alike. Regarding the individual and communal nature of classic blues, Hazel Carby writes, "the blues singers had assertive and demanding voices; they had no respect for sexual taboos or for breaking through the boundaries of respectability and convention, and we hear the 'we' when they say 'I'" ("'It Jus Be's Dat'" 241). In this boastful tale of one woman's power, Spivey reminded Black women that in the imaginary and in life they can wield power too.

Moving beyond the serious and the boastful was "Funny Feather Blues," which Spivey co-wrote with Ruth Naomi Floyd. The recording begins with an upbeat trumpet solo followed by a smooth saxophone response and a trumpet with a mute, after which Spivey begins to sing. Her voice is sassy and playful as she describes a man as a rooster called Funny Feathers who rules the roost. All the chicks want to be with him: "oh, the little chicks call him pa, cause he's a funny feather man . . . , oh he don't kick but he runs them down" (Spivey). Funny Feathers takes advantage of his position. He is good-looking and the only rooster in town. This humorous song is a delightful commentary on good-looking men who capitalize on their attractiveness. They date multiple women with impunity and never think about the consequences of their actions. They love many because they can. When men behave in these ways, the women they leave behind are broken-hearted. It is a standard in blues songs to talk about good-looking unfaithful men whose lovers seek revenge. In "Funny Feather Blues," however, Spivey and Floyd poke fun at the man's charming and philandering ways. Unlike Fauset's perhaps ironically titled novel *Comedy: American Style*, which actually addresses the trauma and pain that can come with being a Black person, the classic blues singers often point to the comic parts of Black life. It is funny to imagine a man as a rooster ruling his flock of women as his charm and good looks convince them to join his harem. Life needs its funny moments too. The blues singers provide this by taking the everyday life experiences of a people often devalued by the broader society and giving them the space to laugh as well as cry. Spivey's imaginative wanderings reflect a people not bound by the dictates of polite society. She employed specular literacy to tell their stories as humorously and forthrightly as she could.

One might think of race work as a high-minded enterprise, which it is. The stakes are high. Yet classic blues singers like Spivey reveal that the work of solving racial problems can encompass both serious and comical dimensions. The blues songs I analyzed in this chapter show the imaginative range of Spivey and some of her cowriters. From the serious to the funny, these blues songs commented on the poor treatment of the ill, the agency of Black women, and the chastisement of men for their sexual exploits. All these issues magnify the daily concerns of a people often forgotten. Moreover, Spivey's blues helped to show that Black women who were from or intimately familiar with the Black working class also turned to that very same community to share language, values, and traditions they all knew and loved. Specular literacy as a lived experience and practice gave Spivey and others the ability to turn inward, then manifest outward to the folk a completeness that valued and affirmed them. That the fullness of the Black self so often rendered second class was made whole in the music of the classic blues is what makes specular literacy so valuable.

CODA

Spectacular Women

The Black women I focus on in this book had a lot to say. They had the courage and the conviction to write at a time when doing so was not easy for any Black woman. At the end of the nineteenth century and into the early decades of the twentieth century, these women had to contend with lynchings, Black Codes, Jim Crow, and myriad other concerns as they wrestled with systemic issues confronting the race. The Black women writers in the late nineteenth century had their own ideas about how to solve the race problem. How could they convince their fellow African Americans that they did not come from inferior people? How could they write themselves into the consciousness of the American people? What writing conventions and genres could they employ persuasively to turn the tide? In many ways, the writers examined here were compelled to do race work from a position of political powerlessness. This did not stop them. In their theories about race and in their creative texts, they had to first prove a negative. That is, they had to convince Black and white audiences that Black people were indeed human and capable of all the feats of success achieved by their white counterparts.

One way this positionality impacted their theoretical positions and artistic approaches was to adopt respectability politics as a political framework. In doing so, these writers armed themselves in theory and practice with a foundation already respected by white gatekeepers. Brittney C. Cooper reminds us that this approach to respectability and race was a "strategic deployment of respectability" (19). It meant, however, that writers such as Anna Julia Cooper, Victoria Earle Matthews, Katherine D. C. Tillman, and Pauline E. Hopkins felt compelled to pursue their persuasive aims by illustrating the links and similarities between Black and white rather than their differences. This does not mean their texts did not challenge white authority. They did. In their texts, Cooper, Matthews, and Hopkins in particular mounted vociferous attacks against white domination. Their literacies challenged and hoped to transform states of being for Black and white alike. These writers did not begin this reformation project. They had their own predecessors working to change the condition of Black people. Yet I chose them as a starting point because they defined the forward movement in ways transparent and profound.

The work started by these late nineteenth-century writers was not finished by the first two decades of the twentieth century. There was more work to be done. Southern rage against Black people did not diminish after Reconstruction, and northern apathy remained a political practice. Enter then Angelina Weld Grimké, Jessie Redmon Fauset, Zora Neale Hurston, and the classic blues singers of the New Negro Era including but not limited to Mamie Smith, Alberta Hunter, and Gertrude "Ma" Rainey. Their worldviews were shaped by laws meant to keep Black people in perpetual second-class status. Undaunted by social custom and legal mandates, these women turned to writing as well to contest the pervasive racism of the first half of the twentieth century. Because they were the creators and beneficiaries of the new modern age, their texts reflected a shifting dynamic among Black women writers, public intellectuals, and singers. While their predecessors were compelled to politicize respectability as a theory and a practice, the New Negro women challenged and rejected respectability politics even as some found value in its application. As well, these New Negro women began to contest a singularity of vision that suggested literacy and education were the great equalizers. Observant of the degree to which white gatekeepers were keeping economic opportunities for African Americans at arm's length, Grimké explored how such realities negatively impacted the lives of the Black professional class. Relatedly, Fauset recognized how the social currency of literacy that affirmed whiteness harmed instead of affirmed. Thus, reducing literacy to a transaction that merely moved Black people away from their racial identity was ill-conceived and destructive. Conversely, soaking in the regional and cultural traditions of her home region, Hurston pointed out that affirmation and contestation were bound together with positive outcomes when Black people valued their ancestral and vernacular practices to live, to love, and to fight against the tide. In so doing, Hurston's visions for Black life were mediated by a specular literacy practice by and of the folk.

The entertainers of the New Negro Era, particularly the classic blues singers, are not always considered an extension of the Woman's Era writers' philosophies on the race or even their New Negro peers. Perhaps fairly, the salacious nature of their music makes this so. However, I situate the classic blues singers on a philosophical continuum with their Woman's Era predecessors and New Negro peers. They too were keen observers of the politics of race. They understood how racism impacted relationships among Black men and women. They understood the intersectional dynamics of race and gender as women traveling on the road and leading bands. In many ways, they were outsiders, even though their music helped to shape the cultural history of the period. Yet it was their outsider status that helped to bring to the fore issues that were meaningful to many members of the Black working class. Love, lust, revenge, violence, intraracial conflict, and same-sex desire are just some of the thematic concerns in classic blues. Relying on dynamic vocals as well as the vernacular of the folk, the classic blues singers affirmed and kept alive the spirit of working-class people long considered fodder for jokes and salacious innuendo. In opposition to modesty and in affirmation of more freedoms, their specular literacy practices provided avenues for validation and attestation. These women's blues shifted the cultural and literacy tide.

BIBLIOGRAPHY

Albertson, Chris. *Bessie*. Yale UP, 2003.
Alexander, Elizabeth. "'We Must Be About Our Father's Business': Anna Julia Cooper and the Incorporation of the Nineteenth-Century African American Woman Intellectual." *Signs: Journal of Women in Culture and Society*, vol. 20, no. 2, 1995, pp. 336–56.
Aristotle. *Rhetoric and Poetics*, translated by Ingram Bywater, Modern Library, 1954.
Babb, Valerie. "'The Joyous Circle': The Vernacular Presence in Frederick Douglass's Narratives." *College English*, vol. 67, no. 4, 2005, pp. 365–77.
Barnett, Timothy. "Politicizing the Personal: Frederick Douglass, Richard Wright, and Some Thoughts on the Limits of Critical Literacy." *College English*, vol. 68, no. 4, 2006, pp. 356–81.
Bassard, Katherine Clay. "Gender and Genre: Black Women's Autobiography and the Ideology of Literacy." *African American Review*, vol. 26, no. 1, 1992, pp. 119–29.
Berlin, James A. *Rhetoric and Reality: Writing Instruction in American Colleges, 1900–1985*. Southern Illinois UP, 1987.
Bloom, Lynn Z. "Freshmen Composition as a Middle-Class Enterprise." *College English*, vol. 58, no. 6, 1996, pp. 654–75.
"'Blues' Mama 'Ma' Rainey Visits Us." *Afro-American*, April 1926, p. 4.
Brandt, Deborah. *Literacy in American Lives*. Cambridge UP, 2003.
Brandt, Deborah, and Kate Clinton. "Limits of the Local: Expanding Perspectives on Literacy as Social Practice." *Journal of Literary Research*, vol. 34, no. 3, 2002, pp. 337–56.
Brooks, Daphne A. *Bodies in Dissent: Spectacular Performances of Race and Freedom, 1850–1910*. Duke UP, 2006.
Burris, Andrew. "Review of *Jonah's Vine Gourd*." *Crisis*, vol. 41, 1934, pp. 166–67.
Carby, Hazel. "'It Jus Be's Dat Way Sometimes': The Sexual Politics of Women's Blues." *Gender and Discourse: The Power of Talk*, edited by Alexandra Dundas Todd and Sue Fisher, Ablex Pub. Corp., 1988, pp. 227–42.
Carby, Hazel. *Reconstructing Womanhood: The Emergence of the Afro-American Woman Novelist*. Oxford UP, 1987.
Carby, Hazel. "They Put a Spell on You." *Cultures in Babylon: Black Britain and African America*, Verso, 1999, pp. 51–63.
Chamberlain, John. "Books of the Times." *New York Times*, 3 May 1934, nytimes.com/1934/05/03/archives/books-of-the-times.
Chapman, Erin D. *Prove It on Me: New Negroes, Sex, and Popular Culture*. Oxford UP, 2012.

Chew, Mable. "Singer Began at Seven Years Old: Bessie Smith Started in Amusement Park Under Direction of 'Ma Rainey.'" *Afro-American*, 27 March 1926, p. 4.

Ciuba, Gary. "The Woman against the Word: The Hermeneutical Challenge in Hurston's *Jonah's Gourd Vine*." *African American Review*, vol. 34, no. 1, 2000, pp. 119–33.

Cobbs, Catherine. "Introduction: Cultures and Practices of U.S. Women's Literacy." *Nineteenth-Century Women Learn to Write*, edited by Catherine Hobbs, UP of Virginia, 1995, pp. 1–33.

Cone, James. *The Spirituals and the Blues: An Interpretation*. Seabury Press. 1972.

Cook-Gumperz, Jenny. "Introduction: The Social Construction of Literacy." *The Social Construction of Literacy*, edited by Jenny Cook-Gumperz, Cambridge UP, 1986, pp. 1–15.

Cooper, Anna Julia. "The Negro As Presented in American Literature." *The Voice of Anna Julia Cooper: Including "A Voice from the South" and Other Important Essays, Papers, and Letters*, edited by Charles Lemert and Esme Bhan, Rowman & Littlefield, 1998, pp. 134–60.

Cooper, Anna Julia. "The Status of Woman in America." *A Voice from the South by a Black Woman of the South*, Negro Universities P, 1969, pp. 127–45.

Cooper, Anna Julia. "Womanhood: A Vital Element in the Regeneration and Progress of a Race." *A Voice from the South by a Black Woman of the South*, Negro Universities P, 1969, pp. 9–47.

Cooper, Brittney C. *Beyond Respectability: The Intellectual Thought of Race Women*. U of Illinois P, 2017.

Crenshaw, Kimberlé Williams. "Mapping the Margins: Intersectionality, Identity, Politics, and Violence against Women of Color." *Critical Race Theory: The Key Writings That Formed the Movement*, edited by Kimberlé Crenshaw et al., The New Press, 1995, pp. 357–83.

Daniels, Melissa Asher. "The Limits of Literary Realism: *Of One Blood*'s Post Racial Fantasy by Pauline Hopkins." *Callaloo: A Journal of African Diaspora Arts and Letters*, vol. 36, no. 1, 2013, pp. 158–77.

Davis, Angela Y. *Blues Legacies and Black Feminism: Gertrude "Ma" Rainey, Bessie Smith, and Billie Holiday*. Vintage Books, 1998.

Davis, Elizabeth Lindsay. *Lifting as They Climb*. National Association of Colored Women, 1933.

Davis, Thadious. "Introduction." *Comedy: American Style*, by Jessie Redmon Fauset, edited by Henry Louis Gates Jr. and Jennifer Burton, G. K. Hall and Co., 1995, pp. xv–xxxv.

Douglas, Ann. *Terrible Honesty: Mongrel Manhattan in the 1920s*. Farrar, Straus, and Giroux, 1995.

Douglass, Frederick. *Narrative of the Life of Frederick Douglass. Frederick Douglass: The Narrative and Selected Writings*, edited by Michael Meyer, Modern Library College Editions, 1984, pp. 3–127.

Du Bois, W. E. B. *The Souls of Black Folk*, edited by Henry Louis Gates Jr. and Terri Hume Oliver, W. W. Norton, 1999, pp. 3–164.

duCille, Ann. *The Coupling Convention: Sex, Text, and Tradition in Black Women's Fiction*. Oxford UP, 1993.

Fauset, Jessie. *Comedy: American Style*. G. K. Hall and Co., 1995.
Fauset, Jessie. "The Gift of Laughter." *The New Negro: Voices of the Harlem Renaissance*, edited by Alain Locke, Simon & Schuster, 1997, pp. 161–67.
Fielder, Brigitte. *Relative Races: Genealogies of Interracial Kinship in Nineteenth-Century America*. Duke UP, 2020.
Foley, Barbara. *Specters of 1919: Class and Nation in the Making of the New Negro*. U of Illinois P, 2003.
Foner, Eric. "Rights and the Constitution in Black Life during the Civil War and Reconstruction." *The Journal of American History*, vol. 74, no. 3, 1987, pp. 863–83.
Foreman, P. Gabrielle. *Activist Sentiments: Reading Black Women in the Nineteenth Century*. U of Illinois P, 2009.
Frazier, E. Franklin. *The Negro Family in the United States*. U of Notre Dame P, 2001.
Gates, Henry Louis, Jr. "Foreword: In Her Own Write." *The Works of Katherine Davis Chapman Tillman*, edited by Claudia Tate, Oxford UP, 1991, pp. xiii–xxxi.
Gates, Henry Louis, Jr. "Writing 'Race' and the Difference It Makes." *"Race," Writing, and Difference*, edited by Henry Louis Gates Jr., U of Chicago P, 1985, pp. 1–20.
Gates, Henry Louis, Jr., and Nellie Y. McKay. "The Blues." *The Norton Anthology of American Literature*, edited by Henry Louis Gates Jr. and Nellie Y. McKay, W. W. Norton, 1997, pp. 22–36.
Gatewood, Willard B. *Aristocrats of Color: The Black Elite, 1880–1920*. Indiana UP, 1990.
Gee, James Paul. "Literacy, Discourse, and Linguistics: Introduction and What Is Literacy?" *Literacy: A Critical Sourcebook*, edited by Ellen Cushman et al., Bedford/St. Martin's, 2001, pp. 525–44.
Gilyard, Keith. *Let's Flip the Script: An African American Discourse on Language, Literature, and Learning*. Wayne State UP, 1996.
Gilyard, Keith, and Adam Banks. *On African American Rhetoric*. Routledge, 2018.
Gilyard, Keith, and Adam Banks. *Voices of the Self: A Study of Language Competence*. Wayne State UP, 1991.
Giroux, Henry. *Schooling and the Struggle for Public Life: Critical Pedagogy in the Modern Age*. U of Minnesota P, 1988.
Glass, Kathy. "Tending to the Roots: Anna Julia Cooper's Philosophical Thoughts and Activism." *Meridians: Feminism, Race, Transnationalism*, vol. 6, no. 1, 2006, pp. 23–55.
Goldsmith, Meredith. "Jessie Fauset's Not-So New Negro Womanhood: The Harlem Renaissance, the Long Nineteenth Century, and Legacies of Feminine Representation." *Legacy*, vol. 32, no. 2, 2015, pp. 258–80.
Goodson, Steve. "Gertrude 'Ma' Rainey (1886–1939), 'Hear Me Talkin' to You.'" *Georgia Women*, edited by Ann Short Chirhart and Kathleen Ann Clark, U of Georgia P, 2014, pp. 148–65.
Graff, Harvey J. *The Legacies of Literacy: Continuities and Contradictions in Western Culture and Society*. Indiana UP, 1987.
Graff, Harvey J. "The Literacy Myth at Thirty." *Journal of Social History*, vol. 43, no. 3, 2010, pp. 635–61.
Graff, Harvey J. "The Nineteenth-Century Origins of Our Times." *Literacy: A Critical Sourcebook*, edited by Ellen Cushman et al., Bedford/St. Martin's, 2001, pp. 211–33.

Grimké, Angelina Weld. *Rachel, A Play in Three Acts*. Cornhill Company, 1920.
Grimké, Angelina Weld. "*Rachel*: The Play of the Month—The Reason and Synopsis by the Author." *The Competitor*, 1920, pp. 51–52.
Gussow, Adam. "'Shoot Myself a Cop': Mamie Smith's 'Crazy Blues' as Social Text." *Callaloo*, vol. 25, no. 1, 2002, pp. 8–44.
Guthrie, John T., and Vincent Greaney. "Literacy Acts." *Handbook of Reading Research: Volume 2*, edited by Rebecca Barr et al., Lawrence Erlbaum Associates, 1991, pp. 68–96.
Hager, Christopher. *Word by Word: Emancipation and the Act of Writing*. Harvard UP, 2013.
Harrison, Daphne Duval. *Blues Queens of the 1920s: Black Pearls*. Rutgers UP, 1988.
Hartman, Saidiya V. *Scenes of Subjection: Terror, Slavery, and Self-Making in Nineteenth-Century America*. Oxford UP, 1997.
Heap, Lauren, and Kate Vieira. "Literacy Can Oppress and Liberate." *(Re)Considering What We Know: Learning Thresholds in Writing, Composition, Rhetoric, and Literacy*, edited by Linda Adler-Kassner and Elizabeth Wardle, Utah State UP, 2019, pp. 37–39.
Heard, Matthew. "'Dancing Is Dancing No Matter Who Is Doing It': Zora Neale Hurston, Literacy, and Contemporary Writing Pedagogy." *College Literature*, vol. 34, no. 1, 2007, pp. 130–55.
Hegamin, Lucille. Performer. "The Jazz Me Blues." *Lucille Hegamin Vol. 1, 1920–1922*. Recorded 1921. Document Records, 2005.
Higginbotham, Evelyn Brooks. "Rethinking Vernacular Culture: Black Religion and Race Records in the 1920s and 1930s." *The House That Race Built: Black Americans, U.S. Terrain*, edited by Wahneema Lubiano, Pantheon, 1997, pp. 155–77.
Higginbotham, Evelyn Brooks. *Righteous Discontent: The Women's Movement in the Black Baptist Church, 1880–1920*. Harvard UP, 1993.
Hobbs, Catherine. "Introduction: Cultures and Practices of U.S. Women's Literacy." *Nineteenth-Century Women Learn to Write*, edited by Catherine Hobbs, UP of Virginia, 1995, pp. 1–33.
Hopkins, Pauline. *Of One Blood; Or the Hidden Self*. *The Magazine Novels of Pauline Hopkins*, edited by Henry Louis Gates Jr., Oxford UP, 1988, pp. 441–621.
Hughes, Langston. "The Negro Artist and the Racial Mountain." *The Anthology of African American Literature*, edited by Henry Louis Gates Jr. and Nellie McKay, W. W. Norton, 2004, pp. 1311–14.
Hunter, Alberta. Performer. "Down Hearted Blues." *Alberta Hunter Vol. 1, 1921–1923*. Recorded 1922. Document Records, 2005.
Hurston, Zora Neale. *Jonah's Gourd Vine: A Novel*. Harper Perennial Modern Classics, 2008.
Hurston, Zora Neale. "To James Weldon Johnson," 8 May 1934. *Zora Neale Hurston: A Life in Letters*, edited by Carla Kaplan, Doubleday, 2002.
James, William. "The Hidden Self." *Scribners Magazine*, vol. 7, no. 3, 1890, pp. 361–73.
Japtok, Martin. "Pauline Hopkins's *Of One Blood*, Africa, and the 'Darwinist Trap.'" *African American Review*, vol. 36, no. 3, 2002, pp. 403–15.
Jensen, Anne Mai Yee. "Under Lynching's Shadow: Grimké's Call for Domestic Reconfiguration in *Rachel*." *African American Review*, vol. 47, no. 2/3, 2014, pp. 391–402.

Jimoh, A. Yemish. "Mapping the Terrain of Black Writing during the Early New Negro Era." *College Literature: A Journal of Critical Literary Studies*, vol. 42, no. 3, 2015, pp. 488–524.

Johnson, Guion Griffis. "Southern Paternalism toward Negroes after Emancipation." *Journal of Southern History*, vol. 23, no. 4, 1957, pp. 483–509.

Jones, Martha S. *All Bound Up Together: The Woman Question in African American Public Culture, 1830–1900*. U of North Carolina P, 2007.

Jones, Sharon L. *Critical Companion to Zora Neale Hurston: A Literary Reference to Her Life and Work*. Facts on File, 2009.

Kaplan, Carla, editor. *Zora Neale Hurston: A Life in Letters*. Doubleday, 2002.

Kunstadt, Len. "Mamie Smith: The First Lady of the Blues." *Record Research: The Magazine of Record Statistics and Information*, vol. 57, 1964, pp. 3, 6.

Kynard, Carmen. "'The Blues Playingest Dog You Ever Heard Of': (Re)positioning Literacy through African American Blues Rhetoric." *Reading Research Quarterly*, vol. 43, no. 4, 2008, pp. 356–73.

Labov, William. "Co-Existence Systems in African American Vernacular English." *African-American English: Structure, History, and Use*, edited by Salikoko S. Mufwene et al., Routledge, 1998, pp. 110–53.

Laguna, Albert Sergio. "On the Comedy of Race." *Cultural Critique*, vol. 111, 2021, pp. 104–32.

Lewis, Vashti Crutcher. "Mulatto Hegemony in the Novels of Jessie Redmon Fauset." *CLA Journal*, vol. 35, no. 4, 1992, pp. 375–86.

Lieb, Sandra. *Mother of the Blues: A Study of Ma Rainey*. U of Massachusetts P, 1981.

Locke, Alain. "The New Negro." *The New Negro: Voices of the Harlem Renaissance*, edited by Alain Locke, Simon & Schuster, 1992, pp. 3–16.

Locke, Alain. "The Saving Grace of Realism: Retrospective Review of the Negro Literature of 1933." *The Critical Temper of Alain Locke: A Selection of His Essays on Art and Culture*, edited by Jeffrey C. Stewart, Garland Publishing, 1983, pp. 222–25.

Logan, Shirley Wilson. "Literacy as a Tool for Social Action among Nineteenth-Century African American Women." *Nineteenth-Century Women Learn to Write*, edited by Catherine Hobbs, UP of Virginia, 1995, pp. 179–96.

Logan, Shirley Wilson. *"We Are Coming": The Persuasive Discourse of Nineteenth-Century Black Women*. Southern Illinois UP, 1999.

Logan, Shirley Wilson. "Victoria Earle Matthews." *American Women Prose Writers, 1870–1920*, edited by Sharon M. Harris, Gale Group, 2000, pp. 272–79.

Lupton, Mary Jane. "Black Women and Survival in *Comedy: American Style* and *Their Eyes Were Watching God*." *The Zora Neale Hurston Forum*, vol. 1, no. 1, 1986, pp. 38–49.

Matthews, Victoria Earle. *Aunt Lindy: A Story Founded on Real Life*. J. J. Little and Co., 1893.

Matthews, Victoria Earle. "Harriet Tubman: Woman's Era Eminent Women Series." *The Woman's Era*, vol. 2, no. 2, 1896.

Matthews, Victoria Earle. "The Value of Race Literature: An Address." *The Massachusetts Review*, vol. 27, no. 2, 1986, pp. 169–91. First published 1895.

May, Vivian A. *Anna Julia Cooper, Visionary Black Feminist: A Critical Introduction*. Routledge, 2012.

May, Vivian A. "Thinking from the Margins, Acting at the Intersections: Anna Julia Cooper's 'A Voice from the South.'" *Hypatia*, vol. 19, no. 2, 2004, pp. 74–91.

May, Vivian A. "Writing the Self into Being: Anna Julia Cooper's Textual Politics." *African American Review*, vol. 43, no. 1, pp. 17–34.

McGinley, Paige A. *Staging the Blues: From Tent Shows to Tourism*. Duke UP, 2014.

McHenry, Elizabeth. *Forgotten Readers: Recovering the Lost History of African American Literary Societies*. Duke UP, 2002.

McMillian, Timothy J. "Black Magic: Witchcraft, Race, and Resistance in Colonial New England." *Journal of Black Studies*, vol. 25, no. 1, 1994, pp. 99–117.

Mitchell, Koritha. *Living with Lynching: African American Lynching Plays, Performance, and Citizenship, 1890–1930*. U of Illinois P, 2011.

Moody-Turner, Shirley. "Gendering Africana Studies: Insights from Anna Julia Cooper." *African American Review*, vol. 43, no. 1, 2009, pp. 35–44.

Morrison, Toni. "Unspeakable Things Unspoken: The Afro-American Presence in American Literature." *Michigan Quarterly Review*, vol. 28, no. 1, 1989, pp. 1–34.

Mullen, Harryette. "African Signs and Spirit Writing." *Callaloo*, vol. 19, no. 3, 1996, pp. 670–89.

Neal, Larry. "The Ethos of the Blues." *The Black Scholar: Journal of Black Studies and Research*, vol. 3, no. 10, 1972, pp. 42–48.

Oliver, Paul. "Can't Even Write: The Blues and Ethnic Literature." *MELUS*, vol. 10, no. 1, 1983, pp. 7–14.

Otten, Thomas J. "Pauline Hopkins and the Hidden Self of Race." *English Literary History*, vol. 59, no. 1, 1992, pp. 227–56.

Pavletich, JoAnne. "'We Are Going to Take That Right': Power and Plagiarism in Pauline Hopkins's 'Winona.'" *CLA Journal*, vol. 59, no. 2, 2015, pp. 115–30.

Peterson, Carla L. *Doers of the Word: African-American Women Speakers and Writers in the North (1830–1880)*. Oxford UP, 1995.

Plant, Deborah G. *Zora Neale Hurston: A Biography of the Spirit*. Rowman & Littlefield, 2011.

Prentiss, Craig. "'Terrible Laughing God': Challenging Divine Justice in African American Antilynching Plays, 1916–1945." *Religion and American Culture: A Journal of Interpretation*, vol. 18, no. 2, 2008, pp. 177–214.

Rainey, Gertrude Ma. "Prove It on Me Blues" Advertisement. *Chicago Defender*, Sept. 1928.

Richardson, Elaine. "'To Protect and Serve': African American Female Literacies." *CCC*, vol. 53, no. 4, 2002, pp. 675–704.

Robbins, Sarah. *Managing Literacy, Mothering America: Women's Narratives on Reading and Writing in the Nineteenth Century*. U of Pittsburgh P, 2006.

Rosenberg, Rosalind. *Jane Crow: The Life of Pauli Murray*. Oxford UP, 2017.

Ross, Michael. "The Supreme Court, Reconstruction, and the Meaning of the Civil War." *Journal of Supreme Court History*, vol. 41, no. 3, 2016, pp. 275–94.

Royster, Jacqueline Jones. "Perspectives on the Intellectual Tradition of Black Women Writers." *The Right to Literacy*, edited by Andrea Lunsford et al., Modern Language Association, 1990, pp. 103–12.

Royster, Jacqueline Jones. *Traces of a Stream: Literacy and Social Change Among African American Women*. U of Pittsburgh P, 2000.

Rudolph, Kerstin. "Victoria Earle Matthews: Making Literature during the Woman's Era." *Legacy*, vol. 33, no. 1, 2016, pp. 103–26.

Ruffin, Josephine St. Pierre, and Florida R. Ridley. "Advertise in the Woman's Era." *The Woman's Era*, vol. 4, no. 1, 1894, p. 7.

Sanborn, Geoffrey. "The Winds of Words: Plagiarism and Intertextuality in *Of One Blood*." *J19: The Journal of Nineteenth-Century Americanists*, vol. 3, no. 1, 2015, pp. 67–87.

Sherrad-Johnson, Cherene. "Introduction." *Comedy: American Style*, by Jessie Fauset, edited by Cherene Sherrad-Johnson, Rutgers UP, 2010.

Shor, Ira. "What Is Critical Literacy?" *Critical Literacy in Action: Writing Words, Changing Worlds*, edited by Ira Shor and Caroline Pari, Boyton/Cook Heinemann, 1999, pp. 1–30.

Simkins, Francis Butler. "Ben Tillman's View of the Negro." *Journal of Southern History*, vol. 3, no. 2, 1937, pp. 161–74.

Smith, Mamie. Performer. "Crazy Blues." *Mamie Smith Vol. 1: 14 February 1920 to 18 August 1921*. Recorded 1920. Document Records, 2005.

Smitherman, Geneva. *Talking and Testifyin: The Language of Black America*. Wayne State UP, 1977.

"Soon This Morning Blues" by Gertrude "Ma" Rainey. Advertisement. *Chicago Defender*, Feb. 1927, p. 7.

Spires, Derrick R. *The Practice of Citizenship: Black Politics and Print Culture in the Early United States*. U of Pennsylvania P, 2019.

Spivey, Victoria. "Blues Is My Business." *Record Research*, no. 53, 1963, p. 12.

Spivey, Victoria. "Dirty TB Blues." *Victoria Spivey Volume 3: 1 October 1929 to 7 July 1936*. Recorded 1929. Document Records, 1995.

Spivey, Victoria. "Dope Head Blues." *Victoria Spivey Volume 1: 11 May 1926 to 31 October 1927*. Recorded 1927. Document Records, 1995.

Spivey, Victoria. "TB Blues." *Victoria Spivey Volume 1: 11 May 1926 to 31 October 1927*. Recorded 1927. Document Records, 1995.

Stewart-Baxter, Derrick. *Ma Rainey and the Classic Blues Singers*. Stein and Day, 1970.

Storm, William. "Reactions of a 'Highly-Strung Girl': Psychological and Dramatic Representations in Angelina Grimké's *Rachel*." *African American Review*, vol. 27, no. 3, 1993, pp. 461–71.

Stuckey, J. Elspeth. *The Violence of Literacy*. Boynton/Cook Publishers, 1991.

Sylvander, Carolyn Wedin. *Jessie Redmon Fauset: Black American Writer*. Whitson Publishing Company, 1981.

Szwed, John F. "The Ethnography of Literacy." *Literacy: A Critical Sourcebook*, edited by Ellen Cushman et al., Bedford/St. Martin's, 2001, pp. 421–29.

Tate, Claudia. *Domestic Allegories of Political Desire: The Black Heroine's Text at the Turn of the Century*. Oxford UP, 1992.

Tate, Claudia. "Introduction." *The Works of Katherine Davis Chapman Tillman*, edited by Claudia Tate, Oxford UP, 1991, pp. 3–62.

Taylor, Carole Anne. *The Tragedy and Comedy of Resistance: Reading Modernity through Black Women's Fiction*. U of Pennsylvania P, 2000.

Tillman, Katherine D. C. *Beryl Weston's Ambition: The Story of an Afro-American Girl's Life*. *The Works of Katherine Davis Chapman Tillman*, edited by Claudia Tate, Oxford UP, 1991, pp. 207–246.

Tillman, Katherine D. C. *Clancy Street. The Works of Katherine Davis Chapman Tillman*, edited by Claudia Tate, Oxford UP, 1991, pp. 251–87.

Torchia, Marion M. "The Tuberculosis and the Race Question." *Bulletin of the History of Medicine*, vol. 49, no. 2, 1975, pp. 152–68.

Turner, Beth. "Colorism in Dael Orandersmith's *Yellowman*: The Effect of Interracial Racism on Black Identity and the Concept of Black Community." *Southern Quarterly: A Journal of the Arts in the South*, vol. 50, no. 3, 2013, pp. 33–53.

Wald, Gayle. *Crossing the Line: Racial Passing in Twentieth-Century U.S. Literature and Culture*. Duke UP, 2000.

Wallinger, Hanna. *Pauline E. Hopkins: A Literary Biography*. U of Georgia P, 2005.

Washington, Booker T. *Up from Slavery*, edited by William L. Andrews, Oxford UP, 1995.

Washington, Forrester B. "Recreational Facilities for the Negro." *Annals of the American Academy of Political and Social Science*, vol. 140, no. 1, 1928, pp. 272–82.

Watkins, James Ray, Jr. *A Taste for Language: Literacy, Class, and English Studies*. Southern Illinois UP, 2009.

Wilkerson, Isabel. *The Warmth of Other Suns: The Epic Story of America's Great Migration*. Random House, 2010.

Williams, Andreá. *Dividing Lines: Class Anxiety and Postbellum Black Fiction*. U of Michigan P, 2013.

Williams, Patricia J. *The Alchemy of Race and Rights*. Harvard UP, 1991.

Wilson, Anthony. "The Music of God, Man, and Beast: Spirituality and Modernity in *Jonah's Gourd Vine*." *Southern Literary Journal*, vol. 35, no. 2, 2003, pp. 64–78.

Winters, Kari J. "On Blues, Autobiography, and Performative Utterance: The *Jouissance* of Alberta Hunter." *Creating Safe Space: Violence and Women's Writing*, edited by Tomoko Kuribayashi and Julie Tharp, State U of New York P, 1998, pp. 201–13.

Woodson, Carter G. *The Mis-Education of the Negro*. Africa World Press, 1990.

INDEX

Africa, 60–62, 66, 68
African American Vernacular English (AAVE), 142. *See also* Labov, William
African occult, 69
Albertson, Chris, 99
A. M. E. Church Review, xiv, 38, 89. *See also* Tillman, Katherine D. C.
American English, edited, 10
American literature, 6–7, 10–11, 13
anti-Black racism, 14
Aristotle, 30, 33
Austin, Lovie, 109

Babb, Valarie, 21, 102
Baltimore Afro-American, 111
Bank, Adam, 30
Barnett, Timothy, 65
Bassard, Katherine Clay, 4
Berlin, James, 5
Binet, M., 59–60
Black Baptist women, 51, 140. *See also* Higginbotham, Evelyn Brooks
Black Codes, 3, 29, 45, 67, 175
Black intelligentsia, 91
Black literature, 28
Black migration, 70
Black periodicals, 33
Black press, 32, 34
Black print culture, xvii
Black professional class, 78
Black rhetorical traditions: signifying, 30, 143–44; speech, 41; vernacular, 28. *See also* Smitherman, Geneva

Bloom, Lynn Z., 67
blues form, 95
blues themes, xi, xviii
blues women, xviii, 100. *See also* classic blues singers
Bradford, Perry, 95. *See also* Smith, Mamie
Brandt, Deborah, 75–76, 78
Britain, 11–12
Brooks, Daphne A., 57
Brown, May, 4
Bruce, E., 34
Burris, Andrew, 168

Carby, Hazel, xvii–xviii, 62, 91, 147–48, 173
Chamberlain, John, 169
Chapman, Erin D., xvii–xviii, 75, 98, 109
Chaucer, 20
Chew, Mable, 111
Chicago Defender, 106, 148. *See also* Rainey, Gertrude "Ma"
Christian Recorder, xiv
classic blues, xviii, 91, 95, 177. *See also* Carby, Hazel
classic blues singers, xvii, xix–xx, xxii; aims and agency, 74, 91, 100, 104; Black womanhood, 90; Black working class, 91; language practices, xvii, 71, 91; race literature, 95, 108; "race record market," 99; race women, 101; secular and spiritual dimensions, 100, 101; shifts and transformations, 90; specular literacy, 91, 94–95, 101, 103, 105, 107–8, 111, 177; thematic concerns, 91
Cinderella, 40

Ciuba, Gary, 160, 162
Civil War, xxvi, 36, 72; amendments, 37, 45
Clinton, Kate, 78
Colored American Magazine, xiv, 38, 89. See also Hopkins, Pauline E.
Cone, James, 105, 142
Cook-Gumperz, Jenny, 41, 53, 100
Cooper, Anna Julia, xii, xxi, xxiv–xxv, xxvii–xxviii, 175; literary imagination, xxvii, 3, 12–13, 20, 36; "The Negro As Presented in American Literature," 4, 10–11; oral and written communication, 10, 19, 21–22; race literature, xiii, 3, 4, 21, 27; transformational literacy, 20–21; *A Voice from the South: By a Black Woman of the South*, 4; white author critiques, 14–18, 36; "Womanhood: A Vital Element in the Regeneration and Progress of a Race," xxiv
Cooper, Brittney C., xiv, 21, 34, 175
Crenshaw, Kimberlé, xxv
critical literacy, 56

Daniels, Melissa Asher, 67
Davis, Angela, xvii–xviii, 92–94, 136
Davis, Thadious, 117
Delany, Tom, 104
discourse, 66. See also Gee, James Paul
Douglas, Ann, 94
Douglass, Frederick, 21, 65, 159
DuBois, W. E. B., 73, 112, 155–57; *The Souls of Black Folk*, 156
duCille, Ann, xvii, xxiii, 105, 148–49
Dunbar, Paul Lawrence, 102; "An Ante-Bellum Sermon," 102; "When Malindy Sings," 102

Egypt, 61
English language. See African American Vernacular English (AAVE); American English, edited; Standard English
Ethiopia, 61, 66, 68–69

Fauset, Jessie Redmon, xiii, xvii, xx, xxviii–xxix, 112, 176; *Comedy: American Style*, xiii, xxi, xxviii; comedy and tragedy, 114;

Henry Louis Gates Jr., xiii–xiv, 24, 27, 73–74, 92, 113; literacy and education, 120, 134, 136; literacy outcomes, 136; passing, 117, 123–24, 127; racial absurdities, 114–15; racial hierarchy, xx, 115; transactional literacy, 113, 119, 123–24, 128
Fielder, Bridgett, 115
First National Conference of the Colored Women of America, xv, 4, 22
Fisk Jubilee singer, 59, 63
Fisk University, 63
Floyd, Ruth Naomi, 174. See also Spivey, Victoria
Foley, Barbara, 73–74
Foreman, P. Gabrielle, 7
Fortune, T. Thomas, 34
Frazier, E. Franklin, 73
Freedman's Bureau, 36

Gatewood, Willard B., xxvi–xxvii
Gee, James Paul, 66, 83
gender, xxiii, xxv
Gilyard, Keith, 30, 63–64
Giroux, Henry, 41
Glass, Kathy, 10
Goldsmith, Meredith, 136
Goodson, Steve, 141, 146
Graff, Harvey J., 5–6, 9, 121
Grimké, Angelina Weld, xi, xvi–xix, xxviii, 176; Black motherhood, 81, 86–87; education, 76–77, 85; employment discrimination, 78–79; God and religion, 76, 82–83, 86, 88; literacy outcomes, 74, 76–78, 80, 84, 86–87, 89, 104; lynching play, 76, 81–82, 84; *Rachel*, xi, xiii, xvi, xix, xxviii, 74; specular literacy, 74; transactional literacy, 7; white women, 88–89
Grimké, Archibald, 75
Grimké, Francis, 75
Grimké, Sarah, 75
Gussow, Adam, 96, 99
Guthrie, John T. and Vincent Greaney, 47

Hagar, Christopher, 25; *Word for Word*, 25–26
Hale, Sarah Josepha, 7

Handy, W. C., 95
Harlem Renaissance, xvi, 73–74, 92, 95–96, 99, 140
Harper, Francis Ellen Watkins, 7–9; *Iola Leroy*, 8
Harrison, Daphne Duval, xxiii, 148
Heap, Lauren, 31
Heard, Matthews, 170
Hegamin, Lucille, xiii, xxviii, 104; aims and agency, 105, 108; "Everybody's Blues," 104; "The Jazz Me Blues," xxviii, 104, 109; language practices, 107; specular literacy, 105
Higginbotham, Evelyn Brooks, 50, 99, 101, 140
Hobbs, Catherine, 5, 30
Honey, Maureen, xvi, 73
Hopkins, Pauline E., xii, xxviii, 38, 175; *Contending Forces*, 57; expansive and transformational, 63, 65, 68, 70; identity formation, 63; literacy and education, 63; literacy outcomes, 57, 65, 67; *Of One Blood; Or the Hidden Self*, xxviii, 38, 57; racial hierarchies, 69; *Winona*, 58
Horton, George Moses, 113
Howells, William Dean, 14–15, 28; *An Imperative Duty*, 14, 18–19, 28
Huggins, Nathan Irvin, 73
Hughes, Langston, 73, 93, 110–11; "The Negro Artist and the Racial Mountain," 110
Hunter, Alberta, xiii, xxviii, 91, 109, 176; "Down Hearted Blues," xxviii, 109, 110; language practices, 110; specular literacy, 110
Hurston, Zora Neale, xii, xvii, xxix, 73, 93, 150, 176; Du Bois vs. Washington debate, 157; *Jonah's Gourd Vine*, xiii, 151; illiteracy, 161–62; language practices, 150–51, 159, 160–66, 168–70; literacy and education, 154, 155; literacy outcomes, 157, 159; race literature, 170; specular literacy, 151, 159, 163, 167; *Their Eyes Were Watching God*, 15; transactional literacy, 154, 163; transformational literacy, 163–64

Jack and the Beanstalk, 40
Jacks, James, xv
Jacobs, Harriet, 9; *Incidents in the Life of a Slave Girl*, 9
James, William, 59; "The Hidden Self," 59
Jane Crow, xxv
Janet, M. Pierre, 59
Japtok, Martin, 60
Jensen, Anne Mai Yee, 84
Jim Crow, xvii, xxvii, 106, 135, 137, 173, 175
Jimoh, Yemish A., xvi, 72
Johnson, Guion Griffis, 46
Johnson, James Weldon, 93, 169
Johnson, Lonnie, 173. See also Spivey, Victoria
Jones, Martha S., 4
Jones, Sharon L., 160

Kaplan, Carla, 169
Kynard, Carmen, 126

Labov, William, 142, 173
Laguna, Albert Sergio, 130
Levering, Lewis, 73
Lewis, Vashti Crutcher, 119
Lieb, Sandra, 136
literacy, xiii, xx–xxii, xxvii; activities, 42, 48; "domestic," 7; educational purposes of, 5–6; "effective," 30; middle-class conventions of, 4; mid- to late nineteenth-century history of, 5; myth, 121; social functions of, xx; specular, xi, xiii, xx–xxii, 176; transactional, xiii, xx–xxii, 176; transformational, xiii, xx–xxii, xxvii–xxviii, 3, 176. *See also* Graff, Harvey J.; Guthrie, John T. and Vincent Greaney
literary societies, 42. *See also* McHenry, Elizabeth
Little Red Riding Hood, 40
Locke, Alain, xvi–xvii, 73–74, 114; *The New Negro*, xvi, 73; "The New Negro," xvii
Logan, Shirley Wilson, xix, 9, 34, 102
Lupton, Mary Jane, 133
lynchings, 175. *See also* Grimké, Angelina Weld

Matthews, Victoria Earle, xii, xv, xxvii–xxviii, 175; "Aunt Lindy," 14, 26–27; Black authorial responsibility, 30; literary imagination, xxvii, 3, 36; literary vision, 25; Negro dialect, 102; race literature, xxi, 3, 4, 23–24, 27–28, 31, 34; racial hierarchy, 29; "The Value of Race Literature," 4, 22; transformational literacy, 22–23, 35–36; *Woman's Era*, 31; white author critiques, 28–29, 36

May, Vivian A., xxiv, 10, 14–15, 22

McGinley, Paige A., 92–94

McHenry, Elizabeth, 27, 31, 42, 56

McKay, Nellie, 92, 96

McMillian, Timothy J., 145

Mitchell, Koritha, 82

Moody-Turner, Shirley, xxiv

Morrison, Toni, 83

motherhood, white, 6–7

Mullen, Harryette, 153, 163

Murray, Pauli, xxv

Neal, Larry, 92

Negro types: Black types, 27; New Negro, xvii, 75; New Negro woman, 75, 97; old Negro, xvii

New Negro Era, xii, xvi, xviii, xxi, xxiii, 70, 73. *See also* Harlem Renaissance

New Negro Movement, xvi, 73. *See also* Harlem Renaissance

Okey Record Company, 172. *See also* Spivey, Victoria

Oliver, Paul, 95

Osgood, Margaret, 170

Otten, Thomas J., 68

Patton, Venetria, xvi, 73

Peterson, Carla, 13

Phillips, Francis C., 28; "A Question of Color," 28

Plant, Deborah, 167

Plessy v. Ferguson, 37

Prentiss, Craig, 86–87

race records, 94, 106

race theories: retrogression, 45, 47, 56, 70; southern paternalism, 46–47, 56, 70

racial caste, 29, 86–87, 119

Rainey, Gertrude "Ma," xiii, xix–xx, xxix, 91, 107, 112, 176; "Black Dust Blues," 145–46; Black women's agency, 138–39; Black working class, 141; blues themes, 138; "Broken Hearted Blues," 139, 142, 145; language practices, 137–38, 140; "Prove It On Me Blues," 146–47; respectability politics, 140–41; "Rough and Tumble Blues," 142–45; same-sex attractions, xii, 146, 148; "Sissy Blues," 146; "Soon This Morning Blues," 106–7; specular literacy, 137, 139, 143–44, 148; voodoo, 145–46

Rampersad, Arnold, 73–74

Reconstruction, xxvii, 3, 44–45, 63, 68, 70, 176

respectability politics, xii–xv, xviii, xxvii, 175–76

Richardson, Elaine, 79, 131

Ridley, Florida R., 32

Robbins, Sarah, xix, 5–7, 9

Rosenberg, Rosalind, xxv

Royster, Jacqueline Jones, xix, 5, 20, 22, 35, 103

Rudolph, Kerstin, 27, 29

Ruffin, Josephine St. Pierre, xii; *Woman's Era*, xii, xiv–xv

Sanborn, Geffrey, 58

Shakespeare, William, 12

Sherrad-Johnson, Cherene, 133

Shor, Ira, 56

Sigourney, Lydia, 7

Simkins, Francis Butler, 45

Smith, Bessie, 111

Smith, Mamie, xi, 91, 95, 176; Black female agency, 98; "Crazy Blues," xi, xiii, xvi, xviii, xxviii, 74, 95, 96; language practices, 107; specular dimensions, 97, 102

Smitherman, Geneva, 41, 110, 142

social class: Black working class, xvii–xviii, xxiii; Black working-class women, xxiii;

elite Black women, xix; middle-class Black women, xix; politics of, xxvi
specular literacy, xiii, xx–xxii, xxix, 71, 176
Spires, Derrick R., xxii, 156
Spivey, Victoria, xxix, 151, 170; Black working class, 173–74; "Blues Is My Business," 171; blues themes, 151; "Dirty TB Blues," 172; "Dope Head Blues," 173; "Funny Feather Blues," 174; race matters, 171, 174; *Record Research: The Magazine of Record Statistics and Information*, 171; specular literacy, 174; "TB Blues," 171–72
Standard English, proper grammar, 40, 57, 78, 102
Stewart, Maria, 3
Stowe, Harriet Beecher, 12–13, 19, 28, 54–55; *Uncle Tom's Cabin*, 12, 28, 54
Stuckey, J. Elspeth, 85, 122–23, 128, 131
Sylvander, Carolyn Wedin, 135
Szed, John F., xx

Tate, Claudia, 47, 84, 88
Thompson, Maurice, 16; "A Voodoo Prophecy," 16–19, 45
Tillman, Ben, 45–46
Tillman, Katherine D. C., xii, xxviii, 37, 175; *Beryl Weston's Ambition: The Story of an Afro-American Girl's Life*, xviii; *Clancy Street*, xiii, xvii, 37; Christianity, 50, 52–55; literacy activities, 42, 48, 54, 57; literacy and education, 51, 54–56; literacy as transformational, 55; race literature, 46
Torchia, Marion M., 172
transactional literacy, xi, xiii, xx–xxii, 176

transformational literacy, xi, xiii, xx–xxii, xxvii, 176
Tubman, Harriet, 32
Twain, Mark, 28; *Pudd'nhead Wilson*, 28

vaudeville, 91
Vieira, Kate, 31
voodoo, 54. *See also* Tillman, Katherine D. C.

Wald, Gayle, 126
Walker, David, 3
Wallinger, Hannah, 57
Washington, Booker T., 155, 156–57
Washington, Forrester B., 106–8
Watkins, James Ray, Jr., 134
Wells-Barnett, Ida B., 34, 73
Western civilization, 57, 68
Western education, 62
Wheatley, Phillis, xiii, 3, 113
white imagination, 27
white press, 7, 32, 34
white print culture, xv
Wilkerson, Isabel, 73
Williams, Andreá, xxvi
Williams, Patricia J., 135
Wilson, Anthony, 163
Wilson, Harriet E., 9; *Our Nig*, 9
Winters, Kari J., 110
Woman's Era, xvi, xxiii, 3–4, 96
womanhood: Black women, xv, xvi, 75; white women, xiv
Woodson, Carter G., 123, 128, 154; *The Miseducation of the Negro*, 123–25
World War I, 75
Wright, Richard, 65

ABOUT THE AUTHOR

Coretta M. Pittman is associate professor in the Department of English at Baylor University. She teaches undergraduate courses on race and rhetoric and writing and social justice and graduate courses in African American Literature and Critical Literacy Studies. Her research focuses on literacy and rhetoric at the intersections of race, class, gender, and popular culture.

www.ingramcontent.com/pod-product-compliance
Lightning Source LLC
Chambersburg PA
CBHW030622230426
43661CB00053B/2105